2S wrote John
scrumpy w/ John
Atkinson while he was
at Berkeley   roommate at MSCN   By Beautiful Sea

145 roommate at MSCN

1454 (1453) Cleo
w/ Hubert

1-14-61 Hubert dies p187

The Welty Collection

The Welty Collection

A Guide to the Eudora Welty Manuscripts
and Documents at the Mississippi Department
of Archives and History

by Suzanne Marrs

UNIVERSITY PRESS OF MISSISSIPPI
Jackson & London

The paper in this book meets the guidelines for permanence and durability of the Committee on Production Guidelines for Book Longevity of the Council on Library Resources.

Designed by John A. Langston

All illustrations are from the Eudora Welty Collection, Mississippi Department of Archives and History.

Library of Congress Cataloging-in-Publication Data

Marrs, Suzanne.
    The Welty collection : a guide to the Eudora Welty manuscripts and documents at the Mississippi Department of Archives and History / by Suzanne Marrs.
        p.   cm.
        Bibliography: p.
        Includes index.
        ISBN 0-87805-366-2 (alk. paper)
        1. Welty, Eudora, 1909–   —Manuscripts—Catalogs.
    2. Manuscripts, American—Mississippi—Jackson—Catalogs.
    3. Mississippi. Dept. of Archives and History—Catalogs.
    I. Welty, Eudora, 1909–   . II. Mississippi. Dept. of Archives and History.   III. Title.
    Z6616.W454M37   1988
    [PS3545.E6]
    016.813′52—dc19   88-17537
                                                      CIP

British Library Cataloguing in Publication data is available.

C O N T E N T S

PREFACE

In 1957, at the request of Charlotte Capers, Director of the Mississippi Department of Archives and History, Eudora Welty began to donate manuscripts, photographs, correspondence, published works, and secondary works about her fiction to the department. She has continued and will continue to do so, and the result is a valuable, extensive, and expanding Eudora Welty Collection.

In 1985 the Department of Archives and History invited me to reorganize and to write a guide to this collection; Patricia Carr Black, Madel Morgan, Christine Wilson, H. T. Holmes, Karin Den Bleyker, and other members of the archives staff provided me with valuable assistance and advice in this undertaking. Most important, Miss Welty herself generously answered my many questions about her manuscripts, photographs, and correspondence. Her conversations with me inform the introductory essays and annotations in this guide; the opportunity to work closely with Eudora Welty has been the most significant experience of my professional life.

The Welty Collection: A Guide to the Eudora Welty Manuscripts and Documents at the Mississippi Department of Archives and History includes five chapters. Chapter one concerns manuscript holdings in the collection. Here I have listed and described typescripts of Welty's many books as well as typescripts of her uncollected and unpublished works; the annotated entries typically do not delineate the nature of revisions to individual typescripts, but I discuss the revisions at some length in the introduction to chapter one. Chapter two describes the negatives and printed photographs in the Welty Collection and includes commentary about selected photographs. Chapter three provides a calendar of the Welty correspondence, a summary of each letter, and an identification of the correspondents and of individuals mentioned in the letters. Chapter four lists the Welty publications that are part of the collection, and chapter five lists the secondary materials Welty has given to the Department of Archives and History. The guide concludes with appendixes citing other collections that are relevant to the study of Welty's fiction.

This guide should make the Welty Collection readily accessible to scholars. It should also complement existing critical discussions of a remarkable career. Introductory essays to the first three chapters provide background information and comment on the value of the collection. The introduction to the manuscript holdings describes Welty's method of writing and comments on the extent and signficance of her revisions; the introduction to chapter two describes her work as a photographer, the equipment she relied upon, and the relation of her photographs to her fiction; and the introduction to the collected correspondence discusses the biographical significance of correspondence held in the Welty Collection—what it reveals about Welty's career, her friendships, her travels, and her fiction. The other chapters in this guide do not really need introductions. The Welty publications and the secondary materials held in the collection (see chapters four and five) have in large part been described in bibliographies by Noel Polk, Victor Thompson, and Pearl McHaney; those bibliographies also list published materials that are not part of the Welty Collection. Scholars interested in reviews of Welty's fiction, however, will find chapter five of signficance, and those interested in unpublished interviews and in Welty's letters to her friends Lehman Engel and Charlotte Capers will find appendix A useful.

I am indebted to James West, Michael Kreyling, Noel Polk, R. Barbara Gitenstein, and Mary Hughes Brookhart for their advice on the final preparation of this guide, to my students Amy Haggblom, Jennifer Gibbs, and Barbara Adams for assistance in proofreading, to the State University of New York-Oswego for giving me time to complete this project, and to the Mississippi Committee for the Humanities for helping to fund my work.

I am grateful to the Mississippi Department of Archives and History for permission to quote from typescripts in the Eudora Welty Collection, to G. K. Hall for permission to use my essay "Eudora Welty's Photography: Images into Fiction," originally published in a slightly different form in *Critical Essays on Eudora Welty*, as the introduction to chapter two, and to the *Southern Review* and *Notes on Mississippi Writers* for permission to use portions of my essays which they have published.

A final and very special word of thanks goes to Charlotte Capers—for beginning the Eudora Welty Collection, for insuring that it has been carefully preserved and wisely administered, and for sharing her knowledge of it.

The Welty Collection

CHAPTER ONE

Manuscripts

The Eudora Welty Collection includes manuscripts of Welty's fiction, her critical and autobiographical writing, and her dramatic works. Dating from 1925 and extending to 1983, these manuscripts span the entire course of Welty's career and tell us much about her methods of composition and about the importance of revision to her achievements as a writer. Few careers are more fully documented.

As a sixteen-year-old college freshman, Welty typed her first attempt at a novel (see IV.A1), and she has composed at the typewriter ever since. After typing her earliest stories, including those collected in *A Curtain of Green*, she typically made a few holograph revisions to the typescripts and then retyped, sometimes adding more holograph revisions on these subsequent drafts. By the time she wrote *Delta Wedding*, however, Welty was revising more extensively, and in doing so, she began to use the method of revision she would follow for the rest of her career. From this time on, she would type her story, decide upon transpositions to be made, cut up the typescript and move paragraphs about, fixing them in place with pins or paste and adding holograph transitions. Then she would retype the story and start the cut-and-paste or -pin revision process again. In the 1960s, pressed for time, Welty relied upon typists for help with *Losing Battles* and gave her semifinal "paste copy" to a typist in Jackson, who prepared a fair copy for her. But under ordinary circumstances Welty herself prepared the fair copy, which then underwent further holograph or paste revision before going to the Russell and Volkening literary agency for circulation to publishers. Even then Welty's revising did not stop. After a work had gone to Russell and Volkening, been accepted by a publishing house, and been copy-edited, Welty revised her carbons or photocopies of a manuscript, requesting that an editor make parallel revisions to the setting copy. And Welty also made revisions to galleys. These revisions have occasionally been numerous, but they have not typically been of great substantive import; instead they were

3

usually stylistic. A three-page typed insertion for *Losing Battles* may be the lengthiest revision Welty ever made in galleys.

Welty has had many fine editors—John Woodburn, Mary Louise Aswell, William Maxwell, Albert Erskine, and John Ferrone among them. Albert Erskine in the late sixties was the first of Welty's editors to go with her line by line through a novel, a process that Welty found useful and exciting. As Erskine and Welty went through *Losing Battles*, for example, they discussed Erskine's questions about back-country roads and old cars, about the entrances and exits of characters. The galleys of *Losing Battles* show Erskine raising questions he and Welty had overlooked in their meetings and typify the sort of attention he devoted to the novel. Setting copies or galleys of Welty's other works include similar editorial queries about clarity of phrasing or consistency of detail, and Welty typically revised the passage to alleviate the problem her editor had noted.

The wisdom of Welty's editors is further seen in the degree of autonomy they have granted her. Welty has always had final authority over the text of her stories and novels. Though typescript setting copies and galleys at times show revisions and corrections in an editorial hand, these are changes made at Welty's behest and are *not* evidence of editorial tampering (Personal interview with Eudora Welty). Editors have trusted Welty's aesthetic judgment and her craftsmanship. They have also relied upon her assistance with proofreading. When she read galleys or page proof, Welty meticulously corrected printers' errors in spelling or punctuation, even as she coped with more serious problems.

In giving her manuscripts to the archives, Welty has attempted to date them or to put the drafts of individual stories into the order of their composition. At times her dating may be imprecise. After all, she presented her early stories to the archives over thirty years after she wrote them. But if specific dates are sometimes suspect, her ordering of typescripts appears to be quite accurate. Careful examination indicates that apparent discrepancies in their order exist only because different versions of the same story have been donated to the archives at widely different times. Versions of "The Burning," for example, were presented in 1957 and in 1985, so that an identification of a story in 1957 as the second available version was accurate then, but is not today. The dating of typescripts is not always problematic, however. Welty seems to have dated typescripts of *The Shoe Bird*, *Losing Battles*, and *The Optimist's Daughter* as they came from her typewriter, and those dates thus seem reliable.

The typescripts in the Eudora Welty Collection tell us much about Welty's method of composition and about the periods during which she worked on a particular piece of writing. But more important, they document the evolving significance of revision to Welty. In her early stories, many of which were collected in *A Curtain of Green* (1941), Welty revised very little, perhaps because of inexperience and the confidence of youth. When she did undertake substantial revisions, they were designed to provide more detailed descriptions or to solve basic problems in plot. During the 1940s, those years when she was producing *The Robber Bridegroom*, *The Wide Net*, *Delta Wedding*, and *The Golden Apples*, Welty revised more extensively. Though she wrote *The Robber Bridegroom* rapidly and evidently with scant revision, her other works of the forties underwent major transformations in the writing process. The revisions from this period reveal a writer who had become more experimental and innovative, one to whom the possibilities of fiction seemed far larger. Plot in "The Winds," setting in *Delta Wedding*, and character in "Music from Spain," for example, all became more complex and resonant as Welty typed, revised by hand, made cut-and-paste (or -pin) transpositions, and retyped her works. After 1949, it seems, Welty revised even more heavily; the collection contains multiple drafts of her later works, not merely an early draft and a setting copy. Perhaps these many drafts exist because Welty had become a far more self-conscious writer: the reviews she produced in the forties and the critical essays she would write in the fifties, sixties, and seventies show how carefully Welty was thinking about her craft during those decades. It is also possible that more revisions survive today because requests from archives for her typescripts had prompted Welty to preserve them. Or the number of revisions may be due to the increasingly demanding projects that Welty tackled during this period—trying to write about the Civil War, a subject which seemed intractable to her; trying, during very difficult personal times, to write a long novel from a consistently external perspective; and trying to transform the experience of loss into literature shortly after her mother and brother died. "The Burning," *Losing Battles*, and *The Optimist's Daughter* demonstrate how successfully Welty met these challenges.

In 1972 Eudora Welty told interviewer Linda Kuehl,

Well, when I wrote my first stories, I wrote much faster and it failed to occur to me that I could write them any other way, and perhaps better the second time. They show all the weaknesses of the headlong. I never rewrote, I just wrote. The plots in these stories are weak because I didn't know enough to worry about plots. In the dialogue stories, they came into being exactly as the dialogue led them along. I didn't realize their real weakness until I began reading stories in public—and my ear told me. (88)

Welty's judgment of her stories is overly harsh and her recollection of never rewriting is inaccurate, but this statement does reveal the relatively slight attention to revision we find in Welty's early stories. Between May 1940, when Russell and Volkening began to circulate a manuscript collection of Welty stories, the majority of which had been retyped from periodicals (I.A4), and the time she sent a final typescript of *A Curtain of Green* to Doubleday (I.A5), Welty for the most part fine-tuned her stories, seldom adding episodes or radically changing setting. But some revisions were substantial. Welty saw, for instance, that the periodical version of "The Whistle" lacked a central dramatic and emblematic incident, and she revised the story to give it one. In the periodical version, Jason and Sara Morton are summoned from their pallets by a warning whistle that signals a freeze, a freeze that could destroy their crop of tomatoes. They go into the fields, cover the plants with their bedding and even their clothes, and then return to their cabin and burn their last big cherry log. Such was the plot of the story Welty published in *Prairie Schooner*. But in the revised story, after burning their last log, Jason breaks up and burns the only furniture in the Morton's barren, one-room home—a split-bottom chair and a sturdy kitchen table. Welty no longer focuses upon the deadening routine of Jason's and Sara's lives; instead, through the startling incident, Welty establishes a moment of delusive hope and a prospect of absolute misery for Jason and Sara.

Just as Welty felt that she had mismanaged plot in the periodical text of "The Whistle," she found fault with setting in the 1936 *Manuscript* version of "Death of a Traveling Salesman." "This landscape," she has said, "is general, and set down in it, the 'unpainted cabin' appears made-up, invented, though incompletely—I was shy of its interior." And she adds that "I allowed myself to write 'stream' instead of 'creek,' making it audible, although all water that runs in Mississippi is slow, brown, and quiet—nothing makes a noise but the big Mississippi itself" ("Looking Back at the First Story," 753, 754). Some of these "errors" Welty did not correct when she revised the story for book publication—Bowman still hears the stream—but the "unpainted cabin" has become a shotgun house in the "desolate hill country" ("Death of a Traveling Salesman," 232). Though Welty's early revisions were usually not extensive, in this case she did make significant minor revisions to setting.

Another sort of revision appears in a typescript of "Clytie." Welty told Linda Kuehl that in her early stories she

> needed the device of what you call the "grotesque." That is, I hoped to differentiate characters by their physical qualities as a way of showing what they were like inside. . . . It's instinctive for a writer to show acute feelings or intense states of emotion by translating it into something—red hair, if nothing else. But it's not necessary. I believe I'm writing about the same inward things now [1972] without resorting to such obvious devices. (87)

Clytie is surely one of Welty's early grotesque characters, but revisions of "Clytie" show Welty moving away from a two-dimensional portrait of Clytie to a more rounded view. In an early version of the story, Clytie thinks about the faces of her family members and recalls, "It was their faces which had come pushing in front of the face of love, long ago, when she was young. In a sort of arbor, she had laughed, leaned forward . . . and the face of love, which was a little like all the other faces . . .—and yet different, yet far more—this face of love had been very close, almost familiar, almost accessible ("Stories" 7). Clytie, it seems, leads her grotesque, warped existence because she has been denied love, perhaps the love of a particular man. But when Welty concludes the story by having Clytie recognize "the face of love" staring back at her from a rain barrel and by describing Clytie as "sick at heart, as though the poor, half-remembered face of love had finally betrayed her" ("Stories" 13), Welty elicits a startled recognition from her readers. Only at this final moment do readers recognize that Clytie's search for the face of love has been a search for herself. Clytie has not been able to love herself or to give love. In revising her story, Welty relinquishes this moment of ironic revelation in favor of more sustained character development. No longer does Clytie seek the "face of love." Now she seeks "a face"; she seeks to recognize the many bonds that tie her to others. Thus, when this Clytie recognizes her own reflection as the face from which she had become separated, surprise is not the primary effect Welty achieves. Instead the reader feels an understanding and a sympathy that the earlier version had precluded. In failing to communicate and connect with others, the story's ending suggests, Clytie has failed to know herself. In the published story, therefore, Clytie's reunion with herself comes not so much as an ironic revelation as a completed pattern.

Welty, even as a young writer, was an astute editor of her own work, as W. U. McDonald's studies of the early revisions testify. Yet astute though she was, Welty made sparing use of her editorial talents in revising her early stories. Those talents came into full play, however, during the most productive decade of her career—the 1940s. Though the Welty Collection's five typescripts of stories from *The Wide Net* are very close to the published texts of the stories, two very early stories, "The Children" and "Beautiful Ohio," underwent radical alteration before becoming "At The Landing" and "The Winds." In our essay "More Notes on River Country," Mary Hughes Brookhart and I have looked closely at the way Welty changed the rose garden of "The Children" into the densely metaphoric river country of "At The Landing." Of equal interest and significance is the alteration of a simple plot in "Beautiful Ohio" into the complex and suggestive plot of "The Winds."

In "Beautiful Ohio" (IV.A4), Welty describes an event that would become the central incident in "The Winds," but that event—a young girl's trip to a Chautauqua concert—is surrounded by a series of events in the later story. "Beautiful Ohio" begins as a very young Celia and her parents leave home for the evening's Chautauqua concert—Celia's first evening out. The streetcar trip to the Chautauqua seems to promise something out of the ordinary. And something out of the ordinary does occur for Celia—she hears a lady trumpeter play, and the music calls Celia away from home to a life of questing for the beautiful. For the first time in her life Celia feels separate from her parents, an entity unto herself. Celia's mother comes in to tell her good night and Celia begins to cry. "Were you lonely here in the dark by yourself?" her mother asks, but Celia can only say no: "It was as though she wanted to be lonely and could not. Something had come to stay" (9).

These same events and themes are part of "The Winds," but the plot of the later story is far more intricate in design. Instead of providing a straightforward narration, Welty scrambles the chronology of this story. It begins during a storm that signals the coming of autumn. While two children and their parents wait out this storm, the daughter Josie moves in and out of dreams of the summer now past. The events of the stormy night—the empty bed rolling around and squeaking on its wheels, a Tinker-Toy tower falling apart, the house shaking "as if a big drum were being beaten down the street" (119)—signal a change in the season and a change in Josie. And Josie's dreamy memories show us the cause and nature of that change. She recalls interruptions of her childhood fantasies by parents who have "no memory of magic," she remembers playing in the neighborhood park with a friend, and she thinks about the "big" girl Cornella who lives across the street. And all these recollections develop variations on the theme to be established in the Chautauqua incident.

Welty has chosen not to present these events chronologically. Instead we repeatedly move from the night of the storm into dreams of the past, and those dreams come to Josie in a purely associative order. The result is a far more profound story than "Beautiful Ohio" and a narrative method far more complex than can be found in *A Curtain of Green*. "The Winds" deals with memory and the importance of memory as surely as it does with the importance of passion, imagination, and risk-taking. As Welty has written in *One Writer's Beginnings*: "It is our inward journey that leads us through time—forward or back, seldom in a straight line, most often spiraling. As we discover, we remember; remembering, we discover . . . " (102). This is certainly the case with Josie. She has not realized the significance of events as they have occurred. They take on meaning for her only in retrospect—the night of the storm seems "slowly to be waking something that slept longer than Josie had slept" (212). She discovers the most intimate facts about herself only by remembering the Chautauqua concert and placing it in the context of other events in her young life. Such is not the case with Celia in "Beautiful Ohio," and in Welty's transformation of that early story we see her vision and technique grow increasingly sophisticated.

Welty's skill as an editor is even more clearly demonstrated by the revisions that led to the publication of *Delta Wedding*. The Welty Collection includes a short story called "The Delta Cousins" (I.C1) which Welty, at the suggestion of her agent Diarmuid Russell, turned into the novel *Delta Wedding*, and the collection also includes the typescript setting copy of *Delta Wedding* (I.C2), complete with substantial holograph and typed revisions. Though revisions to the setting copy show Welty's sure hand, far more dramatic are the changes made between story and novel. In his book *Eudora Welty's Achievement of Order*, Michael Kreyling discusses at some length the changes in plot, point of view, characterization, and setting that occurred as Welty transformed story into novel. Neither the wedding preparations nor the wedding itself is part of "The Delta Cousins" nor is the incident of the Yellow Dog; Aunt Studney and Root M'Hook and a large cast of black characters are in the novel, but not the short story; and the conflict between George and Robbie plays no part in the story. But perhaps the way the novel expands upon the story is of greater interest than the way it diverges from it. For example, Welty revises one particular setting—the house called Marmion in *Delta Wedding*—so that an isolated locale in the story becomes linked to the major characters and events and themes of the novel.

There is no house called Marmion in "The Delta Cousins," but there is a house that resembles it in almost every physical detail. In this short story, young Laura Kimball and her cousin India Shelton meet a masked beeman who ferries them across the Sunflower River to a house with a dead yellow finch on its front steps and with a foyer that reminds them of "an old, round tower that had not yet fallen" (21). From the top of this tower hangs "a silver chandelier, all covered with melted and burned down candles, each with its black wick blown. The whole seemed to sway, to almost start in the sight, like a pendulum that wants to swing in a clock but no one starts it" (24). The only furniture in the house is a piano which occupies Laura's attention: "She touched a key, and it would hardly sink at the pressure of her finger, but the note sounded after a pause, as if it came from very far away, a little far-off flat sound. The keys were as warm as sun" (25).

This unnamed house plays a metaphoric role in the story. Laura and India seemed to have crossed the river of time and to have come to a very different world. The house is associated with death, with blown wicks and stopped clocks. And just as surely it is associated with sex, with the phallic tower up and around which India runs, and with the beeman who exposes himself to the little girls. But this house is not as integral to the central motifs of "The Delta Cousins" as it would become to the central motifs of *Delta Wedding*.

In *Delta Wedding* the house is the same; the descriptions are almost identical. But in *Delta Wedding* the house belongs not to the sinister beeman but to the Fairchilds. It is Marmion, built in 1890 by James Fairchild, father of Denis, Battle, George, Tempe, Jim Allen, Primrose, and Annie Laurie, and abandoned in the same year after James Fairchild was killed in a duel. Now it is to be the home of Dabney and Troy once they are married. Before Laura ever sees the house in *Delta Wedding*, Dabney comes alone to look across the Yazoo River at the "magnificent temple-like, castle-like house, with the pillars springing naked from the ground, and the lookout tower, and twenty-five rooms, and inside, the wonderful free-standing stair—the chandelier, chaliced, golden in light, like the stamen in the lily down-hanging" (122). Dabney sees the house, or the chandelier at least, in sexual terms, and when she rides away from Marmion, she also sees the river's backwater in these terms. Dabney dismounts from her horse, parts "thronged vines of wild grapes, thick as legs," and looks at snakes in the bayou and at "vines and cypress roots" growing in the water "more thickly than any roots should grow, gray and red," some of which "moved and floated like hair." In "a vertigo of sexual fascination," to use Louise Westling's words (*Sacred Groves and Ravaged Gardens* 80), Dabney then ponders a whirlpool:

> And the whirlpool itself—could you doubt it? doubt all the stories since childhood of people white and black who had been drowned there, people that were dared to swim in this place, and of boats that would venture to the center of the pool and begin to go around and everybody fall out and go to the bottom, the boat to disappear? A beginning of vertigo seized her, until she felt herself leaning, leaning toward the whirlpool. (122–23)

Dabney never describes this experience to anyone, not even to her future husband, though she goes on to associate the tangled vines and the dangerous whirlpool with the mysteries of sex and marriage. After her marriage, Dabney thinks of her love as an untamed river: "In catching sight of love she had seen both banks of a river and the river rushing between—she saw everything but the way down" (244–45). Dabney has troubing seeing "the way down," has trouble trusting her intuition as a guide through uncharted territory. The river, which runs more swiftly by Marmion than it runs elsewhere, thus suggests the sexual initiation that lies ahead for Dabney, an initiation she desires far more than she fears. Marmion, the bayou, and the river are part of one landscape for Dabney, a landscape that holds forth love and marriage.

When Laura and her cousin Roy visit Marmion, the house continues to be an emblem of sexual experience, but that experience is now linked to Dabney's coming marriage, to a life-enhancing act, not to the distorted life of the beeman. Nevertheless, during Laura and Roy's visit, Welty associates the house with death as well as love, and she does so more thoroughly than she had in "The Delta Cousins." At Marmion, Laura and Roy meet Aunt Studney, who is carrying her mysterious sack and will not let the children look inside it. Aunt Studney lives beyond the Deadening, and the location of her home makes her seem an emblem of mortality. Of course, Roy believes her sack is also the place "where Mama gets all her babies" (173). Welty further links Studney to both life and death when at Marmion Studney gives forth "a cry high and threatening like the first note of a song at a ceremony, a wedding or a funeral" (176). And when Roy throws

Laura into the Yazoo River, literally the River of Death, these associations with both life and death are reiterated: "As though Aunt
Studney's sack had opened after all, like a whale's mouth, Laura
opening her eyes head down saw its insides all around her—dark
water and fearful fishes" (178). Laura, whose only previous swim has
been in Jackson's Pythian Castle with the protection of water wings,
is immersed in the river that has been associated with the mysterious
realm of love and death and that is now linked to Studney's sack. She
placidly accepts this experience, and at the end of the novel she holds
her arms "out to the radiant night" (247). She is not disoriented by
the unknown and unknowable. Laura, still a child of course, cannot
achieve the kind of awareness George and Ellen know; but Laura,
who so much wants to belong to the Fairchild family, will be able to
face life's transience and the consequent urgency to love, and she will
not have to use the extended family as a shelter from those enigmas.

Laura's acceptance of life's complexity in *Delta Wedding*, though not
in "The Delta Cousins," is part of her inheritance from her dead
mother. Annie Laurie, who left the Delta in order to marry Laura's
father, has rightfully inherited Marmion, and Marmion therefore
should one day be Laura's. When Annie Laurie makes her young
daughter a doll and names the doll Marmion, she looks forward to
the legacy that will be Laura's. Peggy Prenshaw suggests the link between doll and house. Annie Laurie, she writes,

> makes Laura a baby named Marmion, named for one of the Fairchild plan-
> tation houses near Shellmound. The great empty house is Annie Laurie's
> inheritance and will one day perhaps be Laura's. As her Uncle Battle says,
> "Someday you'll live there like your Aunt Ellen here, with all your chil-
> dren." The gesture of Annie Laurie's handing the doll to her daughter, an
> act of a loving mother, prideful of her skills, is the generational correla-
> tive of "passing the torch" in Julia Mortimer's realm in *Losing Battles*. The
> mother's link forms the human chain, and in *Delta Wedding* the connections
> lead ultimately, even mystically, back to the earth. (51)

Annie Laurie's legacy to Laura is aptly represented by the house, for
her legacy is a knowledge of love and death—the love she has given
her daughter, the love implicit in her making of the doll, but also
death, her own death. Ellen believes that Uncle George is the only
Fairchild who sees "death on its way" (188), but she is wrong. Nine-
year-old Laura shares this perception. In "Delta Cousins" Laura's doll
is Imogene, her mother's death is scarcely mentioned, and the house
belongs neither to the Sheltons nor to Laura. Laura's inheritance of
property and of knowledge, her consciousness of life's great myster-

ies, of love and death, remain to be developed in *Delta Wedding*, and that development comes primarily through Welty's increasingly metaphoric use of setting and through a pattern of associations that tie character, event, setting, and concept inextricably together.

Welty's revisions of *The Golden Apples* produce similar patterns that tie story to story. When she began to write the stories to be collected in *The Golden Apples*, Welty did not realize that she was writing about a single cast of characters and following their lives over more than forty years. That realization came during the composition process and necessitated thorough revision of some stories. Although the Welty Collection includes preliminary drafts of four stories and the complete typescript setting copy of the book, only one early draft held in the Welty Collection was written before Welty had realized the interrelationships that would unite *The Golden Apples*. "The Flower and the Rock" (I.D3) is essentially "Music from Spain," except that its protagonist has no connection with Morgana, Mississippi. When Welty revised the story, however, Francis Dowdie became Eugene Hudson MacLain and gained a background which he had totally lacked. "The Flower and the Rock" gave no indication of Dowdie's home state or of his family relationships, except with wife and daughter. These elements Welty added later. She has said that this story really doesn't comfortably fit in *The Golden Apples* and that she included it because setting the entire collection in Morgana created a claustrophobic atmosphere. But once again, Welty's judgment of herself seems too harsh. Though adding "Music from Spain" to *The Golden Apples* was an afterthought on her part, it was a very well conceived one. The transformation of Francis Dowdie to Eugene MacLain adds depth, texture, credibility to the story.

Changing Francis into Eugene and giving him Eugene's heritage certainly makes his motivation more explicable. Francis Dowdie is a man trapped in a passionless marriage to a woman older than himself. Quite naturally he longs for something more in his life and is attracted to the life of the artist, the foreigner, the wanderer, a life he claims to reject: "He saw himself for a moment as the man in the wilderness in the geography book engraving who touched the traveler's tree, opened his mouth, and the water poured in. What did he really care about the life of an artist—or a foreigner, or a wanderer—all the same thing. He came from a whole line of clock and watch people—they were quite special enough" (15–16). Francis comes from a long line of meticulous, unadventurous people. He longs for excitement but feels compelled to defend the life he leads. Eugene's motivation is similar but is more fully and convincingly developed. His father, the archetypal wanderer King MacLain, inspires both envy and disgust in Eugene. He longs for the freedom his father has known but hates his father for abandoning him and his family. Welty's revisions of "The Flower and the Rock" associate the Spaniard with King MacLain and explain the admiration and hostility Eugene feels toward the Spaniard:

> Eugene saw himself for a moment as the kneeling Man in the Wilderness in the engraving in his father's remnant geography book, who hacked once at the Traveler's Tree, opened his mouth, and the water came pouring in. What did Eugene MacLain really care about the life of an artist, or a foreigner, or a wanderer, all the same thing—to have it all brought upon him now? That engraving itself, he had once believed, represented his father, King MacLain, in the flesh, the one who had never seen him or wanted to see him. (180)

This association of the Spaniard and King MacLain is again apparent when the two men walk toward the ocean. In "The Flower and the Rock," Francis views his outing with the Spaniard as part of a trick he has played on his wife, a trick that began when he slapped her face: "He looked up at the Spaniard and took an expansive breath, like a demonstration. The Spaniard breathed deeply also, and seemed to increase in size. Dowdie let out his breath smiling. A joke had been played on Emma, that was it—a little trick, a persuasion simply, which was still going on" (23). Francis here focuses upon his wife and his feelings of guilt about striking her. His feeling of release as they near the open sea is only vaguely linked to the Spaniard in this passage. Eugene's feeling of release, however, is directly linked to his companion. He experiences both freedom and a symbolic reunion with his father: "He looked up at his Spaniard and drew a breath also, perhaps not really a sympathetic one, but he seemed to increase in size. Eugene watched his great fatherly barrel of chest move, and had a momentary glimpse of his suspenders, which were pink trimmed in silver with little bearded animal faces on the buckles" (188). Eugene's freedom from Emma, his freedom from the routine and deadly life that is his, comes through his association with the Spaniard, who is so "fatherly." And Eugene's freedom, like his father's, comes at the expense of his wife, a fact that does not bother him at this moment but that repeatedly torments him during the story.

Just as mention of his father makes Eugene's motivation clearer, so does mention of his twin brother Ran MacLain. At one point in "The Flower and the Rock" Francis feels "all at once the secret tenderness toward himself that he might have felt toward a lover; for considering that he might have done a reprehensible thing, then he would himself need the gravest and tenderest handling" (22). Here Francis continues to be obsessed with the fact that he has struck Emma, and he pities himself as a result. But Eugene MacLain directs his tenderness not toward himself but toward his brother: "And Eugene felt all at once an emotion that visited him inexplicably at times—the overwhelming, secret tenderness toward his twin, Ran MacLain, whom he had not seen for half his life, that he might have felt toward a lover. Was all well with Ran? How little we know! For considering that he might have done some reprehensible thing, then he would need the gravest and tenderest handling" (187). Ran, in fact, has done a reprehensible thing—he has caused Maideen Sumrall's suicide—and he does need tender handling. Ran has had a tragic affair and a troubled marriage, and he feels the same longing for freedom, for the life of his father, that Eugene feels. Their difficulties are twin ones, and Eugene's intuitive concern for Ran may in part be a concern for himself. But Eugene is less self-absorbed than Dowdie, less self-indulgent, more sympathetic.

Eugene's memories of his Mississippi home also help to establish his motivation and to make it credible. We do not know where Dowdie is from. He may be from New York City—at one point he longs "for cryptic cold streets in New York that ended in the highest walls" (8)—but there are no other references to his origins. He may even be a native of San Francisco. Whatever the case, there is no real contrast between his provincial origins and his sophisticated, exotic new home in San Francisco. There is that contrast, however, in "Music from Spain." Eugene has left Morgana, Mississippi, for life in the most European of American cities; he has become a wanderer. But in San Francisco he has settled down into a life that he could as well lead in Morgana, a life of routine with a woman who is more like a mother than a lover. Even so, he feels dispossessed in San Francisco; he feels cut off from home, from the world that defines him. And at one point he longs "for that careless, patched land of Mississippi winter, trees in their rusty wrappers, slow-grown trees taking their time, the lost shambles of old cane, the winter swamp where his own twin brother, he supposed, still hunted" (169). For Eugene, the rural, unthreatening, familiar, yet wintery landscape of home is opposed to the urban, impersonal, yet vital world of San Francisco, and the contrast between these worlds helps to define the key issues he faces—the need for freedom and adventure, the need for stability and continuity, and the difficulty of fulfilling or reconciling those desires.

In transforming "The Flower and the Rock" into "Music from

Spain," Welty thus does far more than create an artificial connection between stories she would group together for publication. Her revisions of the early story enrich it. Neither this story nor her other fiction of the forties could be accused of the "weaknesses of the headlong." During this decade, Welty proved to be a master at her craft.

In the fifties, sixties, and seventies, Welty's concern for craftsmanship became more intense. *The Ponder Heart* she wrote quickly and effortlessly she recalls, but *The Bride of the Innisfallen, Losing Battles,* and *The Optimist's Daughter* she repeatedly revised. In these works the revisions are not typically so radical as those in her books of the forties, but they record a more persistent attention to detail than Welty had ever before demonstrated and occasionally show substantial alteration of character or setting or incident. Welty's rendering of character in these works is of special interest. Her characters have always grown more complex in the process of revision—Clytie, Josie, Laura, and Eugene MacLain all illustrate that fact. But the gradual process by which characters became more complex, more mysterious, more human is clearest in Welty's late works because the multiple typescripts of this period show characters being reworked and reworked and reworked again.

The Welty Collection includes drafts of all seven stories in *The Bride of the Innisfallen* and multiple drafts of five of them. The one complete and one incomplete typescript of "No Place for You, My Love" in the collection unfortunately do not document the transformation Welty describes in her essay "Writing and Analyzing a Story," the transformation of a young woman caught in the "monotonous life of her small town" and in "a prolonged and hopeless love affair" into a woman from Toledo who, along with a stranger, encounters the primeval landscape south of New Orleans. The collection does, however, include many revisions of "The Burning," a story with which Welty has never been satisfied. Albert Devlin discusses these revisions in his book *Eudora Welty's Chronicle*, but Devlin recommends that more detailed study be made. A look at the transformation of Florabel into Delilah confirms the validity of Devlin's suggestion and establishes the crucial nature of each detail Welty chooses to include in her story.

In an early version of the story, titled "The Ghosts" (I.F4), the slave Florabel is an essentially passive character who has been denied a real identity of her own and who faces a perilous freedom. After she sees the Yankees burn the plantation house where she is a slave and witnesses the double suicide of the white sisters who have owned her, Florabel is confused. When she leaves the ruins of the plantation, she longs to take the parlor mirror with her because "it could see like Miss Theo—it had seen Miss Theo" (20). She is reluctant to give up her reliance on her mistress. But she also thinks of the mirror as being free: "The mirror was by itself, like her—free, fortunate, not destroyed—but belonging to nobody" (21). Ultimately, however, she abandons the mirror, thinking that "even if that allowed to be her own papa bottled up inside, she wouldn't take it" (21). She seems to think she is totally abandoning her past—her papa and Miss Theo both— but she carries her life as a slave with her. Florabel leaves the plantation, walking in Miss Myra's shoes, carrying Miss Theo's, wearing Miss Myra's willing rings, carrying the keys to their house on her belt, and balancing the Jubilee cup on her head. Perhaps she has merely provided for her physical well-being, but perhaps she continues to be as dependent as the slave system has taught her to be. She leaves with no mementos of a personal past, only with remembrances of her servitude. Her freedom is a kind of emptiness.

In the revised typescript published as "The Burning" in _Harper's Bazaar_ (I.F6), Florabel is a more complex individual. As a slave she is "earth's most detached visitor" (18), yet this detached visitor loves Phinny, who now seems to have been her son—"she worshiped him still, though it was long ago he had to be given up" (17). She may have been compelled to surrender Phinny to her mistresses, she may have watched while the Yankees burned the plantation house with Phinny in it, but her outward acquiescence does not betoken an inner blankness. This Florabel searches for Phinny's bones before she leaves the ruins of the house, and this Florabel leaves without any bounty from the sisters—no shoes, no rings, no keys, no Jubilee cup. These actions suggest that Florabel has reclaimed her personal past and that she has left behind her life as a slave. This rather sanguine prospect needs qualification, however, for it does not prepare us for the darkness of the story's final paragraphs. At the story's close, Florabel takes no thought of danger as she crosses the Big Black River; though she carries Phinny's bones high above her head as she wades through the water, she never considers that she "might step too deep and the river smile and take her" (19). Phinny's death has brought Florabel no sense of her own mortality. She does not face the bleak future that lies ahead when she reaches the soldiers who have nominally come to free her.

Welty found a more appropriate and metaphoric action with which to close her final version of the story. Delilah, like the _Harper's Bazaar_ Florabel, searches for Phinny's bones and takes them with her. But she also walks in Myra's shoes and carries Theo's. Delilah's memory is comprehensive and credible. She goes into the future bearing reminders of Phinny's tragic life and death and of her own servitude. Still, Delilah, whose very name suggests a kind of resourcefulness that Florabel lacked, seems more realistic than dependent in providing for herself, in taking the shoes and the jewelry and a silver cup. And when Delilah crosses the river, she does not go mindlessly forward. She trusts in her intuition or knowledge of natural signs. She knows that it won't rain until Saturday and that the river is low. The events of the story have affected and changed her. She journeys into danger, but she seems far more capable of dealing with the future than did Florabel. "The Burning" ends on this ambivalent, thoroughly convincing note, a note achieved only through repeated revision.

Repeated rewriting certainly characterized the composition of *Losing Battles*, for it was written over a nine year period while Welty lectured, reviewed books, taught, and dealt with family responsibilities. Welty described this time-consuming process in an interview with Charles Bunting:

> I think normally I would have just written it and finished it, the way I do everything else. But owing to personal responsibilities, I couldn't work at it with any sustainment or any regularity, so that what I did was mostly make notes and write scenes and tuck them in a box, with no opportunity to go back and revise, but writing a scene anew instead of revising it, so that the work prolonged itself. I don't mind any of this, because I was teaching myself all this time. And the fact that it stayed alive in my head over a period of years cheered me up because I thought that it must have some spark of vitality or it would have just faded away. But it kept staying with me; I only kept thinking of more and more scenes. So then when I did have time to work on it, I just had boxes full of scenes. (719)

Those boxes of scenes, of course, eventually became drafts of the novel. The Welty Collection includes a 1961 draft of Part 2 of the novel, a 1963 draft of Part 2, a 1964 draft of Part 6, 1965 drafts of Parts 1 and 2, a 1968–1969 draft of the complete novel, and the typescript setting copy of the novel (I.H). The drafts show that the basic lines of development in *Losing Battles* were set very early on. Though Welty does cut some scenes and add others in the course of rewriting her novel, more often she uses rather subtle revisions to alter the course of individual episodes, the look of the landscape, and the nature of key characters.

For example, Welty ultimately depicts Judge Oscar Moody as a man who confronts and comes to terms with the fact of human mortality. In all versions of Part 2, the judge flees this knowledge, but in the complete typescripts of the novel he eventually stops running and deals with the reality of death. In the 1961 and 1963 drafts, Judge Moody does not wish to pay his last respects to Florence Hand or Vera Thrasher, in the 1965 draft he is loath to visit Ida Moorehead, who lies near death, and in 1968–1969, he isn't "anxious enough" to visit the ailing Julia and "find out what had happened to her" (114). Significantly, the mask each judge wears against the dusty Boone County roads serves as an emblem of his reluctance to face his former mentor and the death that has claimed or soon will claim her. Mary Anne Ferguson has persuasively argued that an "association of dust and death" pervades *Losing Battles* (316), and Judge Moody in 1961 and 1963 dons a dust mask when he learns of the teacher's death. Only in the 1968–1969 draft and subsequent drafts does he remove the mask when her death is announced: "Judge Moody, out in the road, put his hands to his cheeks and rolled the tied-on handkerchief up into a ring around his forehead, and now there was his naked face" (252). The announcement of Julia's death brings this judge out from behind his mask and forces him to acknowledge life's transience, to acknowledge man's inevitable return to the dust from which he came. Judge Moody does put the mask back on as he and his wife proceed to the Renfro-Beecham reunion, but this Judge, unlike his forebears, has recognized "time's deepest meaning" ("Some Notes on Time in Fiction" 168). A minor revision thus signals this new concept of the judge and prepares us for his future actions. He will go on to read Miss Julia's will to the assembled reunion, to recount the story of his relationship with Julia, and sorrowfully to recall the ways in which he "betrayed" her. And paradoxically these wounding memories are a mark of triumph for Moody. As Laurel Hand and Eudora Welty know, "The memory can be hurt, time and again—but in that may lie its final mercy. As long as it's vulnerable to the living moment, it lives for us, and while it lives, and while we are able, we can give it up its due" (*The Optimist's Daughter* 179).

Welty wrote *The Optimist's Daughter* in a fraction of the time she spent on *Losing Battles*. She wrote the story as published in the *New Yorker* in less than a year, and she seems to have completed the typescript setting copy for Random House within a year and a half after she began revising the *New Yorker* story. Helen Hurt Tiegreen has discussed the differences between story and novel; the Welty Collection now permits scholars to consider four drafts leading to the story and two leading to the novel (I.I). Most of the revisions to story and novel are subtle and undramatic, but they show Welty's meticulous attention to detail, the attention that makes *The Optimist's Daughter* a seamless whole. One change, however, is very striking—the addition of the character Philip Hand and the consequent modification of the character Laurel Hand.

In an incomplete typescript that dates from February 1967, Welty attempted to incorporate Philip Hand into the story she would publish in the *New Yorker*, but unable to do so, she put the material into a folder with a note instructing herself, "Omit this part for now" ("An Only Child"—omitted pages); she intended to return to this character before publishing her story as a book. In these omitted pages, Philip is an artist who fills his sketchbook with drawings of the birds he loves; Laurel too is an artist, but she gives up painting for design after her husband, who has become a wartime pilot, is shot down over the Pacific Ocean. Though this Laurel's memories of Phil are idealized, they are not locked away. "The reminder of loss was still part of her conscious effort to live," Welty writes, "but was familiar now, almost in the nature of a comfort. Losing your love was like being given a compass, though too late for the journey" ("An Only Child"—omitted pages). For this Laurel, memory seems to provide consolation but never joy. She is like the Laurel of the other early drafts in her vision of absurdity and futility and in her self-doubt. Neither her constant openness to the memory of Philip nor her response to that memory are appropriate to the Random House novel. Welty thus had to alter her concept of Philip and his effect upon Laurel, and in revising the *New Yorker* text, Welty included much more information about the new Phil than she could ultimately keep. An excited, portentous meeting of Laurel and Phil at the Art Institute in Chicago, specific examples of Phil's practical abilities—these are passages that Welty later omitted from the novel, for they merely reiterate facts established elsewhere and are therefore unnecessary. Other passages, crucial to the novel's consideration of memory, remain. With Philip, Welty tells us, Laurel has falsified the past—put it in a silver frame, refused to acknowledge what pain might have come their way, refused to recognize how desperately Phil would have wanted life instead of a perfect past. Only when she is able to remember how much Phil would have wanted to live, how much he valued process over product, how fully he accepted the tragic nature of experience is

Laurel able finally to see the true importance of memory, the continuity it provides.

When Laurel is able to recall Philip and the pain of his loss, she gains full access to her past and to her emotional life. By refusing to let memory hurt her, she has denied not only the past but also emotion itself. But after dreaming of Philip and their wedding journey past the confluence of the Ohio and Mississippi Rivers, she awakes to a sense of joy. Now she is free to feel. No longer does she deny emotion. Now she will be able to face Fay, to abandon silence, and to tell Fay what she had done. Laurel in the early part of the novel seems numb, almost unable to feel. She expresses no anger with Fay; she does not display the emotions of grief. But by the novel's end, she has overcome this numbness and is fully alive. Just as Philip, an officer on a mine sweeper, faced *kamikaze* pilots who flew so near his ship that he might have shaken hands with them, Laurel confronts her hatred of Fay: "there is hate as well as love, she supposed, in the coming together and continuing our lives. She thought of Phil and the *kamikaze* shaking hands" (177).

The Eudora Welty Collection thus shows us three major patterns Welty followed in revising her fiction. She evidently wrote her early stories rapidly, published them in periodicals with scant revision, and then fine-tuned them for book publication. She occasionally added a major episode to a story, but typically her revisions were minor. During the 1940s, Welty commonly made sharp changes of direction in revising her stories or novels. The entire plot of "Beautiful Ohio" is but an incident in "The Winds." The wedding, the point of view, the fully developed thematic concern with love and death—all of these elements Welty added to "The Delta Cousins" in transforming it from story to novel. And the interlocking elements of *The Golden Apples* Welty resolved upon in the course of revising. In her works subsequent to *The Golden Apples*, Welty's revisions do not typically loom so large, but she does tend to produce more drafts of these later works than she had of her earlier books. And though she might add a character like Philip Hand in *The Optimist's Daughter*, her persistent rewriting more typically concerns itself with the precise detail so crucial to character development, a long-held concern that seems to have become increasingly important to her.

No such pattern of revision emerges from Welty's autobiographical, critical, and dramatic writing. The Welty Collection's typescripts of *The Eye of the Story*, of numerous uncollected reviews and essays, and of three dramatic works are not heavily revised; the collection includes extensive revision only of *One Writer's Beginnings*. Still, the modification of "Place in Fiction," the various drafts of the 1984 autobiography, the typescript of an essay not previously identified as Welty's, and a screenplay of *The Robber Bridegroom* are particularly interesting because they include Welty's comments about modern fiction, her own fiction, and southern writing.

Welty made few substantial revisions to her critical writings when she set out to compile *The Eye of the Story* (II.C). In fact, the setting copy of this book consists largely of photocopied typescripts and articles. Welty did, however, make stylistic revisions throughout the setting copy, and she deleted two paragraphs from her *South Atlantic Quarterly* essay, "Place in Fiction." And in her galleys of the collection, Welty marked an additional passage for deletion from this essay:

> When we write a novel out of the saturation of place, we have more to draw on than we know, but when we write with no roots struck down, we will have to be explorers snatching the first things that glitter on top . . . .
>
> The bad novel of today is unhappily like the tale told to the analyst. It is not communication, it is confession—often of nothing more than some mild weakness. It is self-absorbed, self-indulgent, too often self-pitying. And it's dull. (Galley 70)

Welty felt that these remarks, as published in 1956, were inappropriate in 1978 as she prepared *The Eye of the Story*. Thus, she wrote to Albert Erskine: "Albert—don't you think the essay could do without any of this? (I'd already cut part of the discussion of this point.) I feel it's dated and weakening probably" (author's galley 70).

Though the Welty Collection holds four distinct typescripts of *One Writer's Beginnings*, the most valuable to the scholar may be the typescript of the William E. Massey Sr. Lectures in the History of American Civilization that Welty delivered at Harvard University (II.E1). The typescript of the lectures contains some biographical information excluded when she actually spoke at Harvard and not published in *One Writer's Beginnings*. This typescript also contains some analyses of her fiction that were cut for book publication.

One Writer's Beginnings includes a vivid description of life in Jackson, Mississippi, in the early part of the century, but that description has been pared back from a fuller description in the Harvard lectures. And some of the cut descriptions are very interesting, especially in terms of Welty's early stories. "Many of my early stories," she writes in the text of her lectures, "are an outgrowth of the mornings and afternoons and evenings and nights when I grew up on North Congress Street, aware of it house by house, and it seemed to me hour by hour. It was *all* visible" (I, 34). Welty then goes on to describe the business activities that occurred before her eyes:

> They spoke to you, the ice man climbing off his wagon with your 25-pound or 50-pound cake of ice in his tongs, the delivery man bringing your groceries from the market, the postman who came to the door, not only speaking but blowing his whistle if you had a letter.
>
> There were knife-grinders, jacks-of-all-trades, the monkey-man cranking his organ with his monkey on a leash holding his cup for pennies, there was the blackberry lady and the watermelon man, all with their calls.
> "Milk, milk,
> Buttermilk,
> New Potatoes, snap beans, green peas
> And buttermilk."
> There was the sassafras man, who just took up a position on the post office steps every March, with his orange roots in cartridge size and strung all over him, like a general in uniform belted and sashed; you could buy these (he intoned to the public) to make sassafras tea and purify your blood after the long winter. And there were the Gypsies, silent. They just moved through you. All were seasonal, all were looked for, and remembered. (I, 34)

A bygone way of life emerges from this passage, and the origins of characters like the organ-grinder in "The Winds" and Fate Raney in *The Golden Apples* are evident here as well. The passage probably was not essential to developing *One Writer's Beginnings*, but one regrets its absence nonetheless.

Welty also cut some comments about her own fiction from the Harvard lectures; books or stories she had discussed fully in interviews, she chose not to discuss in *One Writer's Beginnings*. But her discussion of "Powerhouse" in the lectures is far more thorough than her comments in most interviews have been.

> In "Powerhouse," I tried to turn the impromptu, frantic and abandoned playing together of a jazz pianist and his musicians into an exchange in words—something with its own rhythmic beat and crazy references, in the same onrush of performance. It was an attempt, like any other from a storywriter, to turn one sort of experience into another in order to convey it.
>
> During the 40s I was present at such a concert by Fats Waller; I hadn't dreamed I'd go home after it was over compelled to put down words. The story, all my invention, is nothing but the result of that evening: "Powerhouse" came from Fats Waller, and the story Powerhouse tells sprang from Fats Waller's music, out of his performance that night on stage. It was a one-time thing. I was not musically qualified to write it, but at the time of

writing, I felt I was outside musical qualifications; it was a sort of combustion; I was writing about a demon.

The point of view of this story is floating around somewhere in the concert hall—it belongs to the "we" of the audience. (III 6)

The rhythm and the improvisatory nature of Waller's music, her own attempt to translate it, the point of view of her story—these topics Welty has elsewhere addressed, but not so directly and completely. Though this passage goes over old ground, it provides valuable information and suggests that Welty's Harvard lectures are well worth reading.

The Welty Collection holds six reviews and one essay hitherto unidentified as Welty's own. The reviews of Sylvia Townsend Warner's *Garland of Straw*, of *The Short Novels of Colette*, of Lehman Engel's *Words with Music*, of William Sansom's *Fireman Flower*, of Fritz Peters' *World Next Door*, of Rose Macauley's *The World My Wilderness* are not especially significant, but the typescript of an essay concerning southern literature is. Published in the *Times Literary Supplement* on September 17, 1954, and titled "Place and Time: The Southern Writer's Inheritance," the essay was unsigned as then required by the Supplement (III.D2). It is a longer version of an article later printed in the *Delta Review*, a periodical published in Greenville, Mississippi. In her typescript Welty begins by anticipating the publication of William Faulkner's *A Fable*: "You never know ahead what a new work by Mr. Faulkner will be like—that is one of the joys of living contemporaneously with a genius" (1). And she adds that Faulkner's prose "is indestructibly itself and alive, something passionate and uncompromising, that will never sit still and wait on what anybody thinks, it will never be a possum in the tree. It sheds its light from higher up than any of the boys can shoot it down" (1). Then Welty turns to the nature of southern fiction, asserting that

most of the South's body of memories and lore and states of mind are basically Anglo-Saxon or Celtic—with a dash of Huguenot French here and there—with all of it having passed through Virginia at some time or other, most likely. In the eighteenth or nineteenth century everybody who was coming to the South came, and mostly they stayed. The Civil War and industry have brought its only visitors. And the writing, in a way, communicates out of this larger and older body of understanding, the inheritance that is more felt than seen, more evident and reliable in thought and dream than in present life, in all the racket of the highways with the trucks and the transports bearing down. (5–6)

Finally, Welty looks at the "surge of writers coming out of the South" (1). She writes that *"The Southern Review*, edited in Baton Rouge, La., by Robert Penn Warren and Cleanth Brooks and Albert Erskine—with Katherine Anne Porter, John Crowe Ransom, Allen Tate and others acting in close editorial connection, while some of their finest work was appearing there—was of inestimable help to these new writers in giving them publication in austerely good company, under the blessing of discriminating editing, without ever seeking to alter or absorb them" (8–9). And she adds, in her anonymous voice, "Eudora Welty is an example of the writers who owe publication of their earliest stories to acceptance by *The Southern Review*" (9). Welty goes on to praise the poetry of Robert Penn Warren and the fiction of Katherine Anne Porter and Peter Taylor. She also pays homage to the work of Elizabeth Spencer, Jefferson Young, and Hubert Creekmore, three fellow Mississippians.

Though long a devotee of the theater, Welty has never written a major play. The Welty Collection includes three dramatic works by Welty—a farce, a revue circulated by a Broadway agent, and a screenplay of *The Robber Bridegroom*. None of these works is distinguished, but Welty's work on the 1948–1949 screenplay tells us a good deal about the novel she had published in 1942. Welty wrote the screenplay jointly with her friend John Fraiser Robinson, a Mississippian who was then a graduate student at the University of California at Berkeley. The comments about her novel that Welty addresses to Robinson are perhaps the most interesting aspects of this manuscript. In "Notes on using the locations and props symbolically," Welty writes that the bluff on the Mississippi River "where Ros. goes for herbs" and where "Jamie carries R. off to" and "where Clem. fights the willow tree" is "always the verge and brink of discovery." And in her screenplay synopsis, Welty notes that Jamie is "a man of double-life and an interesting and appealing nature—not too troubled: it is the times. He thinks he is an adventurous opportunist, child of his day, and out after what he can get—but in action he is confounded and diverted too. He is ripe for vision and crisis—obviously for love" (4). Such commentary complements the critical analyses Welty included in her letters to Robinson (See Correspondence Calendar for 1948–1949) and suggests Welty's increasing self-consciousness about her fiction.

The manuscripts composing the Eudora Welty Collection at the Mississippi Department of Archives and History provide a remarkably comprehensive view of Eudora Welty's writing career. In spanning the years from 1925 to 1983, they show her work as fiction writer, as reviewer and critic, as dramatist, and as her own biographer. And they document the routes individual works followed from conception to publication. These manuscripts thus immeasurably enrich our understanding of one of the twentieth-century's finest writers.

2

In time, a barometer was added to our dining room ~~where we~~ also
~~kept the encyclopedia~~ and ~~unabridged dictionary.~~ (We ~~had~~ ready ~~reference~~
~~while we were eating.~~ ~~Our dining room showed up in an entirely~~ different
~~family in my novel Delta Wedding.~~)

My father had the ~~country boy's~~ accurate knowledge of the weather ~~and its~~
skies. He went out and stood on our front steps first thing in the morning
and took ~~a~~ look at it. He was a pretty good weather prophet.

"Well, I'm ~~~~ not," my mother would say with enormous self-satisfacti

He told us children what to do if we were lost in strange country.
"Look for where the sky is brightest along the horizon," he said. "That
reflects the nearest river. ~~Strike~~ out for a river and you will find habita-
tion." Eventualities were much on his mind. In his care for us children
he cautioned us to take measures against such things as being struck by
lightning. He drew us all away from the windows during the severe
electrical storms that are common where we lived. My mother ~~stood apart~~,
scoffing at caution as a character failing. "Why, I always loved a storm!
High winds never bothered me in West Virginia! Just listen at that! I wasn't a bit afraid
of a little lightning and thunder! I'd go out on the mountain and spread
my arms ~~w~~ wide and run in a good big storm!"

So I developed a strong meteorological sensibility. In years
ahead when I wrote stories, atmosphere took its influential role
from the start. ~~A warranted role, I think.~~ Commotion in the weather
and the inner feelings ~~that~~ such a hovering disturbance aroused emerged
connected in dramatic form. [I tried a tornado first.
("The Winds," ~~209-10 Coll. St.~~)]
115-17, 118-20 Josie aroused by the sound of wind in the night, at first mistakes it for the train cries of a...

A page from the 1983 William E. Massey, Sr., Lectures in the History of
American Civilization, which were subsequently published in a revised form
as *One Writer's Beginnings*.

Eudora Welty

Russell & Volkening, Inc.

522 Fifth Avenue, New York City

The Flower and the Rock

One morning at breakfast Francis Dowdie was looking over his paper and
without a thought, when his wife said something innocent to him--"Crumb on
your chin" or the like--he leaned over the dishes on the table and slapped
her face with the flat of his hand. They were in their forties, married
twelve years--she was the older.

He waited for her to say "Francis Dowdie!" Almost leisurely--at least,
he sighed--he got up from the table and walked out of the kitchen, keeping
his paper; usually he deposited it in Emma's hands simultaneously with
kissing her goodbye.

He listened for "Francis Dowdie?" to follow him around the door into the
chill of the hall. He was half smiling as he remembered little Fan's fly-away
habit of answering her mother, and the sticking out of her two plaits behind
her as she ran off, the fair hair screwed up to the first tightenings of
vanity. "That's my name." She had now been dead a year.

He put on his raincoat and hat, and secured his paper under his arm with
two foldings that crackled. Emma was still sitting all the way back in her
chair at the table, with her Chinese robe just now settling in a series of
faint puffs about her, and her too-small, fat feet, as if they had been the
most outraged, apart and outthrust below. He knew from the other room the way

A page from an early version of "Music from Spain"

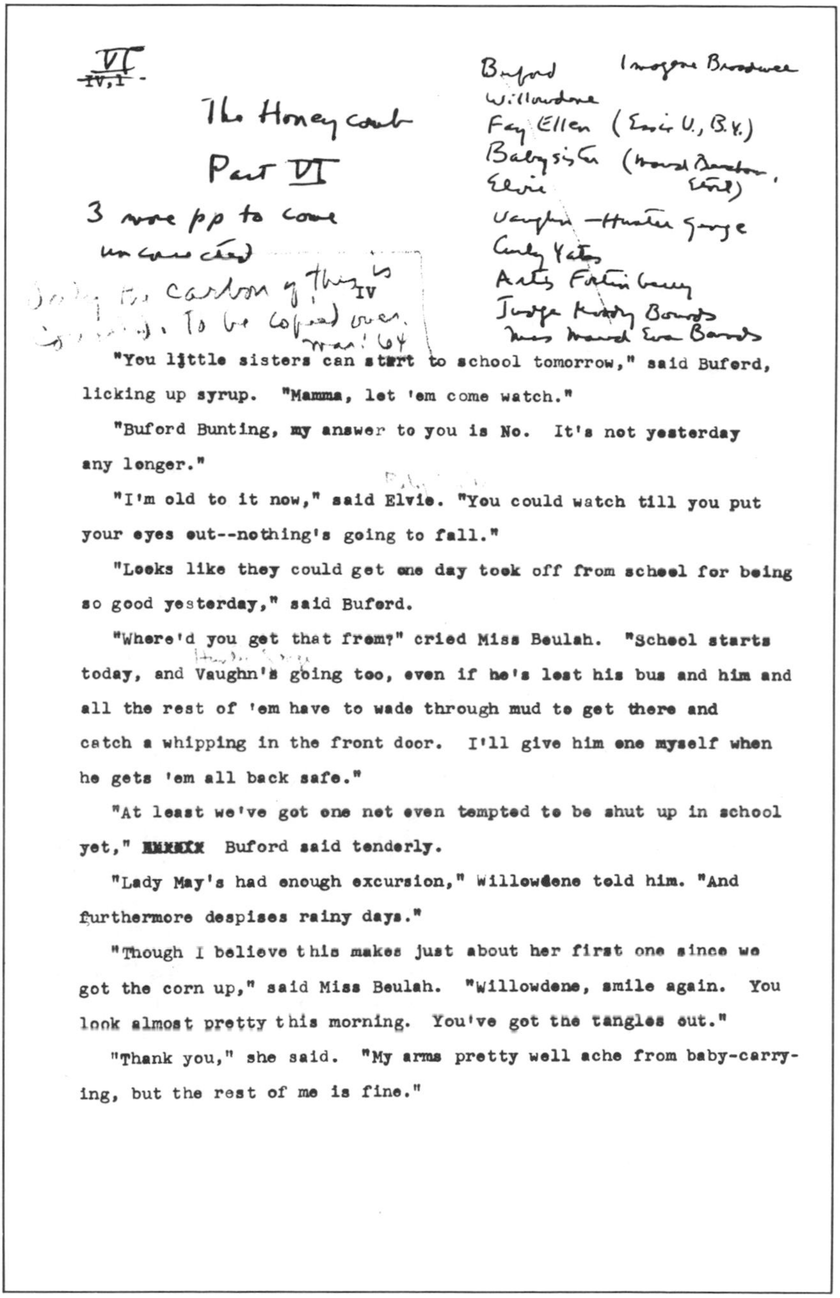

The Honeycomb

Part VI

3 more pp to come
uncorrected

[handwritten, partly illegible] the carbon of this IV
[...]. To be copied over.
Mar. '64

[handwritten character list, right margin:]
Buford — Imogene Broadwax
Willowdene
Fay Ellen (Emir U., B.Y.)
Baby sister (*[illegible]*, *[illegible]*)
Elvie
Vaughn — Hunter Gorge
Curly Yates
Aunt Fortune*[illegible]*
Judge *[illegible]* Bonds
Mrs *[illegible]* Eva Bonds

"You little sisters can start to school tomorrow," said Buford,
licking up syrup. "Mamma, let 'em come watch."

"Buford Bunting, my answer to you is No. It's not yesterday
any longer."

"I'm old to it now," said Elvie. "You could watch till you put
your eyes out--nothing's going to fall."

"Looks like they could get one day took off from school for being
so good yesterday," said Buford.

"Where'd you get that from?" cried Miss Beulah. "School starts
today, and Vaughn's going too, even if he's lost his bus and him and
all the rest of 'em have to wade through mud to get there and
catch a whipping in the front door. I'll give him one myself when
he gets 'em all back safe."

"At least we've got one not even tempted to be shut up in school
yet," Buford said tenderly.

"Lady May's had enough excursion," Willowdene told him. "And
furthermore despises rainy days."

"Though I believe this makes just about her first one since we
got the corn up," said Miss Beulah. "Willowdene, smile again. You
look almost pretty this morning. You've got the tangles out."

"Thank you," she said. "My arms pretty well ache from baby-carry-
ing, but the rest of me is fine."

A page from the 1964 draft of *Losing Battles*

I. BOOKS OF FICTION

Welty's books of fiction are listed chronologically by publication date. Typescripts of each book appear in the order of their composition. Typescripts of stories that Welty has not grouped into volumes appear in the order in which they appeared in the published volume; if there is more than one draft of such stories, the drafts have been placed together in order of composition.

The following abbreviations are used in Chapter One:
EW = Eudora Welty
n.d. = no date
ts = typescript
ms = manuscript

A. A Curtain of Green (1941)
(Archives Series 2)

Drafts of Individual Stories

A1. "Keela the Outcast Indian Maiden." n.d.
Carbon ts; pages [1]–10; almost clean copy.
A2. "Why I Live at the P.O." n. d.
Carbon ts; pages [1]–13; almost clean copy; the text varies substantially from published versions of the story and from the version in "Stories" (A4); holograph note to John Robinson at the head of page 1: "my new theme read it & throw it away." [John Fraiser Robinson is a Delta native, a one-time Jackson resident, EW's longtime friend, and the author of stories published in *Harper's Magazine* and the *New Yorker*.]
A3. "Clytie." n.d.
Carbon ts; pages [1]–13; almost clean copy; holograph note to John Robinson at the top of page 1: "How are you? I've just been to Rodney in a regular Texas wind—Love E-"; EW has drawn a sketch of the wind-blown car and labeled it: "The car from rear"; an arrow extends from label to drawing.

Preliminary Collection

A4. "Stories." ca. 1939/1940

Ts; 2 preliminary pages, 215 subsequent pages, including a title page at the head of each story; the first preliminary page has a Russell & Volkening grey mailing label attached and "STORIES by Eudora Welty" typed on the label; the second preliminary page is a table of contents with holograph notations by Welty, primarily dating the periodical publications of the stories listed; the title "Acrobats in a Park" has been lined out and the holograph title "A Worn Path" substituted; nevertheless, "Acrobats in a Park" is included in the typescript and "A Worn Path" is not. EW appears to have retyped from periodical versions, typically with some alterations, all stories published before 1941; "Clytie," "The Key," "Why I Live at the P.O.," "A Visit of Charity," and "Powerhouse" had not yet been accepted for publication when EW prepared this typescript; holograph notations on the table of contents identify the periodicals where these stories were eventually accepted and suggest a reordering of the stories. It seems likely that this typescript circulated among publishing houses during 1940.

Front matter. n.d. 2 pages.

"Lily Daw and the Three Ladies." n.d.
Title page, pages [1]–13; holograph revisions.

"Clytie." n.d.
Title page, pages [1]–13; numerous holograph revisions.

"A Piece of News." n.d.
Title page, pages [1]–8; numerous holograph revisions.

"Petrified Man." n.d.
Title page, pages [1]–16; holograph revisions.

"Death of a Traveling Salesman." n.d.
Title page, pages [1]–18; numerous holograph revisions.

"The Whistle." n.d.
Title page, pages [1]–7; numerous holograph revisions.

"The Key." n.d.
Title page, pages [1]–12; almost clean copy.

"Why I Live at the P.O." n.d.
Title page, pages [1]–15; holograph revisions.

"A Curtain of Green." n.d.
Title page, pages [1]–8; holograph revisions.

"Keela the Outcast Indian Maiden." n.d.
Title page, pages [1]–10; holograph revisions.

"The Hitch-Hikers." n.d.
Title page, pages [1]–17; holograph revisions.

"Old Mr. Granada." n.d.
Title page, pages [1]–8; numerous holograph revisions.

"Acrobats in a Park." n.d.
Title page, pages [1]–11; a few holograph revisions.

"Flowers for Marjorie." n.d.
Title page, pages [1]–13; numerous holograph revisions.

"A Visit of Charity." n.d.
Title page, pages [1]–7; holograph revisions.

"A Memory." n.d.
Title page, pages [1]–8; holograph revisions.

"Powerhouse." n.d.
Title page, pages [1]–14; almost clean copy.

Typescript Setting Copy of Collection

A5. "A Curtain of Green." 1941.
Ts; 7 preliminary pages; pages [1]–220, including individual title pages for all stories except "Lily Daw and the Three Ladies"; after the first story, the pages have been renumbered so that pagination is continuous; numerous editorial corrections; a few holograph revisions by EW; an occasional editorial query and authorial response.

Front matter. 1941. 7 pages.
"Lily Daw and the Three Ladies." Pages [1]–13.
"A Piece of News." Pages 14–22.
"Petrified Man." Pages 23–40.
"The Key." Pages 41–54.
"Keela, the Outcast Indian Maiden." Pages 55–65.
"Why I Live at the P.O." Pages 66–82.
"The Whistle." Pages 83–90.
"The Hitch-Hikers." Pages 91–110.
"A Memory." Pages 111–119.
"Clytie." Pages 120–134.
"Old Mr. Marblehall." Pages 135–144.
"Flowers for Marjorie." Pages 145–157.
"A Curtain of Green." Pages 158–166.
"A Visit of Charity." Pages 167–175.

"Death of a Traveling Salesman." Pages 176–192.
"Powerhouse." Pages 193–208.
"A Worn Path." Pages 209–220.

B. THE WIDE NET (1943)
(Archives Series 3)

Drafts of Individual Stories

B1.   "The Wide Net." n.d.
Ts; pages [1]–25, blue cover and green end pages; a few holograph corrections; a holograph note on page [1]: "To John [Robinson] who told it to me to begin with-."
B2.   "A Still Moment (An Imaginary Encounter)." n.d.
Carbon ts; pages [1]–7, 9–15; because of misnumbering, there is no page 8, almost clean copy.
B3.   "Asphodel." 1942.
Carbon ts; pages [1]–12; almost clean copy.
B4.   "The Purple Hat." n.d.
Carbon ts; pages [1]–9; a few holograph corrections.
B5.   "At the Landing." 1942.
Carbon ts; pages [1]–23; almost clean copy; one major transposition of material is yet to be made.

C. DELTA WEDDING (1946)
(Archives Series 4)

Preliminary Story

C1.a.   "The Delta Cousins." [1942].
Ts; pages [1]–36, title and end pages; the title page is on grey Russell and Volkening letterhead construction paper; a few holograph revisions and corrections; also listed as IV.A5.a.
C1.b.   "The Delta Cousins." 1942.
Carbon ts; pages [1]–36 (pages [1]–6, 8–35 are on recto and verso sides of 17 sheets of paper) and an 11.05. [1942] holograph note from EW to John Robinson; carbon of C1.a above; at the time of donation, EW dated this ts as 1942; it may, however, date from 1943; a few holograph additions and corrections; holograph notes to Robinson on pages 14 and 16; also listed as IV.A5.b.

Typescript Setting Copy of Novel

C2. "Delta Wedding." 1945.
Ts; pages 1–239 plus pages 31A, 120A, 137A, 142A, 228A, 229A, 2 carbons inserted to substitute for pages 132–35, 2 blank pages, and an MDAH title page; paste-overs and holograph revisions; the carbon substitutes for pages 132–35 call for changes in the galleys; editorial corrections; some editorial comments or queries and some authorial responses.

D. THE GOLDEN APPLES (1949)
(Archives Series 5)

Drafts of Individual Stories

D1. "Golden Apples." n.d. [Later titled "June Recital."]
Carbon ts; pages [1]–81, plus 66A, front and rear cover pages; page 77 is a paste copy; holograph revisions scattered throughout the typescript; on the construction paper cover EW has written in ink "Golden Apples" and in pencil "Extra copy—carbon."
D2. "Sir Rabbit." n.d.
Carbon ts; pages [1]–12, 14–15; there is no page 13; the text varies substantially from the published version of the story; at the head of the ts a holograph note to John Robinson reads: "I realize all is risked on every sentence—let me know if you think it works—or not—Please—Yours, E-Suddenly all aweary-."
D3. "The Flower and the Rock." 1947. [Later titled "Music from Spain."]
Carbon ts, incomplete; pages [1]–34; the final pages of the story are missing; a few holograph revisions and corrections. Sent to John Robinson, 1947.
D4. "The Humming-Birds." n.d. [Later titled "The Wanderers."]
Carbon ts, incomplete; pages [1]–9; a few holograph revisions and corrections.

Typescript Setting Copy of Collection

D5. "The Golden Apples." n.d.
Ts; pages 8–309, as renumbered; holograph revisions and corrections; at least one addition in an editorial hand.

> "Shower of Gold." Pages 8–26; some pages in elite type, others in pica.

"June Recital." Pages 27–111; header "Golden Apples" has been lined out; typed in pica.

"Sir Rabbit." Pages 112–127; typed in pica.

"Moon Lake." Pages 128–178; typed in pica.

"The Whole World Knows." Pages 179–206; use of italics called for by pencilled underlining.

"Music from Spain." Pages 207–255; primarily in elite type but including two pica pages.

"The Wanderers." Pages 256–309; typed title "The Kin" has been deleted and holograph title "The Wanderers" added; header "The Kin" is erased on some pages while header "The Humming-Birds" is erased on some others; some pages in elite type, others in pica.

Galleys

D6. "The Golden Apples." 1949.
Galleys 1–78; unmarked.

E. THE PONDER HEART (1954)
(Archives Series 6)

Preliminary Drafts

E1. "The Ponder Heart." n.d.
Ts; 1 preliminary page, pages [1]–42, 44–55, 57–96, plus 1A, 29A, 40A, 53A, 4 unnumbered pages or partial pages, an extra page numbered 57, an extra page numbered 59; pages 43 and 56 are missing; pages 44–51 are carbons; numerous holograph revisions; on the preliminary page EW has written "The Ponder Heart my copy -Corrected version Some pages missing or on carbon."

E2. "The Ponder Heart." n.d.
Carbon ts; title page, pages [1]–105, plus pages 43A, 51A, rear cover; pages 43A-51, 67, 92, 102 are ribbon pages; holograph title page in red pencil, "The Ponder Heart"; scattered holograph corrections throughout; incorporates revisions made in E1 above.

Mimeographed Typescript
Prepared for Book-of-the-Month Club

E3.a. "The Ponder Heart." 1953. 1 item.
Pre-publication, mimeographed copy; soft-bound by publisher; 2

preliminary pages, pages 1–141; holograph corrections scattered throughout; "a novel by" on title page has been lined out; table of contents has a penciled "X" over it; the headings "Chapter 1," etc., have been lined out in pencil; EW has written on cover "Corrected Copy|My copy|Eudora."

E3.b. "The Ponder Heart." 1953. 1 item.
Pre-publication, mimeographed copy; soft-bound by publisher; 2 preliminary pages, pages 1–141.

Galleys

E4. "The Ponder Heart." 1953.
Galleys 1–41; a few editorial corrections in margin; no authorial corrections; dated Sept. 24.

F. The Bride of the Innisfallen (1955)
(Archives Series 7)

Drafts of Individual Stories
"NO PLACE FOR YOU, MY LOVE"

F1. "No Place for You, My Love." n.d.
Ts; pages [1]–24 plus a second version of page 2; numerous holograph revisions, including revision of the title from "The Gorgon's Head" to "No Place for You, My Love."

F2. ["No Place for You, My Love."] n.d.
Ts, incomplete; pages 8, 11, a page headed "Galley 14," pages 12, 12, 14, 17–18, 20 insert, 20–21, 23–25; 2 pages are carbons; numerous holograph revisions; incorporates the changes EW calls for in F1 above.

F3. "No Place for You, My Love." 1952.
Tear sheets from *New Yorker* 20 Sept. 1952: 37–44.

"THE BURNING"

F4.a. "The Ghosts." n.d.
Ts; pages [1]–22 and cover page on grey Russell and Volkening letterhead construction paper; holograph revisions; seems to be the earliest version of the story; holograph note from EW on the cover: "Published in another version as 'The Burning.' Published in another altered version in *Collected Stories*."

F4.b.   "Harm's Way?" n.d.
Carbon ts; pages [1]–22; a carbon of "The Ghosts," described in F4.a above; holograph title; a few holograph revisions.
F5.   "Miss Theo, Miss Myra, Florabel." n.d.
Carbon ts; pages [1]–19; holograph title; holograph revisions.
F6.a.   "The Burning." n.d.
Carbon ts; pages [1]–19, an additional page 17; holograph revisions; incorporates changes suggested in "Miss Theo, Miss Myra, Florabel" (F5 above); EW's holograph notation on page 1 reads: "2nd version published *Harper's Bazaar*."
F6.b.   ["The Burning."] n.d.
Carbon ts, pages 15–19; clean copy; another carbon of pages 15–19 as described in F6.a above, but sent to John Robinson with item described in F5 above.
F7.   "The Burning." n.d.
Carbon ts, pages [1]–20, plus page 2A; almost clean copy; a few revisions and corrections; EW's holograph notation on page 1 reads "Not last version."
F8.a.   "The Burning." n.d.
Ts; pages [1]–20, plus page 2A; pages 1–14 are ribbon originals of the carbons described in F7 above; pages 15–16 vary from the carbons because of cut/paste revisions; pages 17–20 are newly typed sheets; numerous holograph revisions; EW's holograph notation at head of the ts reads: "Last version (?)."
F8.b.   ["The Burning."] n.d.
Carbon ts; pages 17–20; carbons of pages 17–20 described in F8.a above; uncorrected.

"THE BRIDE OF THE INNISFALLEN"

F9.   ["The Bride of the Innisfallen."] n.d.
Carbon ts, incomplete; pages 13–42, with an additional page 20; holograph revisions to this draft typed into subsequent drafts.
F10.a.   "The Bride of the Innisfallen." n.d.
Ts; pages [1]–42; a few holograph revisions; EW's signature at the top of page [1].
F10.b.   "The Bride of the Innisfallen." n.d.
Carbon ts; pages [1]–42; pages 1–35 are purple carbons, pages 36–42 are black carbons; purple carbons are carbons of pages [1]–35 described in F10.a above; holograph revisions to black carbons conform to typed text in F10.a above.

F11.   "The Bride of the Innisfallen." n.d.
Tear sheets, the *New Yorker* 1 Dec. 1951: 53–56, 58, 60, 62, 64, 66, 68, 70–84; numerous holograph revisions.

"LADIES IN SPRING."

F12.   "Ladies in Spring." n.d.
Carbon ts; pages [1]–19; holograph and typed revisions; one addition in a hand other than EW's; holograph title revised three times: the penciled phrase "The Ladies of" has been added to the ink title "Spring," and the entire title has then been rejected; the title "The Ladies are Coming" has also been rejected in favor of "Ladies in Spring."

"CIRCE"

F13.   "Circe." n.d.
Carbon ts; pages [1]–11; a few holograph revisions; EW has written "Last version" at the head of page [1].

"KIN"

F14.a.   "Kin." n.d.
Ts; pages [1]–44, plus pages 17A, 37A, 40A; holograph revisions.
F14.b.   "Kin." n.d.
Carbon ts; holograph title page, pages [1]–44, plus 17A, 37A, 40A; carbon of ts described in F14.a above, except for title page and page 22; holograph and typed alterations are designed to make this version conform to version in F14.a above, though some changes have not been made; queries in a hand other than EW's.
F15.   "Kin." n.d.
Ts, incomplete; pages 1, 43, 44, 45, 46, 50, 51; numerous holograph revisions which typically conform to the text of the story in *The Bride of the Innisfallen*, an indication that these pages were written after those described in F14.a and F14.b above.
F16.   "Kin." 1952.
Tear sheets from the *New Yorker* 15 Nov. 1952: 39–48, 50, 52–54, 56, 58–60, 62, 64–67.

"GOING TO NAPLES"

F17.a.   "The Mother of Us All." n.d.
Ts; pages [1]–59 plus pages 41A, 52A, cover and end pages; a few holograph revisions; the grey Russell & Volkening cover contains the title and EW's holograph note: "Early version of 'Going to Naples.'"

F17.b. "The Mother of Us All." n.d.
Carbon ts; pages [1]–59, plus 22A, 41A, 52A, and an additional page 45; identical to ribbon ts listed in F17.a above, except for page 22A and the additional page 45; a few holograph alterations designed to make this version conform with the version described in F17.a above; a manila envelope stored with this draft has EW's holograph notation, "Carbon of original of 'Going to Naples.' "
F18. ["Going to Naples."] n.d.
Carbon ts; pages [1]–53; two titles have been typed in ribbon and then rejected—"The Pitcher at the Fountain" has been lined out in ink, "Going to Naples" lined out in pencil; holograph revisions.

G. THE SHOE BIRD (1964)
(Archives Series 9)

Preliminary Drafts of Book

G1. "Pepe, the Shoe-Bird " 1963
Carbon ts; pages 1–23, 25–84, 12A, cover and end pages; pages 62 & 63, 73 & 74 are single pages; page 24 is missing; EW has dated this ts as April 1963; though EW has noted that this carbon is uncorrected, there are holograph corrections and revisions in the text.
G2. "The Shoe Bird." n.d.
Carbon ts; pages [1]–83, plus 14A, 18A, 28A, 45A, 47A, 72A, 82A; variant pages 81, 81A, and 82 have been stapled together; holograph name and address on page [1]; holograph revisions.
G3. "The Shoe Bird." 1964.
Carbon ts; pages [1]–97, title page, envelope in which ts was stored; on envelope EW notes that this version of the story was typed from her corrected carbon (see G2 above), March 1964; EW also notes that she sent the ribbon copy to *Why Not*.

Typescript Setting Copy of Book

G4. "The Shoe Bird." n.d.
Ts; pages 1–83, plus pages 18A, 28A, 45A, 69A, 82A, and carbon of page 32; authorial and editorial holograph revisions.

Galleys

G5. "The Shoe Bird." 1964.
First proof; galleys 1–28; EW's holograph revisions and corrections;

galleys dated April 6, 1964; EW's holograph note on reverse of galley 28 reads "my set|Corrected April 12, 1964."

G6. "The Shoe Bird." 1964.

Second proof and carbon ts; galleys 1–28, pages [1]–3; galleys dated May 4, 1964; a few holograph revisions and corrections; three carbon pages list the revisions and corrections to be made in galleys.

H. LOSING BATTLES (1970)
(Archives Series 11)

Incomplete Drafts

H1. "Losing Battles," Part 2. 1961.

Carbon ts; pages [1]–80, plus page 18-A, 12 unnumbered pages, 3 small pieces of paper, and envelope in which ts was stored; one page is numbered "52 & 53"; numerous holograph and typed revisions; a holograph note on the envelope reads, "Part II of Losing Battles |1961|corrected carbon of my original|91 pages"; a small green piece of paper contains the holograph notation: "Part II 'Losing Battles' '61 |This carbon|is obsolete|corrected carbon of my original, 91 pages."

H2. "Losing Battles," Part 2. 1963.

Ts; 122 pages, 2 slips of paper, and envelope in which ts was stored; two pages are carbons; a few holograph revisions; written in episodes which are typically numbered with a coded heading ("II,ul,3," for example, refers to the third page of the "up leap" episode); one of the slips of paper stored with typescript reads, "Pages un-numbered but in sequence|This version of Chapter II is out-of-date Oct:63"; the episodes are largely out of sequence despite Welty's note to the contrary; a holograph note on the envelope reads, "Part II of Losing Battles| 1963, my typed original|120 pages, unnumbered but in|sequence."

H3. "Losing Battles," Part 6. 1964.

Ts; pages [1]–63 and envelope in which ts was stored; holograph revisions; a holograph note on the envelope reads, "Part VI of Losing Battles ('The Honeycomb')|1964 My original|uncorrected|63 pages"; list of character names on page [1].

H4. "Losing Battles," Part 1. 1965.

Ts; pages s1-s78 plus pages 2-a, 3-a, 27-a, 29-a, 41-a, 50-a, 53-a, 60-a, and pages j1-j42, 2 blue pages, 1 slip of paper, and envelope in which ts was stored; one page is both j20 and j21; numerous typed revisions pasted to sheets and numerous holograph revisions; a holograph note on the envelope reads, "From Part I of Losing Battles, '65|old chapter

2 78 pages|old chapter 3 42 pages|Original"; on the first blue page EW
dates the old chapter 2 typescript as "'65 or '66."

H5.   "Losing Battles," Part 2. 1965.

Ts; pages 1–173, plus pages 2-A, 42-A, 76-A, 101-A, 109-A, 127-A,
162-A, 165-A, an additional page numbered 59, an additional page
numbered 60, one unnumbered page, a typed insert numbered 115,
11 variant pages, and envelope in which ts was stored; variant pages
appear at the head of the typescript; numerous typed revisions
pasted onto sheets; numerous holograph revisions as well; a holo-
graph note on the envelope reads, "Part II of Losing Battles|1965|184
pages, my typed original|numbered, as sent to a typist."

Complete Draft

H6.a.   "Losing Battles." [1968]–1969.

Ts; pages 1–341, IV 1-IV 119, V 1-V 90, VI 1–59, VI 61-VI 92, VI 95-VI
110, plus pages 328-a, 332-a, IV 87-A, IV 116-A, V-3A, VI 94-A, VI 98-
A, VI 105-A, VI 105-B, title page, 31 variant pages, 1 slip of paper, 1
MDAH envelope, 1 folder, and 2 Eaton's Berkshire Typing Paper box
lids; one page in Part I is numbered 93 & 94; pages VI 60, VI 93, and
VI 94 are missing; numerous revisions are typed and pasted to sheets;
numerous holograph revisions have been made; a slip of paper contains a typist's note; on the first box lid EW has written: "*Losing Bat-
tles*|pages|1-|252|my original|1969"; on the second she has written:
"My Original (Pasted Copy)|as sent|to typist|not in final revision|
From p. 252|(in II)|to end of V"; on folder EW has written "Losing
Battles|Part VI 107 pages|Paste Copy|my orig."

H6.b.   "Losing Battles." 1968–69.

Ts, photocopy; pages 1–341, IV 1–81, IV 83, IV 85-IV 119, V 1-V 67,
V 69-V 90, VI 33-VI 92, plus pages 328-a, 332-a, IV 87-A, V 41-A, 37
variant pages, and 6 envelopes in which ts was stored; pages 93 &94
are one page; pages IV-82, IV-84, V-68 are missing; Part VI contains
only pp. 33–92; primarily a photocopy of the ts described in H6.a
above; some pages are carbons; others are typed or photocopied
sheets which are not identical to the ribbon pages described in H6.a;
many holograph revisions which tally with the revisions to ribbon ts
(H6.a), others which have not been made there; some revisions to the
ribbon ts (H6.a) have not been made here; on the first envelope is
the holograph note, "Losing Battles|Xerox of my original|Part I-151
pages|Lacks final revisions November '68"; on the label attached
to the second envelope is the holograph note, "Losing Battles|Part

II|Xerox of my original sent to typist|Lacks final revisions 115 pp November '68"; on the label attached to the third envelope is the holograph note, "Losing Battles|Xerox of my original|Part III|Lacks final corrections 74 pp Jan. '69"; on the fourth envelope is the holograph note, "*Losing Battles*|Xerox of my original|Lacks final revisions"|Part IV|A. 1–50 pp.|B. 51–85|C. 86–119|add 82, 84, 87-A"; on the fifth envelope is the holograph note: "*Losing Battles*|Part V Xerox of my Original|Lacks final corrections 120 pp"; on the sixth envelope is the holograph note, "*Losing Battles* Xerox of my original|Part VI, in part|beginning and ending included in|Xeroxed substitute pages."

Typescript Setting Copy and Carbons

H7.a. "Losing Battles." 1969.
Ts; pages 1–782 plus page 43A and an additional page 12; pages 1–782 renumbered in the lower right-hand corner of each page; 8 preliminary pages, 6 pages identifying sections of the novel, 770 pages of text; some pages are photocopies; numerous revisions, occasionally in EW's hand but more typically in an editorial hand or hands.

H7.b. "Losing Battles." [1969].
Carbon ts; pages [1]–750, plus pages 12-A, 25-A, 28-A, 33-A, 59-A, 71-A, 79-A, 86-A, 118-A, 151-A, 182-A, 230-A, 232-A, 238-A, 252-A, 281-A, 320-A, 343-A, 347-A, 354-A, 354-B, 376-A, 382-A, 530-A, 630-A, 651-A, 6 preliminary pages, and an additional page 12; one page is numbered 190 & 191; another is numbered 296–297; primarily a carbon of the ts described in H7.a above; some pages are ribbon pages or photocopies; numerous revisions, primarily in EW's hand, but occasionally in an editorial hand; numerous deletions.

H7.c. "Losing Battles." [1969].
Carbon ts; pages [1]–677, 679–750, plus pages 12-A, 25-A, 28-A, 33-A, 59-A, 71-A, 79-A, 86-A, 118-A, 151-A, 182-A, 230-A, 232-A, 252-A, 281-A, 320-A, 343-A, 354-A, 354-B, 444-A, 444-B, 444-C, 530-A, 651-A, 3 preliminary pages, 2 pages with holograph comments, and 14 variant or duplicate pages; one page is numbered 190 & 191; another is numbered 296–297, 298; pages 376-A and 678 are missing; primarily a carbon of the ts described in H7.a above; some pages are photocopies; numerous holograph revisions, some of which do not appear in the setting copy or the previous carbon but which will be incorporated into the galleys and the novel; two holograph pages concern additions, the other acknowledges a missing page.

Materials from the Printer

GALLEYS

H8.a. "Losing Battles." 1969.

Galleys 1–172, plus galley 8B, an extra galley 133, and envelope in which galleys were stored; labeled "E's set" in an editorial hand on galley 1; numerous holograph revisions and corrections; editorial queries and EW's responses; the envelope is addressed to EW, Jackson, with return address, "Erskine|Random House|201 E 50 New York 10022," postmarked 12.22.1969. [Albert Erskine was EW's editor at Random House.]

H8.b. "Losing Battles." 1969.

Galleys 1–172, galley 8B, an extra galley 8, an unnumbered galley, and 3 typed pages; master set, proofed and corrected, Nov. 6–13, 1969; corrections in an editorial hand; alterations in an editorial hand in accord with EW's instructions; one insert of 14 typed lines on galley 31 concerns burning of courthouse; insertion of pp. 444A, 444B, 444C on galley 104-A concerns Dr. Carruthers's attendance at the birth of Jack Renfro.

H8.c. "Losing Battles." [1969].

Galleys 70, 92, 121, 125, 139, 164; pencilled note on galley 70 reads: "Added corrections, pages 12/29–30"; EW's holograph corrections.

H8.d. "Losing Battles." [1969].

Galleys 8 and 8B, unmarked.

H9.a. "Losing Battles." [1969].

Photocopies of galleys; 3 copies of galley 8, three copies of galley 8A, three copies of galley 8B.

H9.b. "Losing Battles." [1969].

Ts, photocopy; 8 photocopies of typed insertion for galley 31 (see H8.b above).

PAGE PROOF

H10.a. "Losing Battles." 1969.

92 unnumbered galley pages and one typed page; identified as "Master Set 12/19/69," but the set is incomplete; includes pages 160–436 of novel's text, except that the galley containing pages 316–318 is missing; the typed page is headed "About the Author" and dated 12.10.1969; corrections in an editorial hand.

H10.b. "Losing Battles." 1969.

56 unnumbered galley pages; identified as "Master Set 12/23/69"; 10

preliminary pages and pages [1]–159 of the novel; corrections, instructions in an editorial hand.

MECHANICALS

H11. "Losing Battles." 1969. 9 pieces.
Ad card and false title, title page, title page art, logo for title page, map, pmt map #1, pmt map #2, rules for half title and part title pages, art for part title pages.

REPROS

H12. Memorandum concerning "Losing Battles" repros. 1970.
Bland Simpson to Book Press, 01.30.1970.
H13.a. "Losing Battles." 1970.
22 repro sheets (4 pages to a sheet), a photocopy of the publication information page (vi); repros include pages ii-27 (9 sheets), 44–47, 84–87, 104–107, an additional repro of pages 20–23, 3 repros of pages vi, 23, 26, 45, and 3 repros of pages 86 and 105.
H13.b. "Losing Battles." 1970.
108 repro sheets which include preliminary pages, pages 1–19, 28–43, 48–83, 88–437, and pages 432–35 on two half-sheets; pages 20–27, 44–47, 84–87 are missing; some autograph instructions to the printer on the preliminary pages.
H13.c. "Losing Battles." [1970].
111 repro sheets which include 2 preliminary sheets and 109 subsequent sheets containing pages [1]–431, 436–37; the sheet containing pages 432–35 is missing; some autograph notations on the preliminary pages; a note on a cardboard divider reads "Gave Bob Or page 432–435."

BLUES

H14.a. "Losing Battles." 1969. 6 pieces.
Blues of title page art, map, part title page art, photocopy of part title page art, a blank page, and a 12.29.1969 letterhead memorandum from Harry Conover, Random House, to Book Press.
H14.b. "Losing Battles." 1970.
1 signature, including 10 preliminary pages, page [1] which is a part title page, page [2] which is blank, and pages 3–22 of text.

I. The Optimist's Daughter (1972)
(Archives Series 12)

THE NEW YORKER Story

EARLY DRAFTS AND WORKING PAPERS

I1. "Baltimore." n.d.

Ts; pages [1]–5, 7–18, 20–21, 23–41, plus page 30a, an additional page 9, and a slip of paper; pages 6, 19, and 22 are missing; the holograph title, "An Only Child," is written above the typed title, "Baltimore"; holograph revisions; slip of paper following page 29 contains a holograph note: "Use carbon to correct this part by."

I2. "An Only Child." n.d.

Carbon ts; pages [1]–43, plus 37 unnumbered pages, 13 variant pages (hand-numbered pages 31–34 and 9 unnumbered pages), and a folder in which the ts was stored; holograph revisions; a holograph note on page [1]: "77 pp. (Carbon of earlier version, end missing) Later *The Optimist's Daughter*"; a holograph note on the folder, "*An Only Child*|early draft"; seems to be a later version of "Baltimore."

I3. "An Only Child." 1967. 17 pieces.

Carbon and ribbon pages from a draft or drafts of "An Only Child" plus folder in which pages were stored and a holograph note; many of the pages have pin-ons; numerous holograph revisions; EW has written on the folder: "The Changes|An Only Child|Feb. '67|as typed."

I4. "Poor Eyes." n.d.

Ts; pages [1]–96, plus 4A, 6A, 16A, 39A, 86A, 3 variant pages, a small yellow sheet of paper, and the envelope in which the ts was stored; pages 66 and 67 are one sheet; title "Poor Eyes" is a holograph revision of typed title, "The Optimist's Daughter"; holograph revisions throughout; many paste-overs; the pencil markings in the margins of this draft indicate parallel pages in the *New Yorker* typescript setting copy (I5.a); revisions and corrections to this draft typically have been incorporated into the *New Yorker* typescript setting copy (I5.a); on a small sheet of yellow paper enclosed with the ts is a holograph note, "My Original Typescript of *The Optimist's Daughter*."

TYPESCRIPT SETTING COPY AND CARBON

I5.a. "Poor Eyes." 1967.

Ts; pages [1]–114 of text, a page with holograph note, "Original New Yorker MS," and a page describing the ts, partially in EW's hand;

originally titled "The Optimist's Daughter," but the title has been lined out and the title "Poor Eyes" written above it; holograph revisions, editorial changes throughout; revisions tend to be minor, involving the change of a word or phrase.

I5.b.   "The Optimist's Daughter." 1967.
Carbon ts; pages [1]–114, title page, and pink folder with holograph title; carbon of I5.a above; on the title page, the typed title "The Optimist's Daughter" has been lined out; "Poor Eyes" is written above in ink and lined out; "The Optimist's Daughter" is written above that in pencil; a pencilled question mark occurs next to the original typed title; holograph revisions.

GALLEYS

I6.   "The Optimist's Daughter." 1967.
Galleys 1–70 and envelope in which they were stored; last pink galleys of "The Optimist's Daughter" for the *New Yorker*; dated June 13, 1967; a few holograph corrections and revisions; editorial corrections; on the *New Yorker* envelope addressed to Mrs. C.W. Welty is EW's holograph note: "The Optimist's Daughter|Pink galleys (last)."

The Random House Novel

COMPLETE DRAFT

I7.   "The Optimist's Daughter." n.d.
Ts; pages 1–41, 43–167, plus 25A, 35A, 52A, 110A, 114A; there is no page 42; holograph revisions throughout, primarily of words or phrases; substantial deletions; expands upon the *New Yorker* version; many paste-overs, often using photocopied sheets.

TYPESCRIPT SETTING COPY AND AUTHOR'S DUPLICATE COPY

I8.a.   "The Optimist's Daughter." n.d.
Ts, photocopy; pages 8–181, 7 preliminary pages; though this is the setting copy used at Random House, it is a primarily a photocopy of I8.b below; pages 8 and 160 are photocopies of pages 1 and 146 in the ts described in I7 above; there are stamped page numbers in the bottom right-hand corner of each page; legal size paper; holograph revisions; notes from EW to Albert Erskine, her editor; an editorial hand has recopied some of EW's revisions, probably to make them legible; some transpositions, insertions, and deletions not made in the ts described in I7 above.

I8.b.   "The Optimist's Daughter." 1971.
Ts, photocopy; pages 1–167, plus pages 25A, 35A, 52A, 110A, 114A, envelope in which ts was stored, and 3 small yellow pages of notes (encapsulated as one); pages 41 & 42 are one sheet as are pages 148 & 149; a photocopy of the ts described in I7 above, except that pages 1 and 146 are photocopies of pages 8 and 160 in the ts described in I8.a above; identical to Random House setting copy except for some holograph revisions which will be incorporated in the galleys; on the envelope in red ink is the holograph note, "The Optimist's Daughter|only Xerox|as typed up, August, Sept. 1971|to be corrected," and in black ink is the holograph note, "corrected & revised, Oct. 1971"; in the three holograph pages of notes, EW has matched page numbers from the galleys and the ts with some descriptions of revisions.

MATERIALS FROM THE PRINTER

Galleys

I9.a.   "The Optimist's Daughter." [1971].
Galleys 1–58 and envelope in which galleys were returned to FW; EW's holograph revisions and corrections; editorial corrections; numerous queries from Albert Erskine to EW and from EW to Erskine, with their respective replies; most revisions involve only a word or phrase; one deletion of several lines.

I9.b.   "The Optimist's Daughter." 1971.
Galleys 1–58 with photocopy of a 12.30.1971 ts letterhead memo from Ines Alfano, Random House, to Pam Pierce, Book Press, attached to back of galley 58; the galleys are identified as "Master Set 12/2/71"; the memo provides instructions for producing page proof; revisions and corrections suggested by EW in her set of galleys (I9.a) have been made here in an editorial hand.

I9.c.   "The Optimist's Daughter." [1971].
Galleys 1–58; unmarked.

Page Proof

I10.a.   "The Optimist's Daughter." 1972.
95 galley sheets (preliminary pages, pages 3–180, a concluding biographical page), a photocopied page concerning layout, and a photocopy of a 01.28.1972 ts letterhead memo from Barbara Lauster, Random House, to Pam Pierce, Book Press (layout page and memo encapsulated as one); the page proof is identified as "Master Set 1/14/

72"; the memo concerns the production of blues; editorial corrections, primarily of punctuation; two marginal notes in EW's hand.

I10.b. "The Optimist's Daughter." [1972].
95 galleys sheets; unmarked.

Repros

I11.a. "The Optimist's Daughter." [1972].
48 repro sheets which include preliminary pages and pages 3–181; some printer's markings.

I11.b. "The Optimist's Daughter." [1972].
48 repro sheets which include preliminary pages and pages 3–181; slip-sheeted.

Blues

I12. "The Optimist's Daughter." 1972.
6 signatures (10 preliminary pages, pages 3–180 of text, concluding biographical page), 2 dittoed copies of a "Change Order," dated 03.02.1972 and giving instructions to check margins, to set new lines for CR page, and to have that new set-up approved; the only editorial markings on the blues appear on the copyright page and page 25.

Final Signatures

I13. *The Optimist's Daughter.* 1972.
Unbound, typeset copy; 6 signatures (10 preliminary pages, pages 3–180 of text, concluding biographical page); unmarked.

J. ACROBATS IN A PARK
(This very early story was published in a limited, collector's edition by Lord John Press in 1980.)

J1. "Acrobats in a Park." ca. 1934.
Ts; pages [1]–11; pages 5–11 are carbons; holograph revisions. EW has dated the ts as "1934 (?)." This ts is part of Archives Series 1; see III.A1.

J2. "Acrobats in a Park." n.d.
Ts; title page, pages [1]–11; a few holograph revisions; included in an early version of the book to be titled *A Curtain of Green*. This ts is part of Archives Series 2; see I.A4.

K. The Collected Stories of Eudora Welty (1980)

Typescripts of Individual Stories Not Previously Collected

"where is the voice coming from?"
(Archives Series 8)

K1.a.   ["Where is the Voice Coming From?"] [1963].
Ts; pages [1]–8, plus additional pages numbered 3, 5, 6, 7; the typed title *"From the Unknown*|A Voice from a Jackson Interior|June 14" is lined out; two holograph titles, "It Ain't Even July Yet" and "Voice from an Unknown Interior," are also lined out; EW has written in parentheses "All discarded titles"; numerous holograph revisions, some of them changing names of actual people and places to fictitious ones; holograph comments in margins; EW labels this ts "1st Original" on page [1]; EW may have made holograph marginal comments for use by John Kuehl in preparing *Write and Rewrite: A Study of the Creative Process* (New York: Meredith Press, 1967).
K1.b.   *"From the Unknown*|A Voice from a Jackson Interior|June 14." [1963].
Carbon ts; pages [1]–7; a few holograph revisions; pages 1, 2, and 4 are carbons of pages described in K1.a; pages 5, 6, and 7 are carbons of the second versions of pages described in K1.a; the actual names of individuals and places are still included.
K2.   ["Where is the Voice Coming From?"] [1963].
Ts and carbon ts pages [1], [1], [1], [1], [1], 3, 3, 3, 4, 4, 5, 5, 5–7, 8, 8, 8; ribbon and carbon page [1], with holograph title "From my Room" on ribbon copy; carbon page [1] with title *"Where is the Voice Coming From?"* and with several holograph alternative titles; carbon page [1] with title *"Where is That Voice Coming From?"*; carbon page [1] with title "Where Is the Voice Coming From?"; ribbon and two carbon versions of page 3; ribbon and carbon page 4; ribbon and carbon page 5; carbon pages 5–7; ribbon and carbon page 8; carbon of another page 8; holograph revisions.
K3.a.   "Where is the Voice Coming From?" [1963].
Ts; pages 1–8; typescript setting copy for the *New Yorker*; a few holograph revisions.
K3.b.   "Where is the Voice Coming From?" [1963].
Carbon ts; pages 1–8; carbon of the ts described in K3.a above, except for page 1 which is a ribbon copy; holograph corrections; some revisions not made on *New Yorker* setting copy; EW's holograph marginal

comments; this version and the one described in K1.a. may have been used by Kuehl in preparing *Write and Rewrite: A Study of the Creative Process.*

K4.   "Where is the Voice Coming From?" [1963].
Galleys 1–10; galleys for the *New Yorker*, dated June 26, 1963; a few editorial corrections.

"THE DEMONSTRATORS"
(Archives Series 10)

K5.   "The Demonstrators." [1966].
Carbon ts; pages 1–22, plus 19a and folder in which ts was stored; holograph revisions; holograph title; some paste-overs; the folder contains holograph notes concerning the revision of *Losing Battles*.

Page Proof of Entire Collection
(Archives Series 13)

K6.   "The Collected Stories of Eudora Welty." [1980].
333 galley sheets which include 18 preliminary pages, pages 3–622, and duplicates of pages 306–31; holograph revisions and corrections; one substantial typed revision on page 185; duplicates of pages 306–13 bear EW's holograph notation "My copy."

L. RETREAT
(This early short story was published in a limited, collector's edition by
Palaemon Press in 1981.)

L1.   "Retreat." ca. 1936.
Ts; pages [1]–7; clean copy. Welty has written at the top of page 1, "This was published in River (1936) (?)"; actually published in *River* in 1937. This ts is part of Archives Series 1; see III.A5.

II. OTHER BOOKS

Books are listed chronologically by publication date. Drafts of books appear in the order of their composition. Typescripts of essays that Welty has not grouped into volumes appear in the order in which they appeared in the published volume. If there is more than one draft of an essay, the drafts have been placed together in the order of composition.

A. One Time, One Place (1971)
(Archives Series 14)

Draft of Foreword

A1. Foreword to "One Time, One Place." n.d.
Ts, photocopy; pages [1]–2, 4–7, and a page misnumbered as 2 but actually page 3.

Materials from the Printer

GALLEYS

A2. Foreword and photograph captions for "One Time, One Place." n.d.
Galleys 1–6; corrected by EW.

MECHANICALS

A3. "One Time, One Place." n.d.
14 preliminary pages, pages 3–114, enlarged copy of preliminary page listing "Books by Eudora Welty" and enlarged copy of preliminary page giving publication information and acknowledgments; pictures on pages iv, 19, 47, 68, and 82 are missing; there are editorial instructions for the printer to shoot or reshoot four of the missing pictures.

BLUES

A4.a. "One Time, One Place." n.d.
8 signatures; 14 preliminary pages, pages [1]–114; directions to printer made in pencil and in blue and red ink; stamped "OK to print as corrected."
A4.b. "One Time, One Place." n.d.
8 signatures; 14 preliminary pages, pages [1]–114; a few directions to printer; stamped "OK to print as corrected."

FINAL PAGES

A5. "One Time, One Place." n.d.
One large sheet of uncut, unfolded pages containing 31 photographs for *One Time, One Place*; includes photographs appearing on pages 64, 53, 56, 61, 72, 77, 69, 80, 68, 81, 73, 76, 57, 60, 52, 65, 96, 85, 88, 93, 104, 109, 101, 112, 100, 113, 108, 105, 92, 89, 84, 97.

B. Fairy Tale of the Natchez Trace (1975)
(Archives Series 15)

Preliminary Speech

B1.   Untitled speech. 1975.
Ts; pages 1–23; some pages are partially carbons; numerous holograph revisions; paste-overs, pin-ons; long quotations from *The Robber Bridegroom* have been photocopied from the book and pasted to sheets of typing paper; the speech was delivered to the Mississippi Historical Society in Jackson, Miss.; the March 1 date assigned to the speech is an error, for the speech was delivered on March 7, 1975.

Draft of Essay

B2.   "Fairy Tale of the Natchez Trace." 1975.
Ts; pages [1]–19, 3 preliminary pages; holograph revisions.

Typescript Setting Copy

B3.   "Fairy Tale of the Natchez Trace." 1975
Ts, photocopy; pages [1]–19, 2 preliminary pages; photocopy of B2 above.

Materials from the Printer

GALLEYS

B4.   "Fairy Tale of the Natchez Trace." 1975
Galleys 1–6; unmarked.

PAGE PROOF

B5.   "Fairy Tale of the Natchez Trace." 1975
Pages 7–27, 4 preliminary pages, a colophon; unmarked.

FINAL PAGES

B6.a.   "Fairy Tale of the Natchez Trace." n.d.
1 sheet containing pages 19–21 as printed; on reverse of page 21 is a description of the printing as done by Heritage Printers, Inc. of Charlotte, N.C.
B6.b.   "Fairy Tale of the Natchez Trace." n.d.
1 sheet containing pages 19–21 as printed; on reverse of page 21 is a description of the printing as done by Heritage Printers, Inc. of Charlotte, N.C.; identical to B6.a above.

C. The Eye of the Story (1978)
(Archives Series 16)

Typescripts of Individual Essays and Reviews

"THE RADIANCE OF JANE AUSTEN"

C1. Untitled. 1968.
Ts; pages 1–12, plus corrected carbon of page 7; a speech delivered at Millsaps College, Jackson, Miss.; clean copy except for holograph revision on carbon.

C2. "Jane Austen." n.d.
Carbon ts; pages [1]–5; an essay for *Atlantic Brief Lives*, ed. Louis Kronenberger (Boston: Little, Brown, 1971); holograph revisions.

C3. "Jane Austen." 1970.
Galleys [15]–17; an essay for *Atlantic Brief Lives*, ed. Louis Kronenberger; a few holograph revisions and corrections; returned to EW by Atlantic Monthly Press, 05.15.1970.

"HENRY GREEN: NOVELIST OF THE IMAGINATION"

C4. "Novelist of the Imagination." 1961.
Ts, photocopy; pages [1]–14, 16–20, page 15 is missing; published in *Texas Quarterly* 4 (1961): 246–56.

"KATHERINE ANNE PORTER: THE EYE OF THE STORY"

C5. "The Eye of the Story." 1965.
Ts; pages [1]–11 plus pages 5A and 6A; numerous paste-ons and holograph revisions; EW's holograph notation reads, "Draft Sept. 29, 1965"; published in *Yale Review* 55 (1965): 265–74.

"THE HOUSE OF WILLA CATHER"

C6. "The Physical World of Willa Cather." 1973.
Ts, photocopy; pages [1]–8, plus page 4A; beneath title is an identification of the essay, "Taken from a talk delivered at an International Seminar on 'The Art of Willa Cather' at the University of Nebraska at Lincoln. (Oct. 1973)"; later published in *NYTBR* 27 Jan. 1974: 19, 20, 22; EW's holograph notation reads, "Use complete version in book."

"WRITING AND ANALYZING A STORY"

C7. "Writing and Analyzing a Story." 1955.
Ts, photocopy; pages [1]–5; notation reads, "From *The Virginia Quarterly Review*, Vol 31, No. 2, Spring 1955 Revised in part from 'How I Write'"; pages [1]–4 are photocopies of the carbon typescript pages

described in C19 below; page 5 is a photocopy of part of page 5 described in C18 below and of ribbon page 116 in C19 below.

"WORDS INTO FICTION"

C8.a.   "The Opening Sentence." n.d.
Ts; pages [1]–15 and a new first paragraph on separate sheet; some pages are carbons; some pages use paste method; numerous holograph revisions; EW's holograph notation reads, "Use SR version"; published as "Words into Fiction." *SoR* I n.s. (1965): 543–53.
C8.b.   "The Opening Sentence." n.d.
Ts, photocopy; incomplete; photocopy of ts described in C8.a.
C8.c.   "Words into Fiction." n.d.
Ts, photocopy; pages 1–15, plus ribbon ts of page 15; pages 1–14 are photocopies of ts described in C8.a; holograph revisions and instructions to typist or printer.

"MUST THE NOVELIST CRUSADE?"

C9.   "An Interior Affair." 1966.
Ts; pages [1]–3, 5–8, plus a variant page 3 and an unnumbered page; a lecture given at Millsaps College, Jackson, Miss.; appeared in the *Atlantic Monthly* as "Must the Novelist Crusade?" (*Atlantic Monthly* Oct. 1965: 104–08).
C10.   Untitled. n.d.
Ts; 16 full sheets of paper and two parts of sheets; some sheets are numbered, but they are not in sequence; working papers for "Must the Novelist Crusade"; a few holograph comments or revisions.

REVIEWS

C11.   *The Western Journals of Washington Irving.* 1944.
Carbon ts; pages [1]–3; published under title "Skies without a Cloud." *NYTBR* 24 December 1944: 3.
C12.a.   *Granite and Rainbow. Essays by Virginia Woolf.* 1958.
Ts, photocopy; pages [1]–4; primarily a photocopy of the carbon ts described in C18 below; published under title "Uncommon Reader." *NYTBR* 21 September 1958: 6.
C12.b.   *Granite and Rainbow. Essays by Virginia Woolf.* 1958.
Ts, photocopy; pages [1]–3, incomplete; primarily a photocopy of the carbon ts described in C18 below; published under title "Uncommon Reader." *NYTBR* 21 September 1958: 6.
C13.   *Charlotte's Web.* By E. B. White. 1952.
Carbon ts; pages [1]–4; a carbon of the ts described in C19 below;

published under title "'Life in the Barn Was Very Good.'" *NYTBR* 19 October 1952: 49.

C14. *Marianne Thornton: A Domestic Biography, 1797–1887.* By E. M. Forster. 1956.
Carbon ts, page 6, incomplete; published under title "The Thorntons Sit for a Family Portrait." *NYTBR* 27 May 1956: 5.

C15.a. *Baby, It's Cold Inside.* By S. J. Perelman. 1970.
Carbon ts; pages [1]–5; cut and paste revisions; published under title "S. J. Perelman Should be Declared a Living National Treasure." *NYTBR* 30 August 1970: 1, 25.

C15.b. *Baby, It's Cold Inside.* By S. J. Perelman. 1970.
Ts, photocopy; pages [1]–5; published under title "S. J. Perelman Should be Declared a Living National Treasure." *NYTBR* 30 August 1970: 1, 25.

"SOME NOTES ON RIVER COUNTRY"

C16. "Some Notes on River Country." 1943.
Carbon ts; pages [1]–21; mailed to John Robinson overseas; holograph note to Robinson on page 1; a few holograph corrections and additions; published in *Harper's Bazaar* Feb. 1944: 86–87, 150–56.

Projected Front Pages of Collection

C17. "Projected Front Pages for 'The Eye of the Story.'" n.d.
Ms and ts; 13 pages; a three-page holograph list of "Times Book Reviews to Xerox"; a two-page holograph list of reviews to be photocopied; a two-page carbon ts of contents for *The Eye of the Story*, with holograph revisions; a two-page ts (photocopy) outline or plan for *The Eye of the Story*, with holograph revisions and with citations for previously published essays; a ts (photocopy) page of acknowledgments, thanking editors of various publications for permissions to republish; a three-page carbon ts of "Specific Credits" for the essays to compose the collection; a manila folder with holograph notation, "Projected|Front pages for|'The Eye of the Story.'"

Author's Copy of Collection

C18. "Xerox & Carbon Copies of Non-fiction 1944–1976 (selected)." n.d.
Carbon ts, photocopied ts, original pages from published essays and reviews, photocopies of published items; 277 pages; the table of contents lists four pieces that will be deleted from *The Eye of the Story*—1)

Rev. of *A Haunted House*. By Virginia Woolf (1958); 2) Rev. of *Henry Green: Nine Novels and an Unpacked Bag*. By John Russell (1961); as well as 3) "From Where I Live" (1969); 4) "Fairy Tales" (published as "And They All Lived Happily Ever After," *NYTBR* 10 Nov. 1963, sec. II: 3); no copy of "Fairy Tales" is included with this ts; several pieces included in *The Eye of the Story* are not here—"The House of Willa Cather," "Reality in Chekhov's Stories," the review of *Names on the Land* by George R. Stewart, "A Sweet Devouring," and "The Flavor of Jackson."

"THE EYE OF THE STORY. Contents." n.d.
Carbon ts; 2 pages; table of contents; holograph question mark about deleting the V. Woolf review; a delete symbol is next to the Russell review.

"The Radiance of Jane Austen." n.d.
Ts, photocopy; pages [1]–13; published in shorter form in *Shenandoah* 20 (Spring 1969): 3–7 and in *Atlantic Brief Lives*, ed. Louis Kronenberger (Boston: Little, Brown, 1971), 23–25; C19 describes another photocopy of the ts.

"Henry Green|A Novelist of the Imagination." n.d.
Photocopied from *Texas Quarterly* 4 (Autumn 1961): 246–56.

"The Eye of the Story." n.d.
Photocopied from *Yale Review* 55 (1965): 265–74.

"Looking at Short Stories." n.d.
Ts, photocopy; pages [1]–20; photocopies of some typed, some printed, and some combined pages; printed pages copied from *Three Papers on Fiction* (Northhampton, Mass.: Smith College, 1962); a photocopy of ts described in C19 below; an essay originally delivered in another form as a lecture titled "Some Views on the Reading and Writing of Short Stories" (University of Washington, 1947); then published in a shorter form as "The Reading and Writing of Short Stories," *Atlantic* Feb. 1949: 54–58, March 1949: 46–49; subsequently published in full in a limited edition as *Short Stories* (New York: Harcourt, Brace and Company, 1949).

"Writing and Analyzing a Story." n.d.
Ts, photocopy; pages [1]–10; a photocopy of the ts and carbon ts pages described in C19 below; revised in part from "How I Write," *VQR* 31 (1955): 240–51.

"Place in Fiction." n.d.

Photocopied from *SAQ* 55 (1956): 57–72; some deletions have been made.

"Words into Fiction." n.d.

Photocopied from *Three Papers on Fiction*, pages 16–25.

"Must the Novelist Crusade?" n.d.

Photocopied from *Atlantic* 216 (Oct. 1965): 104–108.

"'Is Phoenix Jackson's Grandson Really Dead?'" 1974.

Carbon ts; pages [1]–5; holograph revisions; C19 describes a photocopy of this carbon ts; published in *Critical Inquiry* I (1974): 219–21.

"Some Notes on Time in Fiction." n.d.

Ts, photocopy; pages [1]–13; C19 describes another photocopy of the ts; published in *MQ* 26 (1972–73): 483–92.

"Skies Without a Cloud." Rev. of *The Western Journals of Washington Irving*. n.d.

Photocopied from *NYTBR* 24 Dec. 1944: 3.

Rev. of *A Haunted House, and Other Short Stories*. By Virginia Woolf. 1944.

Carbon ts; pages [1]–4; published under title "Mirrors for Reality," in *NYTBR* 16 April 1944: 3.

Rev. of *Granite and Rainbow. Essays by Virginia Woolf*. 1958.

Carbon ts; pages [1]–4; there are photocopies of this carbon ts described in C12.a, C12.b, and C19; published under title "Uncommon Reader," in *NYTBR* 21 Sept. 1958: 6.

Rev. of *The Letters of Virginia Woolf, Vol. II: 1912–1922*. n.d.

Ts, photocopy; pages [1]–12; a photocopy of the carbon ts described in C19 below; published in *NYTBR* 14 Nov. 1976: 1, 10, 12, 14, 16, 18, 20.

Rev. of *Charlotte's Web*. By E. B. White. n.d.

Ts, photocopy; pages [1]–4; a photocopy of the ribbon ts described in C19 below; published under title "'Life in the Barn Was Very Good,'" in *NYTBR* 19 October 1952: 49.

"In Yoknapatawpha." Rev. of *Intruder in the Dust*. By William Faulkner. n.d.

Photocopied from *Hudson Review* I (1949): 596–98.

Rev. of *Selected Letters of William Faulkner*. 1977.

Carbon ts; pages [1]–9; a carbon of the ribbon ts described in C19 below; published in *NYTBR* 6 Feb. 1977: 1, 28–30.

Rev. of *Marianne Thornton: A Domestic Biography, 1797–1887*. n.d.
Ts, photocopy; pages [1]–6, plus "new page 6"; primarily a photo-copy of carbon ts described in C19 below; C14 above describes a carbon of old page 6; holograph revisions; published under title "The Thorntons Sit for a Family Portrait," in *NYTBR* 27 May 1956: 5.

Rev. of *The Life to Come and Other Stories*. By E. M. Forster. n.d.
Ts, photocopy; pages [1]–8; a photocopy of carbon ts described in C19 below; published under title "A Collection of Old New Stories by E. M. Forster," in *NYTBR* 13 May 1973: 27–28, 30.

Rev. of *Henry Green: Nine Novels and an Unpacked Bag*. By John Russell. 1961.
Carbon ts; pages [1]–5; page 5 is a ribbon page; C19 below de-scribes a photocopy of this carbon ts; published under title "Life's Impact is Oblique," in *NYTBR* 2 April 1961: 5.

Rev. of *The Most of S. J. Perelman*. 1958.
Carbon ts; pages [1]–5; C19 below describes a photocopy of this carbon ts; published under title "All is Grist for His Mill," in *NYTBR* 12 October 1958: 4, 14; a holograph note on page 5 reads, "Add from review of 'Baby, It's Cold Inside' 1970."

From rev. of *Baby, It's Cold Inside*. By S. J. Perelman. n.d.
Ts, photocopy; pages [1]–2; photocopy of ribbon ts described in C19 below; a shortened version of published review; published under title "S. J. Perelman Should be Declared a Living National Treasure," in *NYTBR* 30 August 1970: 1, 25.

Rev. of *The Saddest Story, A Biography of Ford Madox Ford*. By Ar-thur Mizener. n.d.
Ts, photocopy; pages [1]–11; a photocopy of the carbon ts de-scribed in C19 below; a few holograph revisions; published un-der title "The Saddest Story," in *NYTBR* 2 May 1971: 1, 14, 16, 18.

Rev. of *The Underground Man*. By Ross Macdonald. 1971.
Clipped from *NYTBR* 14 Feb. 1971: 1, 28–30, and pasted to two sheets of paper; published under title "The Stuff that Nightmares Are Made Of."

Rev. of *Last Tales*. By Isak Dinesen. 1957.
Carbon ts; pages [1]–3; C19 describes a photocopy of this carbon ts; published under title "A Touch That's Magic," in *NYTBR* 3 Nov. 1957: 5.

Rev. of *The Cockatoos*. By Patrick White. n.d.
Ts, photocopy; pages [1]–6; a photocopy of the carbon ts described in C19 below; published under title "Life's Possibilities Are Those Very Things Once Felt as Dangers," in *NYTBR* 19 Jan. 1975: 4, 37.

Rev. of *Pictures and Conversations. Chapters of an Autobiography. With other collected writings*. By Elizabeth Bowen. 1975.
Carbon ts; pages [1]–9; C19 below describes a photocopy of this carbon ts; holograph revisions; published under title "As If She Had Been Invited into the World," in *NYTBR* 5 January 1975: 4, 20.

"Some Notes on River Country." n.d.
Photocopied from *Harper's Bazaar* Feb. 1944: 86–87, 150–56.

"Fairy Tale of the Natchez Trace." n.d.
Ts, photocopy; pages [1]–19; a copy of the ts described in II.B2; C19 below describes another photocopy of the ts; substantial deletions; originally a paper delivered to the Mississippi Historical Society 7 March 1975; published by the Society in 1975.

"Pageant of Birds." n.d.
Photocopied from *New Republic* 25 October 1943: 565–67.

"From Where I Live." 1969.
Original page from *Delta Review* 6 (Nov./Dec. 1969): 69.

"The Little Store." n.d.
Ts, photocopy; pages [1]–10; a photocopy of the carbon ts described in C19 below; holograph revision of title; published under title "The Corner Store," in *Esquire* Dec. 1975: 161, 212, 215.

"Ida M'Toy." n.d.
Photocopied from *Accent* 2 (Summer 1942): 214–22; holograph revisions.

Foreword to *One Time, One Place*. n.d.
Ts, photocopy; pages [1]–2, 4–7, and a page misnumbered as 2 but actually page 3; II.A1 describes another photocopy of the ts; published as foreword to *One Time, One Place* (New York: Random House, 1971).

Setting Copy of Collection

C19. "The Eye of the Story." n.d.
Ts, carbon ts, photocopied ts, original pages from published essays and reviews, photocopies of published items; 366 pages; pages

1–349, plus 12 preliminary pages, pages 86a, 166a, 204a, 271a, and an unnumbered page; a few holograph revisions; includes "From Where I Live," "Fairy Tales," and reviews of *A Haunted House* and *Nine Novels and an Unpacked Bag*, all of which were ultimately deleted from the collection.

Front matter. 12 pages.

I. On Writers

"The Radiance of Jane Austen." n.d.
Ts, photocopy; pages 1–13; C18 above includes another photocopy of the ts.

"Henry Green: Novelist of the Imagination." 1961.
Original pages from the *Texas Quarterly* 4 (Autumn 1961) have been pasted to sheets of typing paper; pages 14–24.

"Katherine Anne Porter: The Eye of the Story." 1965.
Original pages from the *Yale Review* 55 (1965) have been pasted to sheets of typing paper; pages 25–34.

"The House of Willa Cather." 1974.
Ts; pages 35–60; the text of an address given at the University of Nebraska for an international seminar on "The Art of Willa Cather"; the ts is dated 1974, but the seminar was held in 1973.

"Reality in Chekhov's Stories." 1977.
Ts, photocopy; pages 61–86.

II. On Writing

"Looking at Short Stories." n.d.
Ts and printed pages; pages 87–106; some typed, some printed, some combined pages; printed pages are from *Three Papers on Fiction* (Northhampton, Mass.: Smith College, 1962); C18 includes a photocopy of this ts.

"Writing and Analyzing a Story." n.d.
Ts and carbon ts; pages 107–116; pages 107–110 are carbons; remaining pages are ribbon copies; C19 above includes a photocopy of this ts.

"Place in Fiction." n.d.
Photocopy; pages 117–132; copied from *South Atlantic Quarterly* 55 (1956); two paragraphs have been marked for deletion.

"Words into Fiction." n.d.
Photocopy; pages 133–143; copied from *The Southern Review* I n.s. (1965).

"Must the Novelist Crusade?" n.d.
Photocopy; pages 144–148; copied from *The Atlantic* Feb. and March, 1949.

"'Is Phoenix Jackson's Grandson Really Dead?'" n. d.
Ts, photocopy; pages 149–153; a photocopy of the carbon ts described in C18 above.

"Some Notes on Time in Fiction." n.d.
Ts, photocopy; pages 154–166; C18 above describes another photocopy of the ts.

III. Reviews

"The Western Journals of Washington Irving." n.d.
Photocopy; page 167; copied from *NYTBR* 24 Dec. 1944.

"George R. Stewart's *Names on the Land.*" n.d.
Photocopy and nine typed lines; pages 168–172; copied from *NYTBR* 6 May 1945: 1, 14, 15.

"Virginia Woolf's *A Haunted House.*" n.d.
Photocopy; pages 173–174; copied from *NYTBR* 16 April 1944.

"Virginia Woolf's *Granite and Rainbow.*" n.d.
Ts, photocopy; pages 175–178; primarily a photocopy of carbon ts described in C18 above.

"The Letters of Virginia Woolf, Volume II." 1976.
Carbon ts; pages 179–190; pages 189 and 190 are photocopies; a photocopy of this ts is described in C18 above.

"E.B. White's *Charlotte's Web.*" 1952.
Ts; pages 191–194; a carbon of this typescript is described in C13 above; a photocopy of this ts is described in C18 above.

"William Faulkner's *Intruder in the Dust.*" n.d.
Photocopy; pages 195–197; copied from *Hudson Review* I (1949).

"Selected Letters of William Faulkner." 1977.
Ts; pages 198–205; C18 above describes a carbon of this ts.

"E. M. Forster's *Marianne Thornton.*" 1956.
Carbon ts; pages 206–211; page 211 is a ribbon copy; four different paper stocks are part of this ts; C18 above describes a photocopy of this carbon ts.

"E. M. Forster's *The Life to Come.*" 1973.
Carbon ts; pages 212–219; C18 above describes a photocopy of this carbon ts.

"John Russell's *Nine Novels and an Unpacked Bag*." n.d.
Ts, photocopy; pages 220–224; a photocopy of carbon ts described in C18 above.

"*The Most of S. J. Perelman*; S. J. Perelman's *Baby, It's Cold Inside*." n.d.
Ts, photocopy; pages 225–231; pages 225–229 are photocopies of carbon pages described in C18; pages 230–231 are ribbon pages; C18 describes carbons of pages 230–231.

"Arthur Mizener's *The Saddest Story*." 1971.
Carbon ts; pages 232–242; C18 above describes a photocopy of this carbon ts.

"Ross Macdonald's *The Underground Man*." n.d.
Ts, photocopy; pages 243–253; page 251 is a carbon.

"Isak Dinesen's *Last Tales*." n.d.
Ts, photocopy; pages 254–256; C18 above describes a carbon of the ts.

"Patrick White's *The Cockatoos*." 1975.
Ts and carbon ts; pages 257–262; pages 257–258 are ribbon copies; pages 259–262 are carbons; C18 above describes a photocopy of this ts.

"Elizabeth Bowen's *Pictures and Conversations*." n.d.
Ts, photocopy; pages 263–271; a photocopy of the carbon ts described in C18 above.

IV. Personal and Occasional Pieces

"*A Sweet Devouring*." 1957.
Photocopy; pages 272–278; copied from book published by Albondocani Press (New York, 1969).

"*Some Notes on River Country*." n.d.
Photocopy; pages 279–288; page 288 is a typed page; copied from *Harper's Bazaar* Feb. 1944.

"*Fairy Tales*." n.d.
Photocopy; pages 289–90; copied from *NYTBR* 10 Nov. 1963.

"*Fairy Tale of the Natchez Trace*." n.d.
Ts, photocopy; pages 291–309; a photocopy of the ts described in II.B2; C18 above describes another photocopy of the ts.

"*A Pageant of Birds*." 1943.
Carbon ts; pages 310–316.

"From Where I Live." 1969.
Carbon ts; pages 317–320.

"The Flavor of Jackson." n.d.
Photocopy; pages 321–323; copied from *The Jackson Cookbook* (Jackson, Miss.: Symphony League of Jackson, 1971, n. pag.).

"The Little Store." 1975.
Carbon ts; pages 324–333; C18 above describes a photocopy of this carbon ts; holograph revision of title.

"Ida M'Toy." n.d.
Photocopy; pages 334–342; copied from *Accent* 2 (Summer 1942).

"One Time, One Place." n.d.
Photocopy; pages 343–348; page 344 is a typed page; copied from *One Time, One Place* (New York: Random House, 1971).

"About the Author." n.d.
Ts, photocopy; page 349; biographical sketch of EW.

Materials from the Printer

GALLEYS

C20.a.   "The Eye of the Story." n.d.
Galleys 1–194; author's set of galleys; EW suggests deletion of reviews of *A Haunted House* and *Nine Novels and an Unpacked Bag* and of essays titled "From Where I Live" and "Fairy Tales"; a few holograph corrections and revisions; deletions (a three-paragraph deletion from "Place in Fiction," galley 70, a longer one still from "Fairy Tale of the Natchez Trace," galley 169); queries to editor Albert Erskine.

C20.b.   "The Eye of the Story." n.d.
Galleys 1–194; master set of galleys; a few editorial corrections and revisions; substantial deletions, including deletion of four entire pieces: reviews of *A Haunted House* and of *Nine Novels and an Unpacked Bag*, "Fairy Tales," and "From Where I Live"; revisions and deletions as suggested by EW on her set of galleys (C20.a) have been incorporated here.

PAGE PROOF

C21.   "The Eye of the Story." n.d.
Galley pages 1–181; master set; contains 5 preliminary pages and pages 3–357; editorial corrections only.

MECHANICALS

C22.   "The Eye of the Story." n.d.
Mechanicals of title page and of four part title pages; stored with C24.a below.

C23.a.   "The Eye of the Story." n.d.
Photocopies of the various type settings for title, chapter headings, section headings, identification of publisher; 9 pages; master set.

C23.b.   "The Eye of the Story." n.d.
Photocopies of the various type settings for title, chapter headings, section headings, identification of publisher; 9 pages; the word "REVISED" is stamped in blue on this set.

REPROS

C24.a.   "The Eye of the Story." n.d.
183 repro sheets; 178 whole sheets (two book pages per sheet), 5 half sheets; pages vi, x, 85, 177, 276 are on half sheets; there are no pages 82, 84, 174, 176 because these are blank pages; editorial corrections; essay titles pasted at the head of essays; preliminary pages III and IV have the words "Random House" and a device pasted to the repro sheet.

C24.b.   "The Eye of the Story." n.d.
179 repro sheets; sheet containing pages 50–51 is missing; pages 83 and 85 are one sheet as are pages 175 and 177; there are no pages 82, 84, 174, 176 because these are blank pages.

C24.c.   "The Eye of the Story." n.d.
5 repro sheets; 1) title and credits, 2) pages 50–51, 3) page 50 alone on sheet, 4) page 51 alone on sheet, 5) credits alone on sheet; editorial revisions on title and credit pages and on pages 50 & 51.

BLUES

C25.   "The Eye of the Story." n.d.
12 signatures; preliminary pages i–x, pages [1]–355, a blank page, and a biographical page; unmarked.

D. BYE-BYE BREVOORT
(This dramatic sketch was published in a limited collector's edition by New Stage Theatre of Jackson, Mississippi, in 1980.)

D1.   "Bye Bye Brevoort." n.d.
Carbon ts; pages 1–14; part of an unpublished revue containing

sketches written by EW and by Hildegarde Dolson; included in Archives Series 21, IV.B2.a; see also Chapter 5, VII.A9.

D2. "Bye Bye Brevoort." n.d.
Carbon ts; pages 1–15; holograph note reads, "copy 4." This ts is part of Archives Series 21, IV.B2.b; see also Chapter 5, VII.A9.

E. ONE WRITER'S BEGINNINGS (1984)
(Archives Series 17)

William E. Massey Sr. Lectures in the
History of American Civilization, Harvard University

E1. ["One Writer's Beginnings."] 1983.
Ts; Part I, pages 1–42, plus 2A, 10A, 10B; Part II, pages 1–26, 28-[32], plus photocopies of pages 22-[32] and a variant page 10; Part III, pages 1–29; a holograph page identifying this ts and the ts described in E2 below; pages 28 & 29 in Part I are one sheet; lectures given at Harvard University and later revised and published as *One Writer's Beginnings*; holograph revisions and corrections; many pages with additions or revisions pinned or pasted on; some photocopied pages.

Drafts of Book

E2. ["One Writer's Beginnings."] [1983]
Ts,incomplete; Part I, pages 1–40; Part II, pages 1–30, plus section title page and page 8A; Part III, 23 pages; pages 8, 9, 10, and 11 in Part I are one sheet as are pages 21 & 22; paste copy for retyping; some photocopied pages; holograph revisions.

E3.a. "One Writer's Beginnings." [1983]
Ts; 135 pages, including 3 preliminary pages, pages 1–88 (Parts I and II), page 12A, an unnumbered title page for Part II, pages 1–42 (Part III), an unnumbered title page (Part III), and page 15A (Part III); pages 4&5 (Parts I and II) are actually one page as are pp. 53&54 (Parts I and II); holograph revisions throughout, typically involving a word or phrase; a few large deletions; some paste-overs.

E3.b. ["One Writer's Beginnings."] [1983]
Ts, photocopy; incomplete; pages 1–34; photocopy of E3.a above; a few holograph revisions and corrections.

E4.a. "One Writer's Beginnings." [1983]
Ts, photocopy; 135 pages, including prologue, pages 1–53, 55–130, 12A, 40A, 44A, and duplicates of pages 43, 44, 44A; pages 4 & 5 are

one sheet; primarily a photocopy of E3.a above, but some ribbon and carbon pages; two pages not included in E3.a; holograph revisions and corrections; transposition of material.

E4.b. "One Writer's Beginnings." [1983]
Ts, photocopy; 129 pages including pages 1–130, 44A, and a page of prologue; pages 4&5, 34&35, 53&54, 56&57 are single pages; an additional page 92; primarily a photocopy of E4.a above, but there are some variations.

Typescript Setting Copy of Book

E5.a. "One Writer's Beginnings." [1983]
Ts, photocopy; 8 preliminary pages, pages 1–131 as numbered by stamp; pages 45, 65, 66, 73, 105 are ribbon pages; pages 77 and 82 are paste copies with ribbon and photocopied material; pages 1, 2, 71 are also paste copies; numerous holograph revisions, typically of a word or phrase; many authorial and editorial corrections, queries, and responses to queries.

E5.b. "One Writer's Beginnings." 1983.
Ts, photocopy; pages 1–37, 39–132, plus pp. 1A, 12A, 44A (two copies),66A, 71 supplement, 82 supplement, and additional copies of pages 34, 66, 73, 77, 106; there is no page 38; pages 4&5, 53&54, 90&91 are single pages; comments by EW and by copy editor, queries and answers from each are part of this photocopy of E5.a, though printer's instructions are not; holograph label on box containing this ts reads "Xerox of Copy-Edited MS., *One Writer's Beginnings*, '83."

Page Proof

E6.a. "One Writer's Beginnings." 1983.
Master proof; pages 1, 3–39, 41, 43–69, 71, 73–104, plus nine preliminary pages, a cover sheet dated 11.07.1983, and a photocopy of page 41; typeset on 10.03.1983 and 10.20.1983; there are no pages 2, 40, 42, 70, 72 because these are blank pages; EW's holograph corrections and revisions; corrections in an editorial hand; substantial revisions on page 20.

E6.b. "One Writer's Beginnnings." 1983.
Master proof, photocopy; pages 3–39, 41, 43–69, 71, 73–104; there are no pp. 40, 42, 70, 72 because these are blank pages; holograph title on page 3; photocopy of master proof as corrected in E6.a above, though some editorial corrections remain to be made; EW's holograph note on torn slip of paper—"Xerox of master proof as corrected."

E6.c. "One Writer's Beginnings." 1983.
Master proof, photocopy; pages 1, 3–39, 41, 43–69, 71, 73–104; there
are no pages 2, 40, 42, 70, 72 because these are blank pages; a holograph comment in the upper right corner of page 1 reads, "Author's
duplicate—keep"; some authorial revisions made in E6.a have been
photocopied here; other holograph revisions by author in this set of
master proof.
E7.a. "One Writer's Beginnnings." 1983.
One photocopied set of preliminary pages and captions for photo-
graphs in Master Proof; 9 pages; a holograph note from editor Joyce
Backman to EW, promising that her staff will proof this material.
E7.b. "One Writer's Beginnings." n.d.
Ts and photographs, photocopy; 20 pages; one photocopied page of
captions for photographs; 19 photocopied pages of photographs.
E8. "One Writer's Beginnings." n.d.
Ts, photocopy; prologue to text; 2 copies.

F. THE LITTLE STORE
(This essay was published in a limited collector's edition by Tamazunchale
Press in 1985.)

F1.a. "The Little Store." 1975.
Carbon ts; pages 1–10; the title *"A Lot for Your Nickel*|(A Memoir of
the Neighborhood Grocery Store)" has been lined out and the holo-
graph title "The Little Store" added; this ts is part of Archives Series
16; see II. C19 above.
F1.b. "The Little Store." n.d.
Ts, photocopy; pages 1–10; photocopy of F1.a above; the title *"A Lot
for Your Nickel"* has been lined out and the holograph title "The Little
Store" added; the subtitle "(A Memoir of the Neighborhood Grocery
Store)" has been preserved; this ts is part of Archives Series 16; see
II.C18 above.

III. UNCOLLECTED WORKS

A. FICTION
(Archives Series 1)

A1. "Acrobats in a Park." ca. 1934.
Ts; pages [1]–11; pages 5–11 are carbons; holograph revisions; EW
has dated the ts as "1934(?)." Also listed as I.J1.

A2. "The Doll." ca. 1936.
Ts; pages [1]–7; almost clean copy; a holograph note on page 1 reads, "This was published in Tanager 1936(?)."
A3. "Magic." n.d.
Ts, incomplete; one page; an early version of the opening of "Magic."
A4. "Magic." ca. 1936.
Ts; pages [1]–10; clean copy; EW has written at the top of page [1], "This was published in Manuscript 1936 (?)."
A5. "Retreat." ca. 1936.
Ts; pages [1]–7; clean copy; EW has written at the top of page [1], "This was published in River (1936) (?)"; actually published in *River* in 1937; also listed as I.L1.

B. REVIEWS
(Archives Series 18)

B1. *Our Daily Bread.* By Enrique Gil Gilbert. Trans. Dudley Poore. 1943. 3 pages.
Carbon ts of review—"Exotic from Ecuador." *NYTBR* 18 July 1943: 6.
B2. *Horse and Shadow.* By Enrique Amorim. Trans. Richard L. O'Connell and James Graham Lujan. 1943. 1 page.
Ts and carbon ts of review—"A Powerful Novel of the Pampas." *NYTBR* 15 August 1943: 4.
B3. *The Land of the Great Image.* By Maurice Collis. 1943. 3 pages.
Carbon ts review—"The Great Buddha." *NYTBR* 29 August 1943: 5, 16.
B4. *A Garland of Straw.* By Sylvia Townsend Warner. 1943. 2 pages.
Carbon ts review—EW's holograph note, "NYT 9-5-43, p. 6" is in error.
B5. *Waters over the Dam.* By Harry Harrison Kroll. 1944. 1 page.
Carbon ts review—"Alabama Farm Boy." *NYTBR* 26 March 1944: 4.
B6.a. *South.* By William Sansom. 1950. 3 pages.
Carbon ts review—"Fireworks in Italy." *Saturday Review* 23 September 1950: 16–17.
B6.b. *South.* By William Sansom. 1950. 3 pages.
Ts (photocopy) review—"Fireworks in Italy." *Saturday Review* 23 September 1950: 16–17.
B7.a. *Short Novels of Colette.* 1951. 3 pages.
Carbon ts review—*New York Post* 30 December 1951: 12M.
B7.b. *Short Novels of Colette.* 1951. 3 pages.
Ts (photocopy) review—*New York Post* 30 December 1951: 12M.

B8.a. *Nine Stories.* By J. D. Salinger. 1953. 3 pages.
Ts review—*NYTBR* 5 April 1953: 4.
B8.b. *Nine Stories.* By J. D. Salinger. 1953. 3 pages.
Carbon ts review—*NYTBR* 5 April 1953: 4.
B8.c. *Nine Stories.* By J. D. Salinger. 1953. 3 pages.
Ts (photocopy) review—*NYTBR* 5 April 1953: 4.
B9.a. "William Hollingsworth Show." 1958. 3 pages.
Carbon ts review of an art exhibition—"Hollingsworth Show is 'Superlative Exhibit.' " Jackson *Clarion-Ledger* 14 September 1958, sec. C: 1, 4.
B9.b. "William Hollingsworth Show." 1958. 3 pages.
Ts (photocopy) review—Jackson *Clarion-Ledger* 14 September 1958, sec. C: 1, 4.
B10.a. *Henry Green: Nine Novels and an Unpacked Bag.* By John Russell. 1961. 4 pages.
Carbon ts review—"Life's Impact is Oblique." *NYTBR* 2 April 1961: 5.
B10.b. *Henry Green: Nine Novels and an Unpacked Bag.* By John Russell. 1961. 6 pages.
Ts (photocopy) and carbon ts review—"Life's Impact is Oblique." *NYTBR* 2 April 1961: 5; two photocopied pages attached to front of carbon ts.
B11.a. *The World of Isak Dinesen.* By Eric O. Johannesson. 1961. 4 pages.
Carbon ts review—"The Acceptance of Life is a Defense of the Story." *NYTBR* 17 December 1961: 6.
B11.b. *The World of Isak Dinesen.* By Eric O. Johannesson. 1961. 4 pages.
Ts (photocopy) review—"The Acceptance of Life is a Defense of the Story." *NYTBR* 17 December 1961: 6.
B12.a. *The Stories of William Sansom.* 1963. 6 pages.
Carbon ts review; holograph revisions—"Time and Place—and Suspense." *NYTBR* 30 June 1963: 5, 27.
B12.b. *The Stories of William Sansom.* 1963. 6 pages.
Ts (photocopy) review—"Time and Place—and Suspense." *NYTBR* 30 June 1963: 5, 27.
B13.a. *The Gayety of Vision; A Study of Isak Dinesen's Art.* By Robert Langbaum. 1965. 7 pages.
Carbon ts review—"Cook, Care for the Mad, or Write." *NYTBR* 7 February 1965: 4, 44–45.

B13.b.   *The Gayety of Vision; A Study of Isak Dinesen's Art.* By Robert Langbaum. 1965. 7 pages.
Ts (photocopy) review—"Cook, Care for the Mad, or Write." *NYTBR* 7 February 1965: 4, 44–45.
B14.a.   *Martha Graham: Portrait of the Lady as an Artist.* By LeRoy Leatherman. 1967. 6 pages.
Carbon ts review—"Movement Never Lies." *Sewanee Review* 75 (1967): 529–33.
B14.b.   *Martha Graham: Portrait of the Lady as an Artist.* By LeRoy Leatherman. 1967. 6 pages.
Ts (photocopy) review—"Movement Never Lies." *Sewanee Review* 75 (1967): 529–33.
B15.   *Words with Music.* By Lehman Engel. 1972. 7 pages.
Carbon ts review—"Everything writers and composers of musicals need to know." *NYTBR* 28 May 1972: 7, 10.
B16.   *The Never-Ending Wrong.* By Katherine Anne Porter. 1977. 7 pages.
Carbon ts review—"Post Mortem." *NYTBR* 21 August 1977: 9, 29. Some holograph corrections.
B17.   *Essays of E. B. White.* 1977. 9 pages.
Ts (photocopy) review—*NYTBR* 25 September 1977: 7, 43.
B18.a.   *Fireman Flower.* By William Sansom. 1945. 2 pages.
Carbon ts review—no information about review publication; the short story collection was published by Vanguard Press in 1945.
B18.b.   *Fireman Flower.* By William Sansom. 1945. 2 pages.
Ts (photocopy) review—no information about review publication. The short story collection was published by Vanguard Press in 1945.

C. Speeches
(Archives Series 19)

C1.   "PRESENTATION TO WILLIAM FAULKNER OF THE GOLD MEDAL FOR FICTION." 1962.
Ts (photocopy); pages [1]–2; presentation remarks 24 May 1962 at the Ceremonial of the American Academy and the National Institute of Arts and Letters; published in *Proceedings of the American Academy of Arts and Letters and the National Institute of Arts and Letters.* Second Series. Number B. New York, 1963. 225–26.
C2.   Untitled. 1980.
Ts; pages 1–6; speech delivered at the inauguration symposium of Mississippi Governor William Winter, 21 January 1980; a few holo-

graph revisions; published in *The Inaugural Papers of Governor William F. Winter.* Ed. Charlotte Capers. Jackson: Mississippi Department of Archives and History, 1980. 21–24.

(Typescripts of six of EW's speeches are listed elsewhere: 1) an untitled speech that would be published as a *Fairy Tale of the Natchez Trace*—see Chapter 1, II.B1; 2) an untitled speech that would be published as "Jane Austen"—see Chapter 1, II.C1; 3) "An Interior Affair," a speech that would be published as "Must the Novelist Crusade?"—see Chapter 1, II.C9; and 4) three lectures that would be published under the title *One Writer's Beginnings*—see Chapter 1, II.E1.)

D. Miscellaneous Works
(Archives Series 20)

D1.   Untitled. 1948.
Ts (photocopy); pages [1]–3; letter to *New Yorker* taking issue with Edmund Wilson's comments about William Faulkner and the South; dated 15 November 1948; published in the *New Yorker* 1 Jan. 1949: 50–51.

D2.   Untitled. 1954.
Carbon ts; pages [1]–12 and envelope; envelope bears EW's holograph notation: "Times Literary Supplement| (unsigned)|in 1950's—"; a few holograph revisions; the essay was published as "Place and Time: The Southern Writer's Inheritance." *TLS* 17 September 1954: xlviii.

D3.a.   "Preface to HANGING BY A THREAD, by Joan Kahn." 1969.
Carbon ts; pages [1]–8; a few holograph revisions; published in Boston by Houghton Mifflin, 1969.

D3.b.   "Preface to HANGING BY A THREAD, by Joan Kahn." 1969.
Ts, photocopy; pages [1]–8.

D4.   "Afterword, *The Great Big Doorstep.*" 1979.
Carbon ts; pages 1–14; afterword to E.P. O'Donnell's novel (1941; rpt. Carbondale, Ill.: Southern Illinois University Press, 1979); a few holograph corrections; a holograph note reads, "Corrected after original mailed—probably not OK."

IV. UNPUBLISHED WORKS

(Within each category below, unpublished works are listed
by date of composition.)

A. FICTION
(Archives Series 1)

A1. Untitled. ca. 1925. RESTRICTED.

Ts; 31 total pages; pages 1–21, single-spaced and hand-numbered
pages 1–10, and four unnumbered, single-spaced pages; there is typing on both the recto and verso sides of page 7; hand-numbered pages
1–4 appear on the recto and verso sides of two legal size sheets,
hand-numbered pages 5 and 6 appear on both recto and verso sides
of a single sheet as do hand-numbered pages 8 and 9 and the two
final unnumbered pages; seems to be a projected novel, for there are
chapter headings; holograph revisions.

A2. "A Ghost Story." ca. 1930.

Ts; pages [1]–3; almost clean copy; EW has dated this story as
"1930?."

A3. "The Children." ca. 1934.

Ts; pages [1]–5; numerous holograph revisions; EW has dated the ts
as "1934(?)."

A4. "Beautiful Ohio." ca. 1936.

Ts; pages [1]–9; holograph revisions; EW has dated the ts as
"1936(?)."

(Archives Series 4)

A5.a. "The Delta Cousins." [1942]

Ts; pages [1]–36, title and end pages; title page is on grey Russell and
Volkening letterhead construction paper; a few holograph revisions
and corrections; see I.C1.a.

A5.b. "The Delta Cousins." 1942.

Carbon ts; pages [1]–36 (on 19 sheets of paper) and an 11.05.[1942]
holograph note from EW to John Robinson; a carbon of A5.a above;
at the time of donation, EW dated this ts as 1942; it may, however,
date from 1943; a few holograph additions and corrections; holograph
notes to Robinson on pages 14 and 16; see I.C1.b.

B. Drama
(Archives Series 21)

B1. "The Waiting Room." ca. 1935.
Carbon ts; pages [1]–21 and a preliminary page describing the set; someone, probably EW, has labeled this "a farce for a Little Theatre" and dated it as 1935; a few holograph revisions.

B2.a. "What Year Is This?" n.d.
Carbon ts; 100 pages and a blue folder; sketches from an unpublished revue by Hildegarde Dolson and Eudora Welty; each author wrote her sketches quite independently of the other; EW's sketches are:

"The New York Times," pages 1–5, clean copy

"Hormones!" pages 1–2, clean copy

"Yes, Dear," pages 1–8, clean copy

"What's Happened to Waltzes like This? (and Taking the Waters with You)," pages 1–5, clean copy

"Fifty-Seventh Street Rag," pages 1–11, clean copy

"Bye Bye Brevoort," pages 1–14, clean copy

"The Feet-Out Blues," pages 1–4, clean copy

"Choo-Choo Boat," pages 1–3, clean copy

("Bye Bye Brevoort" was eventually performed as part of *The Littlest Revue* in 1955 in New York City and was performed by the Little Theatre in Jackson in 1958. It was published in a limited edition in 1980.)

B2.b. "Bye Bye Brevoort." n.d.
Carbon ts; pages 1–15; holograph note reads, "copy 4"; this sketch was part of the revue written by Hildegarde Dolson and EW (B2.a above); also listed in II.D; see also Chapter 5, VII.A9.

B3.a. "The Robber Bridegroom." 1948–49.
Ts; 85 pages; notes for and scenes from a screenplay; written by John Robinson (who was living in San Francisco and DeLisle, Miss.) and Eudora Welty (who was living in Jackson, Miss.); pages typed in pica seem to have been written by EW while those typed in elite seem to have been written by Robinson.

Synopsis of screenplay. n.d.
Ts; pages [1]–22; written by EW.

Notes on *The Robber Bridegroom*. n.d.
Carbon ts; 4 pages; notes on the characters, on using the locations and props symbolically, on the plot, and on plot sequences; written by EW.

List of scenes for screenplay. n.d.
Ts; 3 pages; 45 scenes listed on yellow paper; written by Robinson; holograph revisions by EW.

Description of screenplay. n.d.
Ts; 3 pages; written by Robinson; describes action of the proposed film, scene by scene; yellow paper.

List of scenes. n.d.
Ms; 1 page; EW's holograph list.

Scene 1. n.d.
Ts; pages [1.1]–1.5; written by EW.

Scene 2. n.d.
Ts; pages 2.1–2.5; written by EW.

Scene 6. [1948?].
Ts; pages 6.1–6.4; written by EW; includes her holograph note to Robinson; a few holograph revisions; dated Nov. 29.

Scene 6. n.d.
Ts; pages [6.1]–6.3; another Scene 6; written by EW; a few holograph revisions.

Scene 7. n.d.
Ts; pages [7.1]–7.4; written by EW; holograph revisions in EW's hand and probably in Robinson's as well.

Scene 8. n.d.
Ts; pages [8.1]–8.2; written by EW; a few holograph revisions in EW's hand and probably in Robinson's as well.

Scene 9. n.d.
Ts; pages [9.1]–9.4; written by EW; a few holograph revisions by EW.

Scene 10. n.d.
Ts; pages [10.1]–10.6; written by EW; a few holograph revisions by EW.

Scenes 10 and 11. n.d.
Carbon ts; pages [1]–3; written by Robinson; yellow paper.

Scenes 25 and 26. n.d.
Carbon ts; pages 1–3; written by Robinson; yellow paper.

Scene 26A. n.d.
Ts; pages [26A.1]–26A.3; written by EW; a few holograph revisions.

Scene 27. n.d.
Ts and carbon ts; pages [1]–2; page 1 is a carbon, page 2 a ribbon page; written by Robinson.

Scene 44. n.d.
Ts; pages [1]–4, 44.5–44.8; page 44.5 is a carbon; written by EW; holograph notes to Robinson on pages 1 and 5; a few holograph revisions.

B3.b. "The Robber Bridegroom." 1948–49.
Carbon ts; 62 pages; screenplay written in conjunction with John Robinson; carbons of some items listed in B3.a immediately above; these pages are probably by Welty herself; a few holograph revisions.

Synopsis of screenplay. n.d.
Carbon ts; pages [1]–22; a few holograph revisions.

Scene 1. n.d.
Carbon ts; pages [1.1]–1.5.

Scene 2. n.d.
Carbon ts; pages 2.1–2.5.

Scene 6. n.d.
Carbon ts; pages [6.1]–6.3.

Scene 7. n.d.
Carbon ts; [7.1]–7.4.

Scene 8. n.d.
Carbon ts; [8.1]–8.2.

Scene 9. n.d.
Carbon ts; [9.1]–9.4.

Scene 10. n.d.
Carbon ts; [10.1]–10.6.

Scene 26-A. n.d.
Carbon ts; pages [26A.1]–26A.3.

Scene 44. n.d.
Carbon ts; pages [1]–4, 44.5–44.8; page 44.5 is a ribbon page.

C. Speeches
(Archives Series 19)

C1. Untitled. 1965.
Ts; pages 1–15, plus pages 5A and 7A; speech about William Faulkner delivered at the Southern Literary Festival, April 23, 1965, Oxford, Miss.; holograph and typed revisions; paste-overs and pin-ons.

C2.   Untitled. 1974.

Carbon ts; pages [1]–8; a speech about Nash Burger delivered March 28, 1974, for EW by someone at the *New York Times* as part of a retirement party for Burger; a few holograph revisions; tape available. (Burger, a life-long friend of EW's, graduated from high school in Jackson, Miss., taught high school English there after he finished his college education, and went on to become an editor at the *New York Times Book Review*.)

D. Miscellaneous Works
(Archives Series 20)

D1.a.   Engel, Lehman. Libretto for ballet of *The Shoe Bird*. [1968]
Ts, photocopy; 15 pages; substantial holograph revisions by EW.
D1.b.   Welty, Eudora. "NARRATOR'S LINES for THE SHOE BIRD." [1968]
Ts; 8 pages; rewritten from Engel's version because of EW's familiarity with the choreography (EW was in Jackson, where the production was to be staged; Engel, the composer, was in New York City during the production's preliminary stages); holograph revisions or corrections; a note to Lehman Engel from EW on page 1.
D1.c.   Welty, Eudora. "NARRATOR'S LINES for THE SHOE BIRD." [1968]
Ts, photocopy; 8 pages; most of the holograph corrections in D1.b above had not been made when this photocopy was made; one holograph correction on page 8.

Photographs

Eudora Welty's photographs have long been admired but have too seldom received critical and scholarly attention. Admirers of the photographs have erroneously assumed that Welty used only a rather primitive Kodak camera and that she took all her photographs between 1933 and 1936. Most interviewers of Welty have been unconcerned with her photography, essays about the photographs have inevitably been based on very few remarks by Welty, and scholars have typically examined only Welty's published photographs, not all of the 1063 negatives and 328 prints held by the Mississippi Department of Archives and History as part of its Eudora Welty Collection. As a result, Welty's career as a photographer, the elements of change and continuity that characterize her photographs, and the relationship between Welty's photographs and her fiction require further study.

Eudora Welty grew up taking photography for granted. Her father was a camera enthusiast who took family and travel photographs, developed his own prints, and supported the efforts of two young men to establish the first camera store in Jackson, Mississippi. Christian Webb Welty might have expected his daughter to share his enthusiasm for photography, and indeed she did. For twenty years Welty would take and for many years print her own photographs, and when she ceased being an active photographer, Welty would carefully preserve her prints and negatives and would ultimately present both to the Eudora Welty Collection.[1] She began to take snapshots sometime late in the 1920s, perhaps in the summer of 1929 after she had graduated from the University of Wisconsin and before she became a graduate student at Columbia University. At that time she used a Kodak camera with a bellows, and she continued to use that camera until she purchased a more sophisticated Recomar camera in 1935. The Recomar, however, proved expensive to use. It required film packs (3-by-4-inch negatives), not the more economical 116 film (2 1/2-by-4 1/4-inch negatives) that the Kodak had taken. So late in 1936 she changed cameras once again. She bought a Rolleiflex camera (2 1/4-by-2 1/4 inch negatives) and used it until 1950. In that year she accidentally left the Rolleiflex on a Paris Metro bench, and annoyed with her own carelessness, she refused for many years to replace it. From her graduate student days until 1950, therefore, Welty was busy with a camera.

Welty's activity with her cameras resulted not in one, as has been assumed, but in two New York shows. The first was sponsored by Lugene Opticians at the Photographic Galleries in New York City, the second by the Camera House, also in New York City. We know a good deal about the first show: held from March 31-April 15, 1936, it consisted of forty-five photographs; twenty-nine of the originals are part of the Welty Collection (see Chapter 2, II.A1), and all of the photographs in this show were taken with the Kodak or Recomar camera. Samuel Robbins, who had worked on Welty's first show, contacted her when he moved from the Lugene gallery to the Camera House and proposed a second show of her photographs. He requested photos of "poor whites," and his correspondence with Welty further indicates that this show of March 6–31, 1937, included photos of cemetery monuments (Correspondence: 7.18.1936, 11.9.1936, 12.14.1936). It seems impossible to determine precisely which photographs were exhibited, but a number of mounted original prints held in the Welty Collection seem likely candidates (see Chapter 2, II.A2).

Though publishers as well as galleries were interested in Welty's photographs, book publication of them was long in coming. In 1935 Welty submitted a collection of photographs to Harrison Smith and Robert Haas, Publishers; the book met with praise but was rejected as an unprofitable undertaking (Correspondence: 04.02.1935). In 1937 Covici-Friede rejected a book in which Welty had juxtaposed stories and photographs (Correspondence: 11.01.1937). The juxtaposition, Welty recalls, was artificial; the pictures had not inspired the stories. She hoped that the photographs might interest publishers in her stories, but Covici-Friede foresaw commercial problems with such a combination. And in 1938 the Story Press rejected a collection of Welty photographs, fearing prohibitive production costs (Correspondence: 02.24.1938). It was not until 1971, therefore, that Welty's photographs were published in book form in *One Time, One Place*. Since then three collections of Welty photographs have been issued: *Welty*, edited by Patti Carr Black (Mississippi Department of Archives and History, 1977), *Twenty Photographs* (Palaemon Press, 1980), and *In Black and White* (Lord John Press, 1985).

Despite the publication of four books of Welty photographs, few scholars have chosen to study them, and no one has looked at the evolution of Welty's career as a photographer or at the parallels between her development as a photographer and her development as a writer.[2] Welty's early photographs tend to focus upon encounters, upon small groups of people, while her later photographs more often depict landscapes and townscapes. But her photographs also show unexpected lines of continuity: pictures of parades and carnivals date from her use of the simple Kodak and extend throughout her years as a photographer; pictures of cemeteries date from her use of the Kodak, though the Mississippi Department of Archives and History holds no such negatives, and are prominent among the Recomar and Rolleiflex photographs the department does hold. In fact, Welty once thought of publishing a book of cemetery photos and took many cemetery shots as a result of that persistent notion. More than 20 percent of Welty's photographs fall into these two categories, but her other photographic subjects varied with the years.

Welty's early photographs, those taken between 1929 and 1936 with the Kodak and Recomar cameras, suggest her fascination with the citizens of her native state (see Chapter 2, I.A and I.B). After returning from the University of Wisconsin and then from Columbia University, Welty seemed to rediscover her native land, to find a world of infinite variety close at hand. Overwhelmingly, Welty photographed people, people engaged in street corner conversations, children at play, adults at work. A majority of these people were blacks, oppressed by white authority but free from white social conventions—a situation that prompted Welty the writer to pair black characters with white characters who were artists or wanderers. But Welty's photographs more often depict both blacks and whites as southerners and as people, not as members of particular racial groups.

Welty's Kodak and Recomar photographs, for instance, often focus upon the typically southern stances, gestures, encounters that she noticed after her stay in the North—stances, gestures, encounters that she had probably taken for granted before living outside the South. In 1953 Welty herself used these photographs to provide a picture of the region for Joe Krush, the illustrator of her novel *The Ponder Heart*. She sent him many of her early photographs and made comments on the backs of them (see Chapter 2, II.B4). Some comments refer to white or black poses, but all discuss southern ones. On the reverse of her photograph of a young black girl lying in a porch swing, she wrote: "Good Southern attitude" (#727). On the reverse of a picture of white people eating watermelon on the town square in Pontotoc, Mississippi, she wrote: "Man seated (l) on ground might look like Old Man Gladney—elastic bands on shirtsleeves, etc. big black hat, suspenders, sharp-featured country face" (#975). On the reverse of a snapshot of four black men leaning against a fence, Welty wrote, "attitudes" (#279). And on the reverse of her portrait of a white storekeeper, she wrote: "A country storekeeper, The face & clothes are usual for people on the street (+ hat) (panama) & the telephone is good" (#694). The typical sights of southern life that Welty had documented in her photographs she sent along to Krush. Her fiction, of course, is filled with just such typically southern types. In fact, Welty's famed sense of place in her early fiction is established more through character and social behavior than through description of the physical setting. The three ladies in "Lily Daw" who gather at the post office while one of their number does up the mail might well be images from a Welty photograph as might the conversational grouping of these women and storekeeper Ed Newton as he strings up Redbird tablets in his store. And the depot gathering to bid Lily farewell evokes the photographs also. None of these images emerges directly from the photographs. Welty took her Kodak photographs before she wrote the stories later collected in *A Curtain of Green* (1941), and very few of her early stories bear an explicit relationship to the photographs. But Welty's vision as a photographer and her vision as a story writer were similar: what interested her in one art form interested her in another.

Though the evocation of a region is important, there is a more profound connection between the 1929–1936 photographs and the early stories. Most of Welty's Kodak and Recomar photographs are framed to emphasize relationships between individuals. Even the photograph titles from her Lugene show emphasize this overriding concern. "The Boast" (#971) is simply a picture of three boys sitting on a street corner, but Welty's title bestows a story upon this framed picture. Another picture, one of a young girl leaning against the porch post of her shabby home, Welty has titled "Waiting" (#704), and this girl seems to be waiting for someone she loves or for someone to love. "Small Talk" (#711) is the photo of two men engaged in conversation, both amused by the talk, both perhaps amused by the repetition of an old story that has become more dear in its repeated tellings. "Dolls Alike" (#988), also called "The Dolls," depicts two black girls with white dolls; Welty's title centers not on the obvious irony but on the relationship of the two sisters who have dolls alike. "Sunday Errand" (no negative available) shows two boys carrying home chunks of ice and suggests a story—the work and the pleasure involved in having iced tea and perhaps homemade ice cream once a week. "Spanking" (#477) shows a mother's frustration with her infant child. "Chums" or "The Chum" (#713) depicts the friendship of two young girls. Welty carefully selected what to enclose within the frame of her camera lens, and her "instinct and knowledge," she told a BBC reporter, "was to take a group of people whose being together shows something" (*A Writer's Beginnings*). The same instinct and knowledge, she went on to state, governed her work as a writer. From the first, Welty's stories focus upon relationships—the relationship between Lily Daw and the community of Victory, Mississippi, the relationships between husbands and wives in "Petrified Man," the relationships denied to Clytie, the two marriages of Mr. Marblehall, the relationships of the family members in "Why I Live at the P.O.," of Ruby Fisher and her husband in "A Piece of News," of Sonny and his wife in "Death of a Traveling Salesman." The mood of these stories, however, differs sharply from the mood of the photographs. Few relationships in the stories provide characters with emotional sustenance; few characters can understand or communicate with their friends or family members. As Robert Penn Warren long ago noted, "the fact of isolation, whatever its nature, provides the basic situation" of Welty's early fiction (250). The photographs bear testimony to the need for love—romantic love, parental love, the love of friends—and at times these photographs show the difficulty of finding love and of transcending separateness—"Waiting," for example. But more typically the photographs are affirmative in implication. The Kodak and Recomar photographs and the stories in *A Curtain of Green*, therefore, suggest the poles of Welty's thought—the need for love and the difficulty inherent in loving.

Although the photographs taken in 1935–1936 with the Recomar camera focused upon human interaction as did her earlier Kodak photos, Welty paid greater attention to landscapes and architecture with her second camera than with her first. Her photographs of the Big Black and Pearl Rivers, of antebellum Natchez homes, of Raymond Courthouse, of Charleston, South Carolina, and of New York City suggest a shift in her photographic interests. With her third camera, her Rolleiflex, Welty took still more photographs of landscapes and townscapes (see Chapter 2, I.C). This is not to say that she ceased to photograph people after she bought the Rolleiflex late in 1936—her pictures of Holiness Church members, of Ida M'Toy, of parade watchers and participants, of state fair crowds and acts, and of New Orleans Mardi Gras revelers put that notion to rest. But the Rolleiflex photos focus upon the Old Natchez Trace region of Mississippi—upon the physical appearance of its small towns and upon the land formations and plant life of the region. Sometime in 1940 Welty, having read Robert Coates' *Outlaw Years*, John James Audubon's journals, Lorenzo Dow's sermons and autobiography, and J. F. H. Claiborne's *Mississippi*, went in search of the exotic world these books described. She saw and photographed Hermanville, Rocky Springs, Port Gibson, Grand Gulf, and Rodney, the hills overlooking the Mississippi River and the dense, vine-covered woods of these hills. This locale entranced Welty and became her central photographic subject.

In *A Curtain of Green* locale is important but not central. This work makes economical use of setting to develop the issues of love and separateness. The desolate hill country in "Death of a Traveling Salesman" suggests that R. J. Bowman is literally and figuratively at the end of the road. The flat, monotonous landscape of the Mississippi Delta reflects the nature of Tom Harris's uncommitted life in "The Hitch-Hikers." The stately homes of Natchez reflect the power of convention in "Old Mr. Marblehall." But the physical world claims few lines in these stories.

Of course, Welty was writing the stories to be collected in *A Curtain of Green* even as she was using her Recomar and her Rolleiflex cameras, and a few of these stories show forth the fictional equivalent of her increasing photographic interest in place. The Recomar photographs of New York City, for instance, depict the city's streets, its squares filled with pigeons, its shops and sidewalk markets, and they were taken only a short time before Welty wrote "Flowers for Marjorie," a story in which she made extensive use of the physical environment to emphasize the failure in the marriage of Marjorie and Howard. Though Welty never consulted her photographs when writing, photographs provide exact parallels to descriptive passages in this story. Howard, sitting on a park bench next to other unemployed men, glancing at a drinking fountain a short distance away, looking at pigeons in the square, might be any of the men Welty photographed in New York City's Union Square (#949, 953, 955, 957, 996, 997, 998, 999, 1000, 1004, 1037). And this New York City world has separated Howard from the natural world and from his wife:

> He walked up Sixth Avenue under the shade of the L, and kept setting his hat on straight. The little spurts of wind tried to take it off and blow it away. How far he would have had to chase it! . . . He reached a crowd of

people who were watching a machine behind a window; it made dough-
nuts very slowly. He went to the next door, where he saw another window
full of colored prints of the Virgin Mary and nearly all kinds of birds and
animals, and down below these a shelf of little gray pasteboard boxes in
which were miniature toilets and night jars to be used in playing jokes, and
in the middle box a bulb attached to a long tube, with a penciled sign,
"Palpitator—the Imitation Heart. Show her you Love her." An organ
grinder immediately removed his hat and played "Valencia." (197)

In the city Howard encounters an unchanging environment of steel
and concrete, of tawdry commercialism and unemployment. For him
time seems to have stopped. Although Marjorie lives in the urban setting, she remains part of the natural world, of the world of time and
growth and change. Her pregnancy makes her part of that world. This
difference from Marjorie is unbearable to Howard because he loves
her, and this difference has been precipitated by the young couple's
move to the city. Welty thus places greater emphasis upon the physical world of her story here than she does in most of the *Curtain of
Green* stories. Her photographic interest in the shade of the L (#1002)
and in the shops she describes in "Flowers for Marjorie" (#953) parallels her increasingly emblematic use of place in her fiction.

So too does Welty's photographing of the Natchez Trace landscape
parallel her emblematic use of that area in her fiction. Welty had photographed Natchez' First Pilgrimage in 1933 and had also photographed the great houses of Natchez with her Recomar. But through
the lens of her Rolleiflex Welty looked not at Natchez itself but at the
wilder region along the old trail that led to it. She came repeatedly to
the Old Trace with her Rolleiflex. Her enlargements of photographs
of Rodney's Landing date from 1940, and that year marks both a photographic and a fictional concentration upon the Old Trace. "A Worn
Path," Welty's first published story with the Trace as setting, was included in *A Curtain of Green*, but was written in 1940, considerably
later than most stories in that volume. In this account of Phoenix Jackson's journey to obtain medicine for her grandson, Welty's response
to the Trace landscape was as direct and intense, though not as expansive, as it would be in her later fiction about the region. On the
way to Natchez, Welty tells us, Phoenix walks up through pine trees
that cast dark shadows and down through oak trees. She sees Spanish
moss hanging white as lace in the cold weather. She passes small
fields of dead cotton and corn. She walks between high, green colored banks. This is the beautiful Trace world seen in so many of Welty's photographs (#13 and 1022, for example), and the very real back-
drop of the Trace makes the story believable—we believe in Phoenix

Jackson because we recognize and believe in the world that she inhabits. But setting does far more than lend credibility to the story's action. The natural world of the Trace is Phoenix's home, and its qualities are to some extent her own. Her life has been relatively untouched by "progress." She is not removed from nature but lives naturally. She tells time by turning to nature. As Phoenix sets out on her December trip to Natchez, she knows that it is "not too late" for the mourning dove. As she travels on, she measures her progress by the progress of the sun: "'Sun so high!' she cried, leaning back and looking, while the thick tears went over her eyes. 'The time getting all gone here'" (275). Later as she crosses a field, she is "'Glad this not the season for bulls'" and that "'the good Lord made his snakes to curl up and sleep in the winter'" (276). The rhythms of the day and of the year constitute Phoenix's way of measuring time. Phoenix herself seems almost to be a part of the natural world: "Her skin had a pattern all its own of numberless branching wrinkles and as though a whole little tree stood in the middle of her forehead, but a golden color ran underneath, and the two knobs of her cheeks were illumined by a yellow burning under the dark. Under the red rag her hair came down on her neck in the frailest of ringlets, still black, and with an odor like copper" (274). And Phoenix's love for her grandson, love which sends her on an heroic quest for medicine, is absolutely natural. It is as enduring as the daily and seasonal cycles. Her love is innate. Even when Phoenix momentarily forgets why she had traveled to the doctor's office, she is acting intuitively out of love. And when she remembers her grandson and his ailment, she states: "I not going to forget him again, no, the whole enduring time. I could tell him from all the others in creation" (284). In "Some Notes on River Country" Welty has asserted, "Whatever is significant and whatever is tragic in its story live as long as the place does" (299). "A Worn Path" shows us that Phoenix's love lives as long as its place does; her love is as enduring as the Trace itself. Welty's photographs of this landscape thus parallel her metaphorical use of it in fiction. Her interest had not moved away from relationships but had shifted to the way the external world can serve as a metaphor for those relationships.

The parallel between Welty's photographs of the Natchez Trace and her writing about the region is even clearer in *The Robber Bridegroom* (1942) and *The Wide Net* (1943), two full-length works set primarily in this area. And the parallels are most direct and revealing in "At The Landing," the final story in *The Wide Net* and a story set in Rodney's

Landing and Grand Gulf. A photograph Welty titled "Hamlet" in *One Time, One Place* shows Rodney's Landing—a two-story brick building with a back gallery, two one-story frame structures, and a man walking beside a dirt road carrying a large fish (#49). This image is part of "At The Landing": "Under the shaggy bluff the bottomlands lay in a river of golden haze. The road dropped like a waterfall from the ridge to the town at its foot and came to a grassy end there. It was spring. One slowly moving figure that was a man with a fishing pole passed like a dreamer through the empty street and on through the trackless haze toward the river" (180). The photographic image suggests the town's decay, its lifeless quality, and these suggestions prove appropriate for Welty's story. She intensifies the image—the scarcely perceptible second man in the photograph is gone from the story, and even the man with the fish seems scarcely to exist as he "passes like a dreamer through the empty street." The isolation and lifelessness of the town suggest the threat the town poses to Jenny Lockhart, the story's protagonist.

A second photographic image comes into the story with a similar impact. Welty writes: "The cemetery was a dark shelf above the town, on the site of the old landing place when the ships docked from across the world a hundred years ago, and its brink was marked by an old table-like grave with its top ajar where the woodbine grew. Everywhere there, the hanging moss and the upthrust stones were in that strange graveyard shade where, by the light they give, the moss seems made of stone, and the stone of moss" (184). Welty might well be describing her series of photographs of the Rodney cemetery. The "table-like grave with its top ajar" appears in negatives #482 and 1006 (*Welty*, 9), and the image of hanging moss and upthrust stones calls to mind negatives #32, 387, 748, and 749. Here Jenny's retreat to the cemetery seems a move away from love and life and the riverman Billy Floyd. Similarly, Welty's photo of a stile over a cemetery fence (#27 or 1058; *Welty*, 4) becomes in the story the point of indecision for Jenny: should she cross into the open sun and meet Billy Floyd or should she remain in the dark and shady cemetery where her grandfather permits her to go? She must choose between a lifeless but secure existence and a perilous quest for love.

A rather different image also unites photography and story. Welty's photographs of Mississippi River fishing nets (#750, 1024) suggest this passage in her story: "A great spiraled net lay on its side and its circles twinkled faintly on the sky. Veil behind veil of long drying nets hung on all sides, dropping softly and blue-colored in the low wind, and the place was folded in by them" (212). The beauty of the nets belies, however, the danger they represent—the place seems "folded in by them" and Jenny's journey toward freedom and love is also a journey toward destruction. The photographs carry no such metaphoric suggestion, though the images are the same as the story's.

Still a final image in the story parallels a Welty photograph, but this photograph depicts people more than place. Her picture of a fisherman and his boys throwing knives at a tree, which appears in *One Time, One Place*, seems only slightly sinister. The activity itself is threatening, but it is after all a father-and-son entertainment, and the man and boys appear to be enjoying themselves (#752). Not so in the story. By the last light of day the men throw knives at the tree, and then after dark the boys do: "The younger boys separated and took their turns throwing knives with a dull *pit* at the tree" (214). This image is decidedly sinister. Jenny Lockhart has left the repressive but secure environment of The Landing and has ventured after Billy Floyd and in quest of love; instead, she meets violence and destruction. The river men rape her, and the knife throwing suggests the violence that has become her lot. In "At The Landing" Welty's creation of setting directly parallels her framing vision as a photographer; the increasing importance of place as a way of developing and representing the nature of human relationships seems implicit in Welty's shifting emphasis as a photographer; she continues to photograph people engaged with each other—witness the shantyboaters—but she also sees the physical environment—the town, the cemetery, the fishing nets—in metaphoric terms. And this metaphoric stress upon setting does not vanish from Welty's fiction when she ceases to write about the Trace. The Mississippi Delta, the Irish city of Cork, and the Mediterranean harbor at Naples, for example, would receive similar emphasis and serve similar functions.

What unites all of Welty's photographs and much of her early fiction is scope. The well-framed photographic image is highly selective: it includes relatively little; it captures a single, decisive moment in time. In these terms, Welty's first two story collections seem photographic in nature. The brevity of elapsed time, the small cast of characters, and the taut structure in a short story resemble those very qualities in a photograph. Welty's subsequent fiction would often be more expansive. She would begin to write novels, and her stories would grow much longer. She would deal with multiple plots, with many characters, and with elaborately rendered landscapes, but she would continue to focus on a limited, decisive time span and to use images in her fiction that she had seen through the lens of her camera. In fact, the precise sorts of images that appear throughout Welty's work as a photographer appear throughout her work as a writer.

Welty's interest in cemetery photographs was consistent during her years as a photographer. She took such pictures with all three of her cameras, and images she photographed in the 1930s and 1940s appear not only in the fiction of those years but also in works of the sixties and seventies. The cemetery photographs Welty took with her Kodak—early in the thirties Welty and some friends posed with cemetery monuments and took a few humorous photographs of each other—are not part of her photographic archives. But the cemetery photographs Welty took with her Recomar and Rolleiflex cameras are a major portion of the collection she has donated to the Mississippi Department of Archives and History. Why did Welty photograph so many cemeteries and why did she contemplate a book of cemetery portraits? Certainly she was amused by the Victorian sentimentality and excess to be found in the monuments, but beyond this must lie Welty's concern with time and mortality. "In the most unpretentious snapshot," Welty has written, "lies the wish to clasp fleeting life. Framing a few square inches of space for the fraction of a second, the photographer may capture—rescue from oblivion—fellow human beings caught in the act of living. He is devoted to the human quality of transience" ("A Word on the Photographs"). The many cemetery photographs are eloquent testimony to that same quality of transience and to the same need to rescue human life from oblivion. Time moves inexorably and life is short, Welty's cemetery photographs tell us. One of her earliest stories, "Magic," set in a Jackson cemetery beneath a cemetery angel that Welty had photographed (#791; Devlin 57), conveys a similar message. Here a young girl is seduced; here she becomes a victim of her own illusions about love and is introduced to the reality of time's movement. But monuments Welty had photographed also appear in her fiction of later years. The cemeteries in *Delta Wedding* and *The Golden Apples* specifically parallel actual cemeteries Welty had photographed as do the cemeteries in *Losing Battles* and *The Optimist's Daughter*. In *Losing Battles* Sam Dale Beecham's grave marker "had darkened, its surface like the smooth, loving slatings of a pencil on tablet paper laid over a buffalo nickel, but the rubbed name and the rubbed chain hanging in two, its broken link, shone out in the wet" (427). On Rachel Sojourner's headstone a small lamb "had turned dark as a blackened lamp chimney" (428). And on Dearman's grave is a shaft, "on its top the moss-ringed finger that pointed straight up from its hand in a chiseled cuff above the words 'At Rest' " (428). All of these images we can see in Welty's photographs (#1048, 787, 781). And both in the photographs she took in the thirties and forties and in this novel published in 1970, cemetery monuments are emblems of human mortality, life's one "irreducible urgency" ("Some Notes on Time in Fiction" 168). Jack Renfro knows that cemetery monuments will be worn smooth, blackened, covered with moss; for Jack, life's only source of continuity lies in love, not stone. When he looks at his grandparents' graves, he tells his wife Gloria: " 'There's Mama and all of 'em's mother and dad going by . . . . Yet when you think back on the reunion and count how many him and her managed to leave behind! Like something had whispered to 'em 'Quick!' and they were smart enough to take heed' " (426).

Laurel McKelva Hand's visit to the Mount Salus Cemetery in *The Optimist's Daughter* brings her in contact with monuments very like those Welty had photographed thirty years earlier, and it helps to bring her in contact with a realization similar to Jack Renfro's. The funeral procession for Judge McKelva enters a cemetery

> between ironwork gates whose kneeling angels and looping vines shone black as licorice. The top of the hill ahead was crowded with winged angels and life-sized effigies of bygone citizens in old-fashioned dress, standing as if by count among the columns and shafts and conifers like a familiar set of passengers collected on deck of a ship, on which they all knew each other—bona-fide members of a small local excursion, embarked on a voyage that is always returning in dreams. (89)

The gates of this fictional cemetery recall Welty's photograph of a Port Gibson, Mississippi, cemetery gate (#860). The cemetery itself could well be Jackson's Greenwood Cemetery or the cemetery in Crystal Springs, Mississippi, both of which Welty photographed extensively. Here the old part of the cemetery offers comfort; the citizens of old Mount Salus seem to experience a sense of community in death as well as life. But this quality is entirely lacking in the new part of the cemetery where Fay elects to bury the judge. Its rawness and its location on the edge of the interstate highway provide no sense of continuity or comfort. And Laurel ultimately realizes that life's only continuity and only meaning lies in love and memory.

Carnivals and parades also provide consistent images for Welty the photographer and for Welty the writer. Clearly the arrival of the circus was an exciting event in the life of small-town Jackson, Mississippi. Welty had attended parades and the state fair as a child, and as an adult she went on to photograph these events. Relatively few overt references to circuses and parades enter her fiction, but these few are significant, though they are also far removed from the high spirits and humor that typify the photographs. "Acrobats in a Park," probably written in 1934, deals with the way adultery threatens the solidarity of a circus family. And "Keela, the Outcast Indian Maiden" recalls a circus sideshow in which a club-footed black man is forced to eat live chickens—Welty heard about such a sideshow during her work for the WPA and that anecdote prompted her story. She also photographed many sideshow posters at the annual state fairs in Jackson—"Rubber Man," "Mule Face Woman," "Frog Boy," "3 Legged Man," "Ossified Man" were among the sideshows that played in Jackson (#117, 113, 481, 110, 469). But Welty's amusement with the posters does not betoken the mood of her story. The story deals with victimization. To his kidnappers, to the circus crowds, even to his own family, Little Lee Roy is scarcely human, a victim of the horrifying separateness that can exist among human beings. Welty's photographs of a pin-headed boy are her only carnival shots to suggest this horror (#112, 115, 1011).

Actual parades as well as carnivals play a role in at least two of Welty's works. King MacLain, Katie Rainey tells us in a "Shower of Gold," is fabled to have ridden in Governor Vardaman's inaugural parade—a sign of the grandeur King holds for the home-town folk. More significantly, in *The Optimist's Daughter* Welty uses an image she herself had photographed during a Mardi Gras parade (#925). Laurel Hand and Fay McKelva find themselves in New Orleans in the midst of this festival of indulgence that occurs annually before Lent, before the fasting and penitence that the crucifixion of Christ made necessary. Fay sees two revelers who embody the dark impetus of Mardi Gras: " 'I saw a man—I saw a man and he was dressed up like a skeleton and his date was in a long white dress, with snakes for hair, holding up a bunch of lilies' " (43). But Fay does not see that these emblems of death and the Medusa are the harsh realities that inspire Mardi Gras. She longs for the celebration but cannot see beyond it as Laurel does.

The carnival of "Keela, the Outcast Indian Maiden" and the Mardi Gras costumes of *The Optimist's Daughter* notwithstanding, indirect, oblique, or figurative references to circuses and parades are more typical of Welty's fiction; in fact, they pervade it. In *One Writer's Beginnings* Welty comments on this motif in relation to a circus parade that she, as a child, saw diverted past the house of a sick boy who shortly thereafter "died of what had given him his special privilege." Welty recalls feeling that the boy had been tricked by the parade and that she and the other children of Davis School "had been tricked by envying him—betrayed into it." An "ominous feeling," she concludes, "often attaches itself to a procession." And Welty adds, "in almost every story I ever wrote, some parade or procession, impromptu or ceremonious, comic or mocking or funereal, has risen up to mark some stage of the story's unfolding" (37).

Eudora Welty's career as a photographer is thus intimately related to her career as a writer. Though her photographs did not inspire her stories, though Welty never consulted her photographs when writing her stories, her interests as a photographer parallel the course of her writing career, and taking snapshots left her with a store of indelible memories that would be available when she needed them. Her photographs of encounters prefigure her fictional concern with human relationships, with love and separateness; her increasing emphasis upon locale prefigures her increasingly detailed and emblematic use of setting in her stories and novels; and her photographs of cemeteries and parades prefigure the central role of these images in the symbolic structure of her fiction. Yet there is a side to Welty's fiction that is rarely conveyed by her photographs. She transforms photographic images when she translates them into language. Through what Patti Carr Black calls "the alchemy of Welty's genius and vision" (*Welty* n. pag.), images become words that illuminate life's terrors as well as its consolations. The greatest value of the photographs may thus lie in what they tell us about Eudora Welty's transcendent imagination.

NOTES

1. While she was using her Kodak and Recomar cameras, Welty typically asked Standard Photo (Jackson, Mississippi) to process her film and provide her with negatives. She would then make her own prints. With negatives from her Rolleiflex Camera, Welty seldom did her own printing.

2. Two important essays about Eudora Welty's photographs appear in *Eudora Welty: Critical Essays*. In one Barbara McKenzie attempts to place Welty in the context of two works about the aesthetics of photographs—William Henry Fox Talbot's *The Pencil of Nature* (1844–46) and Susan Sontag's *On Photography* (1977). She also discusses the simi-

larities between photography and fiction as they appear in Welty's work: the symbolic dimension of place, the informal and therefore unconventional way of seeing that characterizes snapshots, the use of light, and a concern with time and mortality. Elizabeth Meese in the same collection reports on her examination of Welty's entire photographic output, categorizes Welty's subjects, discusses the organization of *One Time, One Place*, and explores the role of photography in Welty's creative processes as a writer, arguing that the visual image triggers Welty's narrative impulse and that photography taught Welty the importance of gesture as a defining feature. Charles Mann in a 1982 essay for *History of Photography* briefly comments on Welty's photographs and suggests that her concept of photography allies her with Jean-Luc Godard "who feels that film catches us in the act of dying, and with others who see the photograph as related to death" (149). In the past year two additional essays have focused upon Welty as photographer. In his brief article for *America*, Patrick Samway argues that Welty's photographs provide noteworthy portraits of women and that they tell us much about Welty's concern with human mortality. Louise Westling, in a more ambitious and expansive piece for *Mississippi Quarterly*, also pays special attention to photographs of women. Westling discusses "Welty's place among documentary photographers and writers" (588) and explores the "lyricism, mysticism, intimacy, and celebration" that differentiate her from those photographers (601).

I. CATALOGUE OF WELTY
NEGATIVES/CONTACT PRINTS
(Archives Series 26)

The negatives in the Welty Collection are ordered differently from the contact prints of them, and I have here followed the order of the contact prints, citing negative numbers for the purposes of identification. The contact prints fall into three major groups: those photographs taken before 1935 with an Eastman Kodak camera; those photographs taken in 1935–1936 with a Recomar Camera; and those photographs taken in late 1936 and subsequently with a Rolleiflex Camera. Within these major divisions, the photographs are organized alphabetically according to the locations where they were taken, first within Mississippi, then beyond its borders. Each entry includes a title or brief description, and there is also a citation if the photograph were used in EW's Lugene exhibition or her book publications.

The following abbreviations have been used in the catalogue:

EW. Eudora Welty.

IBW. Welty, Eudora. *In Black and White*. Northridge, Calif.: Lord John Press, 1985.

L. "Eudora Welty," an exhibit of photographs held March 31-April 15, 1936, at the Photographic Galleries, 600 Madison Avenue, New York City, and sponsored by Lugene, Inc. Opticians.

OTOP. Welty, Eudora. *One Time, One Place*. New York: Random House, 1971.

TP. Welty, Eudora. *Twenty Photographs*. Winston-Salem, N.C.: Palaemon Press, 1980.

W. Welty, Eudora. *Welty*. Ed. Patti Carr Black. Jackson, Miss: Mississippi Department of Archives and History, 1977.

Any necessary page references to these works will appear parenthetically after the relevant abbreviation.

A. Volume I
Photographs taken prior to 1935, Eastman Kodak camera with
bellows, 2 1/2" × 4 1/4" negatives

CANTON

973   "In the bag," *OTOP*.

CLINTON

   878   "Yard man," *OTOP*.

COPIAH COUNTY

   982   "To find plums," *OTOP*.

GRENADA

   971   "The Boast," L; "Store front," *OTOP*.
         In her Lugene show Welty cited Grenada as the location of this photograph. In *OTOP* she cites Canton.

   735   "Crossing the pavement," *OTOP*.
   714   "Saturday in town," *OTOP*; "Courthouse Town," *TP*.
   623   Untitled. Cropped copy negative of 714.
  1047   Untitled. The Square.
    45   Untitled. The Square.
   990   "Underwear," L; "Window shopping," *OTOP*.
   992   "Encounter," L; "Making a date," *OTOP*.
   703   "Strollers," L; "Strollers," *OTOP*; "Saturday Strollers," *TP*.
   223   Untitled, *IBW* (38). Two women and a man in conversation on the Square.
   640   Untitled. Old family home of Mary Moore Mitchell, EW's roommate at MSCW.
   200   Untitled. Vi'let, a servant at the Mitchell home.
   182   Untitled. Vi'let.
   189   Untitled. Ellen and her husband, servants at the Mitchell home and former members of Cindy's Band. Cindy, a resident of Grenada late in the nineteenth century, led a group of people known as Cindy's Band. This group believed the end of the world was coming, and its members marched through the streets exhorting people to repent and reform.
   163   Untitled. Ellen of Cindy's Band.
  1062   "Farmer and his Wife," *IBW*. Ellen of Cindy's Band.
   168   Untitled. Ellen of Cindy's Band.
   649   Untitled. Ellen of Cindy's Band.
   205   Untitled. Ellen of Cindy's Band.
   195   Untitled. Ellen of Cindy's Band.
   196   Untitled. Ellen of Cindy's Band.
   648   Untitled. Ellen of Cindy's Band.
   651   Untitled. Ellen of Cindy's Band.
   190   Untitled. Ellen of Cindy's Band.
  1015   Untitled. Ellen's husband.
   219   Untitled. Ellen's husband.
   256   Untitled. Ellen's husband.

647   Untitled. Ellen's husband.

215   "Farmer and his Wife," *IBW*. Ellen's husband.

185   Untitled. Ellen's husband.

158   Untitled. Cindy's apron. Owned by the couple in the previous photos, this apron had once belonged to the religious leader known as Cindy. Cindy made up her own mythology and depicted it on the apron—people with black hearts went to hell, those with gold hearts to heaven.

98   Untitled. Shed at the home of Ellen and her husband.

89   Untitled. Boots belonging to Ellen and her husband.

JACKSON

418   Untitled. Old Capitol, side entrance.

928   Untitled. Old Capitol.

427   Untitled. Old Capitol, front entrance.

288   Untitled. Freight train.

429   Untitled. First National Bank.

no neg.   Untitled. State St.

441   Untitled. Cottonseed mills.

458   Untitled. Cottonseed mills.

419   Untitled. Cottonseed mills.

424   Untitled. Cottonseed mills.

425   Untitled. Cottonseed mills.

689   "The fortune-teller's house," *OTOP*.

183   Untitled. Fortuneteller.

217   Untitled. Fortuneteller and daughter.

218   Untitled. Fortuneteller and daughter.

193   Untitled. Fortuneteller and daughter.

162   Untitled. Fortuneteller and daughter.

155   Untitled. Fortuneteller's daughter with guinea pigs. When EW visited the fortuneteller and had her fortune told, guinea pigs were running all over the floor. The daughter finally caught them by using the celery she holds in the picture as a lure.

1060   "Hat, fan, and quilts," *OTOP*.

1053   Untitled. Hat, fan, quilts.

1061   Untitled. Hat, fan, quilts.

174   "Dancing for Pennies," *IBW*. Boy with tambourine on Town Creek bridge.

161   "Playing for Pennies," *IBW*. Boy with tambourine and man with guitar.

164   Untitled. Boy with tambourine and man with guitar.

968   "Wash Day," L; "Washwoman," *OTOP.*
476   "Dappled," L.
962   "Schoolteacher on Friday Afternoon," L.
725   "The Date," L; "Making a date for Saturday night," *OTOP.*
733   "Mother and Child," L; "Mother and child," *OTOP* (107).
717   "The Porch," L; "Saturday off," *OTOP.*
727   "Swing," L; "Staying home," *OTOP.*
979   "Madonna with Coca Cola," L; "Coke," *OTOP.*
213   Untitled. Girl with Coca-Cola.
151   Untitled. Boy with toy pistol.
266   Untitled. Boys with toy pistol.
194   Untitled. Man with goatee.
197   Untitled. Man with goatee.
972   "Baptist deacon," *OTOP.*
181   "Sunday School Teacher," *IBW.*
221   Untitled. Mother smiling at two children.
477   "Spanking," L.
701   "With the baby," *OTOP.*
224   Untitled. Two women on a front porch.
718   "Hairdressing queue," *OTOP.*
264   Untitled. Mother and two children in porch swing.
265   Untitled. Two boys exchanging a smile.
188   Untitled. Arlene Catchings, also called Rosa, who worked for the Weltys.
172   "Sister and Brother," *IBW.*
1016 Untitled. Man in front of the Jitney Jungle grocery.
985   "Sunday Morning," L; "Sunday School child," *OTOP.*
977   "Author and director of the Bird Pageant," *OTOP.*
742   Untitled. Baby bluebird.
1046 "Baby Bluebird, Bird Pageant," *OTOP.*
984   "Bird Pageant costumes," *OTOP.*
980   "Bird Pageant," L; "Members of a Pageant of Birds," *OTOP.*
1013 Untitled. Pageant of birds.
511   "The Mattress Factory," L.
209   Untitled. Workshop.
210   Untitled. Gathering at the train depot.
267   Untitled. Two women on front porch.
202   Untitled. Three men at a mail box.
638   "Back Street," *IBW.* In *IBW* the location is identified as New Orleans.

381 Untitled. Women crossing railroad bridge. Another contact print from the same negative is numbered 382.
276 Untitled. City Ice and Coal.
271 Untitled. Two men walking by a frame church.
 57 Untitled. Man seated on a fence.
260 Untitled. Three children.
208 Untitled. Children and tricycle.
452 Untitled. Pigeons.
303 Untitled. Chickens.
456 Untitled. Chickens, cropped copy negative of 303.
170 Untitled. Young man feeding the chickens.
204 Untitled. Young man holding a chicken.
659 Untitled. Boy with a pig on a leash.
450 Untitled. Concrete pipe.
 95 Untitled. Porch with plants and rocker.
 88 Untitled. Porch with hanging plant and flower box.
327 Untitled. Porch with lattice work.
435 Untitled. Fence, trees, wall.
436 Untitled. Fence, trees, wall.
421 Untitled. Tree and broken wall.
437 Untitled. Fence, trees, wall.
422 Untitled. Fence, wall, gate.
438 Untitled. Back stairs.
426 Untitled. Pines.
423 Untitled. Trees.

PARADES AND FESTIVALS IN JACKSON

127 Untitled. N.R.A. parade float.
119 Untitled. Parade passing St. Andrews Cathedral.
135 "Negro State Fair Parade Down Capitol Street," *IBW*.
129 Untitled. Parade float—"Plow Deep."
130 Untitled. Parade float—women in white.
722 "Parade Float," L; "Club float, Negro State Fair parade," *OTOP*.
491 Untitled. Parade—horse and buggy.
486 Untitled. Parade float—bathing beauties.
131 Untitled. Parade float.
503 Untitled. Marching band.
118 "Parade Coming," *IBW*.
487 Untitled. State fair—boys looking at a camel.
132 Untitled. Children and maypole.
142 Untitled. Children around maypoles.

MADISON COUNTY
738 "Sorghum Making," L; "Making cane syrup," *OTOP*.
879 "Making cane syrup," *OTOP*.
86 Untitled. Pasture.

MISSISSIPPI RIVER
521 Untitled. Shantyboat.
315 Untitled. Barge.
316 Untitled. Barge.
317 Untitled. Barge.
318 Untitled. River view.

NATCHEZ
no neg. "Home open to the public," *OTOP*.
1 Untitled. Dunleith.
17 Untitled. Dunleith.
15 Untitled. Arlington, front view.
16 Untitled. Arlington, rear view.

PEARL RIVER
461 "High Water," *IBW* (11).
480 Untitled. Father and child on shantyboat.
522 Untitled. Father and child on shantyboat.
519 Untitled. Shantyboat *Fritz*.
520 Untitled. Shantyboat.
549 Untitled. Bridge.
518 Untitled. Looking down from a bridge.

UTICA
165 Untitled. Two men.
1012 Untitled. Woman with cane.
42 Untitled. Gathering in front of the soda parlor.
41 Untitled. Gathering in front of the soda parlor.
198 Untitled. Woman in wide-brimmed hat.
876 Untitled. Telling stories.
711 "Small Talk," L; "Tall story," *OTOP*.
143 Untitled. Five men leaning on a bridge rail.
55 Untitled. Large house belonging to friends of EW.

VICKSBURG/WARREN COUNTY
523 Untitled. Farm machinery.
969 "Chopping in the field," *OTOP*; "Chopping in the Fields," *TP*.
106 Untitled. Woman in cotton field.

YALOBUSHA COUNTY
993 "Home by Dark," L; "Home by dark," *OTOP*; "Home by Dark," *TP*.

963 "Washwomen," L; "Washwomen carrying the clothes," *OTOP*.

156 Untitled. Washwomen.

YAZOO COUNTY

192 Untitled. Family, house, laundry.

207 Untitled. Boy on porch, girl in doorway.

220 "Child Dancing," *IBW*. In *IBW* the location is identified as Jackson.

995 Untitled. Children playing in a ring.

699 "Front yard," *OTOP*.

171 "Saturday Afternoon," *IBW*. In *IBW* the location is identified as Jackson.

154 "Mother Dressing Her Child's Hair," *IBW*. In *IBW* the location is identified as Jackson.

NEW ORLEANS

920 "A Charleston Courtyard," *IBW*. Seems instead to be a New Orleans courtyard.

923 Untitled. House.

916 Untitled. Balcony, a woman watering her plants.

919 Untitled. Banana plant in courtyard.

927 Untitled. Women on balcony above, boy on pavement below.

UNIDENTIFIED

420 Untitled. Pasture scene.

104 Untitled. Houses on a river bank.

105 Untitled. Houses on a river bank.

451 Untitled. Cow.

169 Untitled, *IBW* (43). In *IBW* the location is identified as Utica.

211 Untitled. Four children.

167 Untitled. Meeting at the barber shop.

457 Untitled. Two smiling women.

206 Untitled. Man and woman in conversation.

199 Untitled. Two laughing women.

212 Untitled. Woman with a white collar.

184 Untitled. Man with ice cream cone.

177 Untitled. Babies.

259 Untitled. A drink of water.

222 Untitled. Meeting at the corner.

166 Untitled. Parasol.

216 Untitled. Man in a straw hat.

255 Untitled. Woman helping man to walk.
258 Untitled. Domestic conflict.
175 Untitled. Baby.
191 Untitled. Two children beside a car.
180 "Sisters," *IBW.*
214 Untitled. Four men.
203 Untitled. Woman using a churn.
 97 Untitled. House and field.
no neg. Untitled. Pasture scene.

B. VOLUME II
1935–36, Recomar Camera, 3″ × 4″ Negatives (Film Pack)

BIG BLACK RIVER
548 Untitled. Row boat.
550 "Cypress in the Big Black River near Vicksburg," *IBW.*
551 Untitled. Cypress swamp.
1040 Untitled. Cypress swamp.

CANTON
1009 Untitled. Mule-drawn wagon on the courthouse square.
708 "Saturday arrivals," *OTOP.*
731 "Late Saturday Afternoon," L; "The Store," *OTOP. OTOP* incorrectly locates this photograph in Utica.
 48 Untitled. Street corner.
515 Untitled. Men in front of store windows.
 72 Untitled. Covered wagon.
230 Untitled. Conversation on the courthouse square.

COLUMBUS
1054 Untitled. Nineteenth-century home.

CRYSTAL SPRINGS
960 "Tomato Packers, Recess," L; "Tomato-packers' recess," *OTOP*; "Tomato Packers' Recess," *TP.*
 94 Untitled. Tomato packers on a break.
976 "Farmers in town," *OTOP.*
534 "House by the Railroad," *IBW.*
821 Untitled. Cemetery monument, "Nellie."
769 Untitled. Cemetery monument, "Daisy."
820 Untitled. Cemetery monument, "Lily."
829 Untitled. Cemetery monument, "Lily."
770 Untitled. Cemetery monument, "Mott."
767 Untitled. Cemetery monument, "Mott."

GRENADA

692   "A slave's apron," *OTOP*. This apron belonged to Cindy, a religious leader who believed the end of the world was at hand. It depicts the day of judgment when those with black hearts will be sent to hell and those with gold hearts to heaven.

467   Untitled. Apron.

173   Untitled. Banner used by Cindy's Band.

505   Untitled. Banner used by Cindy's Band.

553   Untitled. Mule-drawn wagon.

HINDS COUNTY

729   "Blind weaver on the WPA," *OTOP*.

721   "Four sisters," *OTOP*.

987   "Mother and child," *OTOP* (110); "Mother and Child," *TP*.

965   "Nurse at home," *OTOP*.

82   Untitled. Grinding cane.

547   Untitled. Making cane syrup.

967   "Boiling pot," *OTOP*.

81   "The Boiling Pot," *IBW*.

989   "To all go to town," *OTOP*; "Saturday Trip to Town," *TP*.

517   Untitled. Child at play.

80   Untitled. Backyard.

552   Untitled. Backyard.

46   Untitled. Tiger Rag Grocery.

JACKSON

no neg.   Untitled. Nash Burger in front of the New Capitol. Jackson native Nash Burger went on to become an editor at the *New York Times Book Review*.

583   Untitled. New Capitol in snow.

584   Untitled. Partial view of New Capitol in snow.

591   Untitled. Old Capitol, entry.

590   Untitled. Old Capitol pillars.

589   Untitled. Clock tower, Lamar Life Insurance Building.

269   Untitled. Eat Shoppe.

273   Untitled. Fresh Water Fish.

268   Untitled. Woman in fish market.

60   Untitled. Coin collectors.

59   Untitled. Coin collectors.

961   Untitled, *OTOP*. My Blue Heaven Lunch Stand.

463   Untitled. State St. by streetcar line.

62   Untitled. Smith's Radio Shop.

287 Untitled. Laundry on fence.
63 Untitled. Laundry.
64 Untitled. Row houses.
533 "Rental Property," *IBW*.
330 Untitled. Black Catholic church.
56 "Looking Across South State Street from Old Confederate Park," *IBW*.
443 Untitled. Statue of Confederate soldier.
751 "Confederate veterans meeting in the park," *OTOP*.
974 Untitled. Confederate veterans in the park.
147 Untitled. Confederate veterans in the park.
68 Untitled. Confederate veterans in the park.
149 Untitled. Two men on a park bench, Confederate Park.
153 Untitled. Choctaw girls.
662 Untitled. Park bench gathering.
148 Untitled. Swimmer in Livingston Park.
294 Untitled. Livingston Park.
988 "The Dolls," L; "To play dolls," *OTOP*.
157 "New Dolls," *IBW*.
470 Untitled. Girls with dolls.
966 "Schoolchildren," *OTOP*.
512 Untitled. School children.
964 "Schoolchildren meeting a visitor," *OTOP*.
159 Untitled. Children playing in a ring.
160 Untitled. Wagon wheels and shadows.
473 Untitled. Splitting wood.
244 Untitled. Splitting wood.
272 Untitled. Splitting wood.
238 Untitled. Three men in conversation.
247 Untitled. Two men in front of Furniture Co.
248 Untitled. Sweeping the yard.
250 Untitled. Children gazing down the street.
249 Untitled. Window shopping.
506 Untitled. Poultry market.
508 Untitled, *IBW* (14). Woman on Fortification St.
1014 Untitled, *W*. Woman on Fortification St.
544 Untitled. Meeting in front of the Manship House.
474 Untitled. Man in overalls and a top coat.
740 Untitled, *OTOP*; "A Woman of the 'Thirties," *TP*. Frontispiece of *OTOP*.
981 "Boy with his kite," *OTOP*.

726   "If it rains," *OTOP*.

704   "Waiting," L; "Home," *OTOP* (38).

246   Untitled. Children in their rockers.

698   "Wild flowers," *OTOP*.

233   Untitled. Children with wild flowers.

650   "Wildflowers," *IBW*.

239   Untitled. Girls in front of a store window.

144   Untitled. Children on a downtown street.

 58   Untitled. Men with feet on a rail.

465   Untitled. Conversation groups.

270   "Looking In The Market Window," *IBW*.

283   Untitled. Coming down the stairs.

282   Untitled. Children and their nurse.

284   "Nurses and Children on State Street," *IBW*.

280   Untitled. Meeting in front of Hunt & Whitaker.

228   Untitled. Meeting in front of Hunt & Whitaker.

285   "Parrish Street," *IBW*. Photograph is inaccurately titled. It should be called "Farish Street."

464   Untitled. Across the street from Hunt & Whitaker.

471   Untitled. Across from Peoples Furniture Co.

231   Untitled. Waiting to cross the street.

545   Untitled. Sitting on railing, Town Creek bridge.

472   Untitled. Meeting at the post box.

274   "Home," *IBW*. In *IBW* the location is identified as Utica.

478   "Children and Their Automobiles," *IBW*.

277   "The Century Theater Colored Entrance," *IBW*.

275   Untitled. Blacksmith at work.

281   Untitled. Wagon in front of Peoples Furniture Co.

107   "High Water," *IBW* (10).

237   Untitled. Man sitting by a store window.

286   Untitled. Conversation in front of Dr. C. R. v.Seutter's office.

460   Untitled. Pigs and laundry on Farish St.

292   Untitled. Mississippi St. yard with pig.

295   Untitled. Pigeons.

279   Untitled. Four boys leaning on a fence.

468   Untitled. Water tower and river.

693   "Preacher and leaders of Holiness Church," *OTOP*; "Preacher and Leaders of the Holiness Church," *TP*. The preacher had heel taps and would use them when he expected the congregation to respond to his questions.

716 "Sunday School. Holiness Church," *OTOP*. EW was invited to take pictures because her friends' servants were members of the church.

178 Untitled. Holiness Church. The holiest members, the matrons, holding Bible, cymbals, tambourine.

656 Untitled. Holiness Church. Leaders with Bible, cymbals, tambourine.

235 Untitled. Holiness Church. Preacher and leaders with guitar, piano, cymbals.

243 Untitled. Holiness Church. Four women and a child.

251 Untitled. Holiness Church. Leaders with cymbals and tambourine.

201 Untitled. Holiness Church. Leaders with cymbals and tambourine.

986 "Baby Holiness member," *OTOP*.

PARADES AND CIRCUSES IN JACKSON

179 Untitled. Parade float, Holiness Church.

126 Untitled. Medical float.

136 Untitled. Women's float.

134 Untitled. Parade car, "Explosives."

137 Untitled. NRA float.

138 Untitled. Parade float with eight women.

139 Untitled. Horseback riders, man with sign advertising "Big Sale at Handelman's."

140 Untitled. School girls.

560 Untitled. Parade car, " . . . Service Power Prover."

120 Untitled. Parade float, "Divine Healing Service."

125 Untitled. Parade float, "Divine Healing Service."

141 Untitled. Parade car, "Collins Burial Association."

124 Untitled. Parade float, "Madam Palmer."

133 Untitled. Woman in nineteenth-century costume.

494 Untitled. Horseback rider with flag.

495 Untitled. Horseback riders with plumed hats.

123 Untitled. Circus wagon, man with trombone.

496 Untitled. Elephants.

488 Untitled. Lion.

500 Untitled. Lion.

499 Untitled. Lion.

498 Untitled. Lion.

121 Untitled. Circus wagon.

502 Untitled. Crowd in front of "Freaks Oddities" banner.

485 Untitled. The big top.
554 Untitled. Sideshow, man with accordion.
686 "Sideshow, State Fair," *OTOP*.
122 "Midway Attractions," *IBW*.
490 Untitled. Sideshow poster, "How Can She Live."
687 "Sideshow wonders, State Fair," *OTOP*. Sideshow poster, "Junie | Cow with A Human Face."
1044 "Sideshow wonders, State Fair," *OTOP*. Sideshow poster, "Siamese Calves."
970 "Hypnotist, State Fair," *OTOP*; "Side Show, State Fair," *TP*.
1041 Untitled. Sideshow banners.
23 Untitled. Merry-go-round.
492 Untitled. Trapeze act.
22 Untitled. Carnival ride.
994 "The Rides, State Fair," *OTOP*.
978 "Beggar at the Fair gate," *OTOP*.
724 "Free Gate, State Fair," *OTOP*.
559 Untitled. Sideshow, "It Tells You Everything."
493 Untitled. Sideshow, "MO . . . . "

JACKSON'S GREENWOOD CEMETERY
36 Untitled. Cemetery angel.
794 Untitled. Cemetery angel.
789 Untitled. Cemetery monument, lady with wreath.
784 Untitled. Cemetery monument, lady with wreath.
814 Untitled. Cemetery monument, robed, kneeling woman.
809 Untitled. Cemetery monument, robed, kneeling woman.
790 Untitled. Cemetery monument, robed, kneeling woman.
791 Untitled. Cemetery angel, "Ellen Moore."
813 Untitled. Cemetery monument, mother and children beneath weeping willow.

LEARNED
314 Untitled. Erosion.
310 Untitled. Erosion.

LOWNDES COUNTY
741 "WPA farm-to-market road worker," *OTOP*.

MADISON COUNTY
713 "The Chum," L; "With a chum," *OTOP*.

MERIDIAN
43 Untitled. Chart of anatomy and physiology at county fair. Next to chart were two plants, one watered with alcohol and one with water, to show the evil effects of drink.

NATCHEZ

7   Untitled. D'Evereux.
19 Untitled. Antebellum house.
5   Untitled. Arlington.
20 Untitled. Arlington.
9   Untitled. Auburn.
12 Untitled. Auburn, back gallery.
2   Untitled. Richmond.
10 Untitled. Richmond.
11 Untitled. Richmond.
18 Untitled. Richmond.
4   Untitled. Ivy-covered house.
13 Untitled. Trees and Spanish moss.
3   Untitled. Rosalie.
8   Untitled. Rosalie.
14 Untitled. Dunleith.
6   Untitled. Cemetery.

CHURCH HILL (NEAR NATCHEZ)

375 Untitled. Church.
637 Untitled. Church.
685 "Country church," *OTOP*.

PEARL RIVER

459 Untitled. Sand bar.
326 "House-Boat on Pearl River," L.
442 "Houseboat on Pearl River." Not an original negative.
484 Untitled. Father and child on Pearl River shantyboat.
983 "Home," *OTOP* (37); "Houseboat Family, Pearl River," *TP*.
304 Untitled. Pearl River shantyboat.
305 "Settled," L.
524 Untitled. Looking down from a bridge.

PONTOTOC

975 "Watermelon on the courthouse grounds," *OTOP*.
621 Untitled. "Keep Off Grass."
913 Untitled. Courthouse crowd.
754 Untitled. Watermelon on the grounds.
753 Untitled. Political speaking, aftermath.
734 "Political speaking," *OTOP*. Not an original negative.
128 Untitled. Political speaking.

RANKIN COUNTY

694 "Storekeeper," *OTOP*.
145 Untitled. EW with storekeeper and his family.
96   Untitled. Tourist court.

448   Untitled. Tourist court.
408   "Backyard," L.
535   Untitled. Flood.

RAYMOND

454   Untitled. Raymond Courthouse.
440   "Courthouse, Raymond," *IBW* (32).
340   "Courthouse, Raymond," *IBW* (33).
445   Untitled. Statue of Confederate soldier.
455   Untitled. Raymond Courthouse.
444   Untitled. Raymond Courthouse.
755   Untitled. Mrs. Willie Spann on courthouse stile.

SMITH COUNTY

736   "Cotton gin," *OTOP*. In *OTOP* EW locates this photograph in Hinds County. On a mounted print prepared in the late 1930s or early 1940s, however, the photograph's location is said to be Smith County.
 83   Untitled. A cotton gin.

UTICA

226   Untitled. Men on bridge.
229   Untitled. Four men.
546   Untitled. Bootlegger.
232   Untitled. Bootlegger.
991   "The bootlegger's house," *OTOP*.
513   Untitled. Sign for "Douglas Shoes."
700   "Negro Boy," L; "With a dog," *OTOP*.
146   Untitled. Three generations.
 47   "Fruit Packer's Recess," *IBW*.
 92   Untitled. Farmers in conversation.
806   Untitled. Cemetery monument, woman with wreath.
783   Untitled. Cemetery monument, woman with wreath.
815   Untitled. Cemetery angel, child.

VICKSBURG

311   "River Edge," L.
466   Untitled. Crane.
501   Untitled. Paddlewheeler.
382   "The Canal Below," *IBW*; "Dredge," L.
483   Untitled. Smokestacks at river's edge.
525   Untitled. Vicksburg—Delta Ferry.

CHARLESTON, S.C.

(EW stopped in Charleston on her way to New York City and took these pictures early one morning before leaving on a bus.)

928   Untitled. Black cat.
929   Untitled, *IBW* (62). Fruit market.
930   Untitled. Street scene.
931   Untitled. Decorative gate.
932   Untitled. House.
933   Untitled. Church.
934   Untitled. Public Market.
935   Untitled. Street scene.
936   Untitled. Street scene.
937   Untitled. Church tower.
938   Untitled. Street scene.
939   Untitled. Women selling flowers.
940   Untitled. Corner house.
941   Untitled. Churchyard.
942   Untitled. Garden.
943   Untitled. Public statue.
944   Untitled. Churchyard.
945   Untitled. Street scene.
946   Untitled. House.
947   Untitled. Cemetery.
948   Untitled. Black cat.

NEW ORLEANS, LA.

no neg.   Untitled. Open shutters.
1007   Untitled, *W.* Children drinking from a fountain.

NEW YORK CITY

949   Untitled. Pigeons in Union Square.
950   Untitled. Front stoops.
951   Untitled. River in winter.
952   Untitled. River in winter.
953   "East Side," *IBW.*
954   Untitled. Union Square.
955   Untitled. Park bench, Union Square.
956   Untitled. Skyscrapers.
957   "The Fence."
958   Untitled. Outdoor stairway.
959   Untitled. Barber shop.
996   Untitled. Feeding the pigeons.
997   "The Unemployed in Union Square," *IBW* (67).
998   Untitled. Conversation groups.
999   Untitled. Union Square.
1000   Untitled. Union Square.

1001   Untitled. Union Square.
1002   Untitled. Under the elevated tracks.
1003   Untitled. Men gazing in windows.
1004   "The Unemployed and the Apple Seller," *IBW*.
1034   Untitled. Man sitting on sidewalk.
1035   Untitled. Roof tops.
1036   Untitled. Plumbing shop.
1037   "The Unemployed in Union Square," *IBW* (66).
1038   Untitled. River in winter.
1039   Untitled. River in winter.

NORTH CAROLINA (NEAR CHAPEL HILL)
(EW may have visited here on the same trip that took her to Charleston, S.C.)
449   "Potter," L.

UNIDENTIFIED
447   Untitled. Grass fire.
439   Untitled. Outdoor market.
338   Untitled. Bottle tree.
87   Untitled. Bottle tree.
85   Untitled. "Old Miss. Slaughter Pen."
84   Untitled. Rolling a cigarette.
93   Untitled. Watermelons.
1017   Untitled. Children at play.
65   Untitled. Cafe interior.
66   Untitled. Wagon on an unpaved street.
51   Untitled. Storefront.
150   "Child on the Porch," *TP*.
504   "Setting up the State Fair," *IBW*. In *IBW* the location is identified as Jackson.
561   Untitled. Sideshow: "Sex Mad."
555   Untitled. Sideshow: "Sex Mad."
293   Untitled. Mare and foal.
792   Untitled. Identical cemetery monuments, angels with fingers pointing heavenward.
793   Untitled. Cemetery monument, woman with hair in bun.
645   Untitled. Woman crossing the street.
646   Untitled. Man in overalls and suitcoat.
514   Untitled. Man riding a mule down a city street.
225   Untitled. Man and woman in conversation.
234   Untitled. Two men at a building's corner.
657   Untitled. Old man in a topcoat.
658   Untitled. Putting up a billboard.

660 Untitled. Putting up a billboard.

252 Untitled. Children at play.

254 Untitled. Portrait of a woman.

489 Untitled. Two women in conversation.

507 Untitled. Woman sitting on sidewalk.

1018 Untitled. Conversation in front of the grocery store.

236 Untitled. Men and shovels.

240 Untitled. Baby.

241 Untitled. Children beside a house.

242 Untitled. Mother and son.

245 Untitled. Two women and a child at the pasture gate.

509 Untitled. Sisters in a rocking chair.

516 Untitled. Picture show.

510 Untitled. Three men in conversation.

475 Untitled. Children beside wagon.

329 Untitled. House with star above balcony.

328 Untitled. House in Carpenter Gothic style.

C. Volume III
Post-1936, Rolleiflex Camera, 2 1/4" × 2 1/4" negatives

BYRAM

324 Untitled. Wooden suspension bridge.

CANTON

54 Untitled. Store fronts.

298 "Cats in a grocery store window," *IBW*.

732 "Town in a store window," *OTOP*.

446 "Store front." Not an original negative.

44 "Store Front," *TP*.

71 Untitled. Plow in store window.

73 Untitled. Lanterns in store window.

77 Untitled. Sidewalk display.

74 Untitled. Store window—rifle, mailbox, bucket.

COPIAH CO.

737 "Hog-killing time," *OTOP*. Location is identified as Hinds County in *OTOP*.

76 Untitled. Hog-killing.

CRYSTAL SPRINGS

70 Untitled. "Tomatropolis."

775 Untitled. Cemetery monument, "Lily."

836   Untitled. Cemetery monument, "Lily."
861   Untitled. Cemetery monument, "Lily."
840   Untitled. Cemetery monument, "Lily."
855   Untitled. Cemetery monument, "Lily."
873   Untitled. Cemetery monument, "Lily."
1049 Untitled. Cemetery monument, "Lily."
847   Untitled. Cemetery.
863   Untitled. Cemetery monument, "Mott."
453   Untitled. Cemetery monument, "Mott."
801   Untitled. Cemetery monument, "Mott."
849   Untitled. Cemetery monument, "Mott."
848   "Churchyard Cemetery," *IBW*.
811   Untitled. Cemetery monument, child with cross.
798   Untitled. Cemetery monument, child with cross.
779   Untitled. Cemetery monument, "Daisy C."
804   Untitled. Cemetery monument, "Daisy C."
808   Untitled. Cemetery monument, "Daisy C."
837   Untitled. Cemetery monument, "Daisy C."
810   Untitled. Cemetery monument, angel with cross.
800   Untitled. Cemetery monument, weeping willow.

FAYETTE

61   Untitled. Men sitting on downtown steps.
404   Untitled. Men sitting on downtown steps.
50   Untitled. Looking out the cafe window.
412   Untitled. Alcorn College.

GRAND GULF

1024 Untitled. Spiral nets.
750   Untitled. Hanging nets.
706   Untitled. Fisherman and his sons.
752   "Fisherman and his boys," *OTOP*.
389   Untitled. Boats at river's edge.
321   Untitled. Boats at river's edge.
705   "Home," *OTOP*.
1056 Untitled, *W*. Shantyboat aground.
462   Untitled. Shantyboat aground.

HERMANVILLE

707   "Village," *OTOP*.
1029 Untitled. The town stores.

HINDS COUNTY

737   "Hog-killing time," *OTOP*.
76   Untitled. Hog-killing.

JACKSON

582   "Old Capitol of State of Mississippi," *IBW*.
581   Untitled. Old Capitol.
586   Untitled. Old Capitol entry, draped in bunting.
592   Untitled. Statue of Jefferson Davis, Old Capitol.
596   Untitled. Old Capitol, draped in bunting.
577   Untitled. New Capitol.
543   Untitled. New Capitol rotunda.
597   Untitled. New Capitol.
578   Untitled. New Capitol.
152   Untitled. Two beauty contestants at the New Capitol. EW took this picture for the Mississippi Advertising Comission, and doing so inspired the story "Hello and Good-Bye." The pose was the girls' idea.
no neg.   Untitled. State Insane Hospital.
no neg.   Untitled. State Insane Hospital.
641   Untitled. State Insane Hospital.
642   Untitled. State Insane Hospital.
643   Untitled. State Insane Hospital.
290   Untitled. Crowd on a boxcar, watching a fire.
278   Untitled. Fire.
289   Untitled. Watching a fire.
691   "Delegate," *OTOP*; "Delegate," *TP*.
291   Untitled. Delegates in front of the Governor's Mansion.
343   Untitled. Tea at the Governor's Mansion.
728   "Speaking in the Unknown Tongue," *OTOP*.
253   "The Unknown Tongue," *IBW*.
720   "Make a joyful noise unto the Lord," *OTOP*.
653   Untitled. Holiness Church.
102   Untitled. Camellia house.
100   Untitled. Camellia house.
no neg.   Untitled. Davis School.
585   Untitled. Davis School.
579   Untitled. Davis School.
337   Untitled. Religious message, train line switch yard. A minister changed the quotations each morning.
580   Untitled. Tourist court, high water.
594   Untitled. Perhaps this is Bailey Junior High School under construction.
595   Untitled. Cottonseed mill.
69   Untitled. Street corner.

587　Untitled. Pampas grass.
593　Untitled. Residential street.
719　"Ida M'Toy," *OTOP*.
730　"Ida M'Toy, retired midwife," *OTOP*.
664　Untitled. Ida M'Toy.
667　Untitled. Ida M'Toy.
676　Untitled. Ida M'Toy.
671　Untitled. Ida M'Toy.
662　Untitled. Ida M'Toy.
663　Untitled. Ida M'Toy.
677　Untitled. Ida M'Toy.
678　Untitled. Ida M'Toy.
679　Untitled. Ida M'Toy.
912　Untitled. Ida M'Toy.
432　Untitled. Ida M'Toy.
257　Untitled. Ida M'Toy.
661　Untitled. Ida M'Toy.
672　Untitled. Ida M'Toy.
675　Untitled. Ida M'Toy.
1005　"Old Midwife (Ida M'Toy)," *TP*.
665　Untitled. Ida M'Toy.
666　Untitled. Ida M'Toy.
668　Untitled. Ida M'Toy.
669　Untitled. Ida M'Toy.
674　Untitled. Ida M'Toy.
680　Untitled. Ida M'Toy.
909　Untitled. Ida M'Toy.
911　Untitled. Ida M'Toy.
670　Untitled. Ida M'Toy and daughter.
673　Untitled. Ida M'Toy and daughter.
910　Untitled. Ida M'Toy and daughter.
877　Untitled. Ida M'Toy's daughter.
302　Untitled. Geese.
300　Untitled. Geese.
301　Untitled. Swans in Livingston Park.
296　Untitled. Baby bat.
297　Untitled. Baby bat.
299　Untitled. Chickens.
399　Untitled. Chickens.
406　Untitled. Chickens.

PARADES AND CIRCUSES IN JACKSON

723 "County float, State Fair parade," *OTOP*.
688 "Church float, State Fair parade," *OTOP*.
563 Untitled. Marching band.
614 Untitled. Capitol Street.
605 Untitled. Marching band.
567 Untitled. Marching band.
575 Untitled. Marching band.
615 Untitled. Marching band.
565 Untitled. Marching band.
616 Untitled. Marching band.
604 Untitled. Marching band in front of Draughon School.
566 Untitled. Filming the parade.
613 Untitled. Boy Scouts.
557 Untitled. The view from a parent's shoulders.
574 Untitled. Church float.
599 Untitled. Fondren Sisters Beauty Salon and School float.
602 Untitled. Parade passing the Governor's Mansion.
603 Untitled. Parade passing the Governor's Mansion.
612 Untitled. Parade float.
598 Untitled. Taylor Cafe parade car.
601 Untitled. Cars in parade.
558 Untitled. Minstrel show.
497 Untitled. Minstrel show.
556 Untitled. Minstrel show.
112 Untitled. Boy in folding chair.
115 Untitled. Boy in folding chair in front of sideshow barker.
1011 Untitled. Boy in folding chair in front of sideshow barker.
607 Untitled. Carnival workers.
609 Untitled. Carnival workers.
608 Untitled. Carnival workers.
562 Untitled. Carnival workers.
610 Untitled. Carnival workers.
611 Untitled. Carnival workers; EW's friend in this picture is Margaret Harmon.
606 Untitled. Carnival workers.
109 Untitled. Carnival worker.
481 Untitled. Sideshow poster: "Frog Boy."
114 Untitled. Sideshow poster: "1000 Reward if she is not Alive."

117　Untitled. Sideshow poster: "Rubber Man."
113　Untitled. Sideshow poster: "Mule Face Woman."
110　Untitled. Sideshow poster: "3 Legged Man."
469　Untitled. Sideshow poster: "Ossified Man."
111　Untitled. Sideshow poster: "Headless Girl."
600　Untitled. Insect circus.
569　Untitled. Rides at the Fair.
576　Untitled. Putting up the tents.
568　Untitled. Sideshow, setting up.
570　Untitled. Sideshow, setting up.
571　Untitled. Sideshow, setting up.
617　Untitled. Sideshow, setting up.
618　Untitled. Sideshow, setting up.
572　Untitled. Sideshow, "Cotton Club Review."
564　Untitled. Sideshow, "Girls for Sale."

JACKSON'S GREENWOOD CEMETERY

851　Untitled. Cemetery monument, man with cane.
870　Untitled. Cemetery monument, man with cane.
786　Untitled. Cemetery monument, "True to the Public Trust."
797　Untitled. Cemetery monument, "True to the Public Trust."
867　Untitled. Cemetery monument, "Onslow Glenmore."
859　Untitled. Cemetery monument, "Onslow Glenmore."
799　Untitled. Cemetery monument, "Onslow Glenmore."
817　Untitled. Cemetery monument, "Onslow Glenmore."
824　Untitled. Cemetery angel.
834　Untitled. Cemetery angel.
532　Untitled. Cemetery angel.
 38　Untitled. Cemetery angel.
 37　Untitled. Cemetery angel.
1023　Untitled, *W.* Cemetery angel.
788　Untitled. Cemetery angel.
768　Untitled. Cemetery monument, robed, kneeling woman.
866　Untitled. Cemetery monument.
818　Untitled. Cemetery monument, mother and children beneath weeping willow.
757　Untitled. Cemetery monument, mother and children beneath weeping willow.
778　Untitled. Cemetery monument, dog on grave.
858　Untitled. Cemetery monument, dog on grave.

MADISON CO.

739 "Making cane syrup," *OTOP* (15).

1045 Untitled. Making cane syrup.

1020 Untitled. Grinding cane.

416 Untitled. Grinding cane.

634 Untitled. Chapel of the Cross.

334 Untitled. Chapel of the Cross, interior.

336 Untitled. Chapel of the Cross, bell tower.

MISSISSIPPI RIVER

no neg. Untitled. Frank Lyell, Helen Lotterhos. Frank Lyell became a Professor of English at the University of Texas; Helen Lotterhos was a Jackson, Miss., artist.

396 Untitled. "Simpson Freshish Peanuts." EW believes she may have taken this photograph in upstate New York.

405 Untitled. Vista of river.

325 Untitled. Vista of river.

313 Untitled. Vista of river.

313a Untitled. Vista of river.

NATCHEZ

358 Untitled. Ruins. EW says this is not Windsor.

21 Untitled. Home with gallery and pillars.

NATCHEZ TRACE AREA

712 "Home Abandoned," *OTOP*. EW's friend John Robinson knew of this house and showed it to her.

341 Untitled. House near Raymond and Clinton.

342 Untitled. House near Raymond and Clinton.

536 Untitled. House near Raymond and Clinton.

537 Untitled. House near Raymond and Clinton.

538 Untitled. House near Raymond and Clinton.

539 Untitled. House near Raymond and Clinton.

540 Untitled. House near Raymond and Clinton.

541 Untitled. House near Raymond and Clinton.

542 Untitled. House near Raymond and Clinton.

627 Untitled. House near Raymond and Clinton.

628 Untitled. House near Raymond and Clinton.

629 Untitled. House near Raymond and Clinton.

630 Untitled. House near Raymond and Clinton.

631 Untitled. House near Raymond and Clinton.

632 Untitled. House near Raymond and Clinton.

633 Untitled. House near Raymond and Clinton.

1052   Untitled. House near Raymond and Clinton.
1022   Untitled, *W.* Road between high banks.
91   Untitled. Dense growth of vines.
103   Untitled. House.
25   Untitled. Town seen from a distance.
29   Untitled. Town seen from a distance.
34   Untitled. Cemetery in Rodney or Rocky Springs.
748   Untitled. Cemetery in Rodney or Rocky Springs.
749   Untitled. Cemetery in Rodney or Rocky Springs.
no neg.   Untitled. Gravestone for Jennie Owen.
40   Untitled. Cemetery, lilies on graves.
33   Untitled. Cemetery, lilies on graves.
846   Untitled. Table-like cemetery monument.

PEARL RIVER

312   Untitled. River's edge.
320   Untitled. River.
323   Untitled. River.
901   Untitled. River seen through trees and vines.
no neg.   Untitled. Helen Lotterhos.
322   Untitled. Man at river's edge.
319   Untitled. Row boat.
893   Untitled. Row boat.
905   Untitled. Sand bar gathering.
904   Untitled. Sand bar gathering.
896   Untitled. Sand bar gathering.
894   Untitled. Sand bar gathering.
902   Untitled. Sand bar gathering.
908   Untitled. Sand bar gathering.
887   Untitled. Sand bar gathering.
884   Untitled. Sand bar gathering.
890   Untitled. Helen Lotterhos wading.
903   Untitled. Sand bar.
898   Untitled. Sand bar.
899   Untitled. Sand bar.
897   Untitled. River seen through trees.
895   Untitled. Looking up through the trees.
900   Untitled. Woods.
906   Untitled. Artist beside river.
907   Untitled. Artist beside river.
885   Untitled. Shoreline.
886   Untitled. Woods.

1008   Untitled. Woods overlooking river.
891   Untitled. Woods overlooking river.
889   Untitled. Woods overlooking river.
888   Untitled. River seen from bridge.
892   Untitled. Sand bar.
307   Untitled. River seen from woods.
619   Untitled. Shantyboat.

PORT GIBSON
697   "Church in Port Gibson," *OTOP*.
417   Untitled. Presbyterian Church.
434   Untitled. Presbyterian Church.
635   Untitled. Presbyterian Church.
431   Untitled. Synagogue.
116   Untitled. Ice cream stand.
860   Untitled. Decorative cemetery gate.
857   Untitled. Cemetery monument, Graeme.

RAYMOND
391   Untitled. Courthouse.
392   Untitled. Courthouse.
394   Untitled. Courthouse.
397   Untitled. Courthouse.
398   Untitled. Courthouse.
414   Untitled. Courthouse.
433   Untitled. Statue of Confederate soldier.
1030   Untitled, *W*. Stile in front of courthouse.

ROCKY SPRINGS
702   "Home," *OTOP* (36).
407   Untitled. Woman in front porch rocker.
409   Untitled. Woman standing by front porch rocker.
403   Untitled. Woman standing by front porch rocker.
410   Untitled. Woman in front porch rocker.
108   Untitled. Calf in front of house.
479   Untitled. Calf in front of house.
1028   Untitled, *W*. Calf.
347   Untitled. House with porch and porch roof precariously propped.
335   Untitled. Deteriorating house.
411   Untitled. Deteriorating house.
no neg.   Untitled. Methodist Church.
400   Untitled. Methodist Church.
401   Untitled. Methodist Church.

402   Untitled. Methodist Church.
413   Untitled. Cemetery.
715   "Country Church," *OTOP* (93).
1043   Untitled. Methodist Church.
261   Untitled. Man on horse.

RODNEY

24   Untitled. Baptist Church.
415   Untitled. Baptist Church.
1026   Untitled. Catholic Church.
386   Untitled. Catholic Church.
368   Untitled. Catholic Church.
384   Untitled. Catholic Church interior.
332   Untitled. Presbyterian Church.
1032   Untitled. Presbyterian Church.
1032   "Village   Church—Rodney,   Miss."   Not   an   original
       negative.
28   "Home, ghost river town," *OTOP*.
1031   Untitled. Shacks and fence.
49   "Hamlet," *OTOP*.
709   Untitled. Fisherman walking into town.
52   Untitled. The road to town.
1055   "Ghost River-town," *TP*.
690   "A village pet," *OTOP*.
1033   Untitled, *W*. Man photographed in 690.
26   Untitled. Man photographed in 690, in cemetery.
27   Untitled. Cemetery stile.
1058   "Cemetery Still [sic]," *IBW*; Untitled, *W*. Cemetery stile.
32   Untitled. Cemetery.
31   Untitled. Cemetery.
482   Untitled. Cemetery, tomb with top ajar.
1006   Untitled, *W*. Tomb with top ajar.
390   Untitled. Cemetery.
387   Untitled. Cemetery.
388   Untitled. Cemetery.
395   Untitled. Cemetery.
369   Untitled. Bethel Church near Rodney.
636   Untitled. Bethel Church near Rodney.
696   "Country Church," *OTOP* (94).

SIMPSON CO.

710   "Home with bottle-trees," *OTOP*; "A House with Bottle
       Trees," *TP*.
1057   Untitled, *W*. Bottle trees.

STAR
    695   "Too far to walk it," *OTOP*.
STRONG RIVER
    309   Untitled. Wooden suspension bridge from below.
    1027 Untitled. Wooden suspension bridge from below.
UTICA
    842   Untitled. Cemetery monument, "Julia."
    852   Untitled. Cemetery lamb.
    853   Untitled. Cemetery monument, "He was an honor to the
          earth on which he lived."
    865   Untitled. Cemetery monument, "Come Ye Blessed."
VICKSBURG
     39   "Monument on a city street in Vicksburg to a newspaper
          editor who fought against the gamblers on the Mississippi
          River steamboats who were plaguing the local citizens and
          was murdered for it," *IBW*.
    393   Untitled. Sun set. Warehouses.
     53   Untitled. Overlooking the town.
     75   Untitled. Brick street.
     67   Untitled. Street scene.
    1019 Untitled. Town seen from river.
    357   Untitled. Courthouse steps.
    361   Untitled. Courthouse.
    745   Untitled. Courthouse.
    746   Untitled. Courthouse.
    350   Untitled. City Hall.
    354   Untitled. City Hall.
    352   Untitled. Cotton Exchange.
    353   Untitled. Cotton Exchange.
    370   Untitled. Cotton Exchange.
    373   "Old Cotton Exchange Building," *IBW*.
    374   Untitled. Lions at entrance to Cotton Exchange.
    371   Untitled. Jail.
     30   Untitled. Statue of a boy on a lamb.
     35   Untitled. Statue of a boy on a lamb.
    101   Untitled. Tricycle that reminded EW of Pegasus.
    348   Untitled. Cedar Grove.
    349   Untitled. Cedar Grove.
    351   Untitled. Cedar Grove.
    359   Untitled. Garden statue, Cedar Grove.
    363   Untitled. Cedar Grove.
    383   Untitled. Cedar Grove.

383 Untitled. Cedar Grove. There are two contact prints numbered "383."
366 Untitled. Boarding house.
367 Untitled. Boarding house.
362 Untitled. Stained glass window.
372 Untitled. Stained glass window.
771 Untitled. Cemetery angel, star in her crown.
795 Untitled. Cemetery monument, "John B. Reid, Jr."
826 Untitled. Cemetery lambs, "Willis."
845 Untitled. Cemetery lambs, "Willis."
827 Untitled. Cemetery angel.
844 Untitled. Cemetery monument, "Shelton."

WINDSOR

331 Untitled. Ruins.
344 Untitled. Ruins.
345 Untitled. Ruins.
346 Untitled. Ruins.
355 Untitled. Ruins.
356 Untitled. Ruins.
376 Untitled. Henry Miller.
377 Untitled. Henry Miller.
378 Untitled. Ruins.
379 Untitled. Henry Miller.
380 Untitled. Henry Miller.
385 Untitled. Ruins.
747 Untitled. Ruins.
1021 Untitled. Ruins.
1050 Untitled. Ruins.
1051 "Ruins of Windsor," *TP*.
1059 "Home after high water," *OTOP*.

NEW ORLEANS, LA.

681 Untitled. Revelers on a balcony.
682 Untitled. Street to balcony conversation.
683 Untitled. Monkey on a leash.
684 Untitled. Shoppers.
914 "Waiting for Parade," *IBW*.
915 Untitled. "424 The Spot 424."
917 Untitled. Mardi Gras crowd.
918 Untitled. Bartender.
921 Untitled. Man and woman meeting.
922 Untitled. Revelers on a balcony.

Jackson, Miss.   Early 1930s   Neg. #0477

Utica, Miss.   Early 1930s   Neg. #0055

Utica, Miss.   Early 1930s   Neg. #0711

Jackson, Miss.   Early 1930s   Neg. #0266

Jackson, Miss.   Late 1930s or early 1940s   Neg. #0113

Jackson, Miss.   Late 1930s or early 1940s   Neg. #0114

Utica, Miss.   Early 1930s   Neg. #0041

Rodney, Miss.   Late 1930s or early 1940s   Neg. #1026

Rodney, Miss.   Late 1930s or early 1940s   Neg. #1055

Utica, Miss.   Late 1930s or early 1940s   Neg. #0853

Jackson, Miss.   Late 1930s or early 1940s   Neg. #0797

New York City   1935 or 1936   Neg. #0953

New Orleans   Late 1930s or early 1940s   Neg. #0925

924 "A doorway in the quarter during Mardi Gras Parade,"
IBW.`

925 "Mardi Gras Celebrations," *IBW*. Mardi Gras costumes,
Death and Medusa.

926 "On New Orleans Street," *IBW*. Mardi Gras costumes.

ROSEDOWN (ST. FRANCISVILLE, LA.)

360 Untitled. Garden statue.

1025 Untitled. Doorway.

UNIDENTIFIED

78 Untitled. Ox-drawn sled.

90 Untitled. Farm house.

306 Untitled. Rural vista.

308 Untitled. Rural vista.

333 Untitled. Rural scene.

365 Untitled. House with gallery.

624 Untitled. Country road.

644 Untitled. Country church.

652 Untitled. Child with raised arm.

655 Untitled. Child with raised arm.

880 Untitled. "Streamline Cafe."

882 Untitled. Coming to church on mules.

883 Untitled. Woods.

833 Untitled. Cemetery monuments.

762 Untitled. Cemetery monument, woman with hair in bun.

765 Untitled. Cemetery monument, woman with hair in bun.

838 Untitled. Cemetery monument, woman with hair in bun.

856 Untitled. Cemetery monument.

776 Untitled. Cemetery monument, "Receive a crown that fadeth not."

761 Untitled. Cemetery monument, "Receive a crown that fadeth not."

1048 Untitled. Cemetery monument, broken chain.

832 Untitled. Cemetery monument, broken chain.

874 Untitled. Cemetery monument, "Louise Eugenia."

807 Untitled. Cemetery monument, "Louise Eugenia."

780 Untitled. Cemetery monument, "Louise Eugenia."

864 Untitled. Cemetery monument, "Louise Eugenia."

773 Untitled. Cemetery monument, woman and broken pillar.

787 Untitled. Cemetery lamb.

764 Untitled. Cemetery monument, "To our Nannie."

760 Untitled. Cemetery monument, woman and cross.

802　Untitled. Cemetery monument.
796　Untitled. Cemetery angel and cross.
803　Untitled. Cemetery monument, dove atop gravestone.
822　Untitled. Cemetery monument, "Shelby."
816　Untitled. Cemetery monument, "Simpson."
819　Untitled. Cemetery monument, "Julia Quin."
823　Untitled. Cemetery monument, "Moguin."
825　Untitled. Cemetery plot, angels at entrance.
831　Untitled. Cemetery monument, "Gayden."
830　Untitled. Cemetery monument, handshake.
828　Untitled. Cemetery monument, fallen tree.
805　Untitled. Cemetery monument, arch.
843　Untitled. Cemetery monument, "Eugene."
835　Untitled. Cemetery monument, "Charlie M."
868　Untitled. Cemetery monument, "Lewis."
854　Untitled. Cemetery monument, "At Rest."
839　Untitled. Cemetery monument, figure kneeling before cross.
841　Untitled. Cemetery monument, "Miller."
871　Untitled. Cemetery monument, robed woman and cross.
850　Untitled. Cemetery monument, dove over gates of heaven.
875　Untitled. Cemetery monument, angel with trumpet.
812　Untitled. Cemetery monument, "Infant Dau. of J.W. & H.M. Barber."
785　Untitled. Cemetery monument, old rugged cross.
782　Untitled. Cemetery monument, "John R. Jackson."
766　Untitled. Cemetery monument, girl with finger to chin.
759　Untitled. Cemetery monument, girl with finger to chin.
862　Untitled. Cemetery monument, girl with finger to chin.
869　Untitled. Cemetery monument, girl with finger to chin.
872　Untitled. Cemetery monument, girl with finger to chin.
772　Untitled. Cemetery monument, overturned basket.
758　Untitled. Cemetery monument, "Langley."
763　Untitled. Cemetery monument, "Perry W."
774　Untitled. Cemetery monument.
777　Untitled. Cemetery monument, harp and wreath.
781　Untitled. Cemetery monument, hand atop gravestone.

GRAND CANYON

(EW remembers visiting the Grand Canyon with her father in the 1920s but recalls no other trip. Since these photographs seem to have been taken with her Rolleiflex camera, she cannot have made them at that time—she did not purchase the Rolleiflex until late 1936. A letter from Lambert Davis refers to a "Far West" trip EW had made early in 1947 or late in 1946; perhaps she took these phographs on that trip or on another trip to the West that she made later in 1947, or perhaps someone else took these photographs.) 526, 527, 528, 529, 530, 531.

D. EW's Photographs Taken with Cameras Other than Her Own

1. 2 1/4" × 3 1/2" Negatives
   - 430   Untitled. Johnson house, N. West St., Jackson, Miss.
   - 743   Untitled. Raymond Courthouse.
   - 1010 Untitled. Elaborate, two-story, white frame house. Vicksburg.
   - 639   Untitled. Vicksburg.
   - 364   Untitled. Nineteenth-century house. Vicksburg.
   - 1042 Untitled. White frame house with plants in front.
   - 339   Untitled. White frame house with metal fence.
   - 744   Untitled. White frame house with porch rockers.
   - 881   Untitled. Farmhouse with screen porch.

2. Taken with Hubert Creekmore's Leica, 1 5/8" × 2 1/2" negatives
   - 573   Untitled. Carnival ride.
   - 625   Untitled. Carnival ride.
   - 626   Untitled. Looking down from the Ferris wheel.
   - 756   Untitled. Ferris wheel.
   - 620   "Smiling Pig." Taken in Mexico, 1937.

E. Photographs Not Taken by EW

1. 2 1/2" × 4 1/4" Negatives
186, 187, 227, 176

2. 2 1/4" × 2 1/4" Negatives
262, 654

3. Photos taken by John Robinson
99, 79, 263

II. CATALOGUE OF WELTY PRINTS
(Archives Series 27)

Each entry provides as much of the following information as can be determined: Neg. #, Title, Description, Camera, Size (in centimeters), Finish, Maker of the Print, Date Printed. All prints made by EW are cited as "original."

A. Prints Mounted and Prepared for Exhibition

1.   EW's one-woman show sponsored by Lugene, Inc., Opticians, at the Photographic Galleries, 600 Madison Ave., New York City, March 31-April 15, 1936. Twenty-nine of the original forty-five prints in the show are included here.

Two copies of the exhibition program. EW's holograph note on the back of one program reads: "Listen to B. Lillie on Fridays at 7:00—I'm going to see Jack Benny broadcast Sun.! Bea talked to garden clubs last Fri.—Called them Public Anemones No. 1."

Neg. #703, "Saturday"—title in EW's hand. Another hand has titled the photo " 'Strollers'. Grenada, Miss." Pencil enhancement, as requested by Photographic Galleries. On the back, partially erased, "l. Strollers|Eudora Welty|Jackson, Miss." Kodak, 31 × 21, matte, original.

Neg. #971, "Doak's"—title in EW's hand. Another hand has titled the photo " 'The Boast'. Grenada, Miss." Pencil enhancement, as requested by Photographic Galleries. On the back, partially erased, "2. The Boast|Eudora Welty|Jackson, Miss." Kodak, 22 × 30, matte, original.

Neg. #731, "Saturday afternoon, Courthouse Town"—title in EW's hand, "Canton, Miss." in another hand. On the back, partially erased, "3. Late Saturday Afternoon|Eudora Welty|Jackson,Miss." Kodak, 31 × 23, matte, original.

Neg. 717, "The Porch"—title not in EW's hand. Kodak, 31 × 21, matte, original.

Neg. #725, "Date"—title in EW's hand; "Farish Street, Jackson" in another hand. On the back, partially erased, "5. The Date|Eudora Welty|Jackson, Miss." Kodak, 31 × 20, matte, original.

Neg. #704, "Waiting for it"—title in EW's hand; "Jackson, Miss." in another hand. On the back, "6. Waiting|Eudora Welty|Jackson, Miss." Recomar, 30 × 23, matte, original.

Neg. #700, "'Negro Boy'—Jackson, Miss."—title not in EW's hand. Recomar, 23 × 30, matte, original.

Neg. #711, "'Small Talk'—Utica, Miss."—title in a hand other than EW's. On the back, "8. Small Talk|Eudora Welty|Jackson, Miss." partially erased. Kodak, 18 × 27, matte, original.

Neg. #511, "'The Arrival of Industry'—Mattress Factory, Jackson." "The Arrival of Industry" is in the lower left-hand corner and is in EW's hand. Remainder of title in another hand. On the back, partially erased, "9. The Mattress Factory|Eudora Welty|Jackson, Miss." Kodak, 20 × 30, matte, original.

Neg. #980—"'The Bird Pageant' Farish Street Baptist Church|Jackson, Mississippi"—title in a hand other than EW's. EW herself has written in the lower left corner, "The Pageant, partial cast." On the back, "10. The Bird Pageant|Eudora Welty|Jackson, Miss" and "(Farish St. Baptist Chu|Jackson)." Kodak, 20 × 31, matte, original.

Neg. #968, "'Work Day'"—title in a hand other than EW's. On reverse of photo, partially erased, "11.Wash Day." Kodak, 18 × 30, matte, original.

Neg. #992, "'Encounter' Grenada, Miss."—title in hand other than EW's. Pencil enhancement, as requested by Photographic Galleries. On the back, partially erased, "12. Encounter|Eudora Welty|Jackson, Miss." Kodak, 31 × 20, matte, original.

Neg. #979, "Coke"—title in EW's hand. "Jackson, Miss." in a hand other than EW's. On the back, partially erased, is original Lugene title: "Madonna with Coca-Cola." Kodak, 30 × 19, matte, original.

Neg. #988, "Dolls Alike"—title is printed, probably by EW. On the back, partially erased, "15. The Dolls|Eudora Welty, Jackson, Miss" and also "(Jackson)." Recomar, 30 × 23, matte, original.

No Neg., "Sunday Errand"—title in a hand other than EW's. In lower left EW (probably) has printed "Hope." On the back, partially erased, "16. Sunday Errand, Eudora Welty, Jackson, Miss." Kodak, 30 × 21, matte, original.

Neg. #477, "'Spanking'—Jackson, Miss."—title not in EW's hand. EW has written "Out Front" in lower left-hand corner. On the back, partially erased, "17. Spanking|Eudora Welty|Jackson, Miss" and "(Jackson)." Kodak, 29 × 21, matte, original.

Neg. #985, "Sunday—Jackson, Miss."—"Sunday" is in EW's hand, "Jackson, Miss." in another hand. On the back, partially erased, "18. Sunday Morning|Eudora Welty|Jackson, Miss" and "(Jackson)." Kodak, 22 × 14, matte, original.

Neg. #722, Untitled. Dated 1941 (date is not correct). Numbered 21 on back. Includes image of a parade float with banner "the blue Prelude Girls." Kodak, 13 × 18, glossy.

Neg. #476, "'Dappled' "—title in a hand other than EW's. On the back is written "23. Dappled|Eudora Welty|Jackson, Miss." Kodak, 29 × 21, matte, original.

Neg. #990, "Teachers Don't Get Paid—Grenada, Miss." Title in EW's hand, place name in another hand. On the back, partially erased, "24. Underwear|Eudora Welty|Jackson,Miss." Kodak, 29 × 20, matte, original.

Neg. #727, "Swing"—title in hand other than EW's. On the back, partially erased, "Swing|Eudora Welty|Jackson, Miss." Kodak, 19 × 31, matte, original.

Neg. #326, "Houseboat on Pearl River"—on the back, title in a hand other than EW's. Recomar, 23 × 31, matte, original.

Neg. #311, "River Edge"—title in a hand other than EW's. On the back, "32. River Edge|Eudora Welty|Jackson Miss." Recomar, 35 × 26, matte, original.

Neg. #382, "Dredge Boat—Vicksburg, Miss."—title in a hand other than EW's. On the back, partially erased, is "33" and a title that is illegible. Recomar, 30 × 26, matte, original.

Neg. #305, "'Settled'"—title in a hand other than EW's. On the back, "34. Settled|Eudora Welty|Jackson Miss." Recomar, 23 × 31, matte, original.

Neg. #408, "'Backyard'—Rankin County"—title in a hand other than EW's. On the back, partially erased, "35. Backyard (Rankin Co.)|Eudora Welty|Jackson Miss." Recomar, 20 × 25, matte, original.

Neg. #713, "Chums"—title in EW's hand. On the back, "39. The Chum|Eudora Welty|Jackson Miss." Pencil enhancement, as requested by Photographic Galleries. Recomar, 29 × 24, matte, original.

Neg. #738, "Sorghum—Copiah County"—title is in EW's hand, place name in another hand. On the back, partially erased, "44. 'Sorghum Making'(Copiah County)|Eudora Welty|Jackson Miss." Kodak, 20 × 32, matte, original.

Neg. #733, "'Mother and Child' "—title in a hand other than EW's. On the back, "E.Welty" in EW's hand, and partially erased, "45. Mother and Child|Eudora Welty|Jackson, Miss" in another hand. Kodak, 30 × 21, matte, original.

2. Prints Mounted and Prepared for Unspecified Exhibitions or for Submission to Publishers.

Eastman Kodak Camera

Neg. #735, "Town"—title in EW's hand. In another hand, "'Crossing the Street'—Grenada, Miss." Kodak, 30 × 21, matte, original.

Neg. #714, "The Square"—title in EW's hand. In another hand, "Grenada,Miss." Kodak, 16 × 26, glossy.

Neg. #303, Untitled. Chickens in a coop. Kodak, 10 × 17, matte.

Neg. #303, "Chickens"—title in EW's hand. Kodak, 20 × 26, matte, original.

Neg. #969, "Chopping Cotton"—title in EW's hand. In a hand other than EW's, "'Girl with a Hoe.'" Pencil enhancement. Kodak, 26 × 31, matte, original.

Recomar Camera

Neg. #692, Untitled. Elsewhere titled "A slave's apron showing souls in progress to Heaven or Hell." Recomar, 13 × 20, glossy.

Neg. #692, Untitled. Elsewhere titled "A slave's apron . . . . " Recomar, 13 × 20, glossy.

Neg. #964, "Looking at You"—on the back, title in a hand other than EW's. Recomar, 18 × 25, glossy.

Neg. #22, "'Death-Defying'"—title in a hand other than EW's on front, in EW's hand on back. Recomar, 26 × 21, glossy.

Neg. #994, "'Free Gate'"—title in a hand other than EW's. Recomar, 20 × 17, glossy.

Neg. #784, Untitled. Cemetery monument of woman with wreath. Recomar, 25 × 21, glossy.

Neg. #314, "'Abandoned'—Hinds County"—title in a hand other than EW's. Recomar, 21 × 26, glossy.

Neg. #637, "Churchyard"—title in a hand other than EW's. Recomar, 16 × 12, matte, original.

Neg. #975, "Political Speaking—Dinner on the Grounds"—title in EW's hand. Recomar, 26 × 21, glossy.

Neg. #734, "Political Meeting—Pontotoc, Miss."—title in a hand other than EW's. Recomar, 22 × 29, matte, original.

Neg. #736, "Cotton Gin—Smith County"—title in a hand other than EW's on front, in EW's hand on back. Recomar, 19 × 25, matte, original.

Neg. #815, Untitled. Cemetery angel. Recomar, 26 × 21, glossy.

Rolleiflex Camera

Neg. #44, "'Store Front'"—title in a hand other than EW's on front, in EW's hand on back. Rolleiflex, 21 × 20, glossy.

Neg. #453, Untitled. Cemetery monument of boy and dog (Mott). Rolleiflex, 19 × 19, matte, original.

Neg. #737, "'Hog Killin' Time'—Copiah County"—title in a hand other than EW's. Rolleiflex, 21 × 20, glossy.

Neg. #707, "'Town of Tin'—Hermanville, Claiborne County"—title in hand other than EW's. On back, EW's holograph title, partially erased, "Town Built of Tin." Rolleiflex, 21 × 19, glossy.

Neg. #302, "Geese"—title in EW's hand. Rolleiflex, 21 × 17, glossy.

Neg. #797, "Cemetary [sic] Portrait"—title in a hand other than EW's. Rolleiflex, 21 × 20, glossy.

Neg. #824, "Cemetary [sic] Angel—Jackson, Miss."—title in a hand other than EW's. Rolleiflex, 21 × 18, glossy.

Neg. #739, "Cane-Syrup Boiling"—title in EW's hand. Rolleiflex, 21 × 20, glossy.

Neg. #1032, "A Church in Rodney's Landing"—title in EW's hand. Rolleiflex, 16 × 16, glossy.

Neg. #695, "Road"—title in EW's hand. Rolleiflex, 21 × 20, glossy.

Neg. #393, "Sun Set"—title in EW's hand. Rolleiflex, 21 × 20, glossy.

Neg. #787, "Cemetery Lamb"—title in EW's hand. Rolleiflex, 21 × 20, glossy.

Neg. #764, Untitled. Cemetery monument, "To our Nannie." Rolleiflex, 19 × 12, glossy.

Other Cameras

Neg. #620, "'Smiling Pig'"—title in EW's hand on back of print. Not printed from an original negative. Leica, 14 × 10, glossy.

B. OTHER PRINTS

1.   Prints Made in 1938–1939.

No Neg., Untitled. Mexican children at streamside. 17 × 12, matte, Standard Photo (Jackson, Miss.)—11.03.1938.

Neg. #997, Untitled. Union Sq., New York City. Recomar, 25 × 20, matte, Standard Photo (Jackson, Miss.)—09.22.1939.

Neg. #999, Untitled. Union Sq., New York City. Recomar, 20 × 25, matte, Standard Photo (Jackson, Miss.)—09.22.1939.

Neg. #609, "Carnival workers." Rolleiflex, 18 × 25, glossy, Standard Photo (Jackson, Miss.)—10.10.1939.

Neg. #968, "Rest." Elsewhere titled "Washwoman." Kodak, 20 × 25, glossy, Standard Photo (Jackson, Miss.)—10.11.1939.

Neg. #717, "Porch." Elsewhere titled "Saturday off." Kodak, 25 × 17, glossy, Standard Photo (Jackson, Miss.)—10.11.1939.

Neg. #477, "Family." Elsewhere titled "Spanking." Kodak, 25 × 20, glossy, Standard Photo (Jackson, Miss.)—10.11.1939.

Neg. #123, Untitled. Parade, man on circus wagon with trombone. Recomar, 25 × 20, glossy, Standard Photo (Jackson, Miss.)—10.11.1939.

2. Prints Made in 1940

Neg. #878, "Yard man"—title in EW's hand. Kodak, 25 × 18, glossy, Standard Photo (Jackson, Miss.)—02.08.1940.

Neg. #687, Untitled. Sideshow poster: "Junie|Cow with A Human Face." Recomar, 20 × 25, glossy, Standard Photo (Jackson, Miss.)—02.08.1940.

Neg. #1044, Untitled. Sideshow poster: "Siamese Calves." Recomar, 20 × 25, glossy, Standard Photo (Jackson, Miss.)—02.08.1940.

Neg. #713, Untitled. With a chum. Recomar, 25 × 20, glossy, Standard Photo (Jackson, Miss.)—02.08.1940.

Neg. #836, Untitled. Cemetery monument, "Lily." Rolleiflex, 25 × 20, glossy, Standard Photo (Jackson, Miss.)—02.08.1940.

Neg. #1011, Untitled. Boy on a folding chair in front of a sideshow barker. Rolleiflex, 25 × 20, glossy, Standard Photo (Jackson, Miss.)—02.08.1940.

Neg. #114, Untitled. Sideshow poster: "1000 Reward if she is not Alive." Rolleiflex, 25 × 20, glossy, Standard Photo (Jackson, Miss.)—02.08.1940.

Neg. #830, Untitled. Cemetery monument, handshake. Rolleiflex, 18 × 20, glossy, Standard Photo (Jackson, Miss.)—02.08.1940.

Neg. #648, "Ellen of Cindy's Band"—title in EW's hand. Kodak, 25 × 20, glossy, Standard Photo (Jackson, Miss.)—02.10.1940.

Neg. #961, "Depression"—title in EW's hand. My Blue Heaven Lunch Stand. Recomar, 25 × 20, glossy, Standard Photo (Jackson, Miss.)—02.10.1940.

Neg. #740, "Negro Woman"—title in EW's hand. Recomar, 25 × 20, glossy, Standard Photo (Jackson, Miss.)—02.10.1940.

Neg. #686, "Mysterious"—title in EW's hand. Sideshow hynotist. Recomar, 25 × 20, glossy, Standard Photo (Jackson, Miss.)—02.10.1940.

Neg. #22, Untitled. Carnival ride. Recomar, 25 × 20, glossy, Standard Photo (Jackson, Miss.)—02.10.1940.

Neg. #326, "Living on the Pearl"—title in EW's hand. Pearl River shantyboat. Recomar, 25 × 20, glossy, Standard Photo (Jackson, Miss.)—02.10.1940.

Neg. #983, Untitled. Father and child on Pearl River shantyboat. Recomar, 25 × 20, glossy, Standard Photo (Jackson, Miss.)—02.10.1940.

Neg. #74, Untitled. Store window with rifle, mailbox, bucket. Rolleiflex, 23 × 20, glossy, Standard Photo (Jackson, Miss.)—02.10.1940.

Neg. #290, Untitled. Crowd on box car. Rolleiflex, 25 × 21, glossy, Standard Photo (Jackson, Miss.)—02.10.1940.

Neg. #116, Untitled. Ice cream stand, Port Gibson. Rolleiflex, 25 × 20, glossy, Standard Photo (Jackson, Miss.)—02.10.1940.

Neg. #332, "Red Facade"—title in EW's hand. Rodney Presbyterian Church. Rolleiflex, 22 × 20, glossy, Standard Photo (Jackson, Miss.)—03.13.1940.

Neg. #1033, "The Village Pet"—title in EW's hand. Rodney, Miss. Rolleiflex, 21 × 20, glossy, Standard Photo (Jackson, Miss.)—03.13.1940.

Neg. #49, "Rodney's Landing"—title in EW's hand. Rolleiflex, 18 × 24, glossy, Standard Photo (Jackson, Miss.)—03.13.1940.

Neg. #1055, "Rodney"—title in EW's hand. Rolleiflex, 25 × 18, glossy, Standard Photo (Jackson, Miss.)—03.13.1940.

3.   Prints Made in 1941

Neg. #121, Untitled. Circus wagon. Recomar, 18 × 11, glossy, Standard Photo (Jackson, Miss.)—05.01.1941.

Neg. #550, "Something to Drain"—title in EW's hand. Big Black River. Recomar, 12 × 18, glossy, Standard Photo (Jackson, Miss.)—05.02.1941.

Neg. #358, Untitled. Ruins seem to be in Natchez, but on reverse EW has written "Windsor." Rolleiflex, 21 × 19, glossy, Standard Photo (Jackson, Miss.)—05.02.1941.

Neg. #635, "The Way From Port Gibson to Heaven"—title in EW's hand. Port Gibson Presbyterian Church, another view. Rolleiflex, 18 × 13, glossy, Standard Photo (Jackson, Miss.)—05.02.1941.

Neg. #30, "Image in a Meadow"—title in EW's hand. Statue of boy on a lamb. Rolleiflex, 17 × 12, glossy, Standard Photo (Jackson, Miss.)—05.02.1941.

Neg. #356, "Windsor"—title in EW's hand. Rolleiflex, 20 × 19, glossy, Standard Photo (Jackson, Miss.)—05.02.1941.

Neg. #360, Untitled. Garden statue, probably at Rosedown. Rolleiflex, 20 × 19, glossy, Standard Photo (Jackson, Miss.)—05.02.1941.

No Neg. "The Burr Oaks"—title in EW's hand. 18 × 12, glossy, Standard Photo (Jackson, Miss.)—05.02.1941.

Neg. #706, "Grand Gulf on Mississippi River"—title in EW's hand.
Rolleiflex, 12 × 17, glossy, Standard Photo (Jackson, Miss.)—
05.08.1941.

Neg. #710, "Bottle trees"—title in EW's hand. Rolleiflex, 20 × 23,
matte, Standard Photo (Jackson, Miss.)—05.08.1941.

4. Prints used in 1953 by Joseph Krush, illustrator of *The Ponder
Heart*, and in 1955 by Ben Edwards, set designer of the Broadway play
based upon *The Ponder Heart*. EW's holograph comments on the backs
of the prints were addressed to Krush.

Neg. #973, Untitled. In the bag. EW's holograph note, "Men's hats on
colored women's heads the usual." Kodak, 6 × 11, glossy, Standard
Photo (Jackson, Miss.).

Neg. #878, Untitled. Yard man. EW's holograph note, "Big John, in-
tact." Kodak, 11 × 6, glossy, Standard Photo (Jackson, Miss.).

Neg. #982, Untitled. To find plums. Kodak, 11 × 6, glossy, Standard
Photo (Jackson, Miss.).

Neg. #971, Untitled. Doaks. Kodak, 6 × 11, glossy, Standard Photo
(Jackson, Miss.).

Neg. #971, Untitled. Doaks. Kodak, 6 × 11, glossy, Standard Photo
(Jackson, Miss.)—09.08.1953.

Neg. #735, Untitled. Crossing the pavement. EW's holograph notation, "hats & dresses. Rummage sale visitors." Kodak, 11 × 6,
glossy, Standard Photo (Jackson, Miss.)—09.08.1953.

Neg. #714, Untitled. Grenada town square. Kodak, 6 × 11, glossy,
Standard Photo (Jackson, Miss.)—09.08.1953.

Neg. #714, "Town"—title in EW's hand. Town square, Grenada. Kodak, 19 × 28, matte, original

Neg. #1047, "Town Square (Grenada, Mississippi)"—title in EW's
hand. Kodak, 14 × 24, glossy.

Neg. #703, Untitled. Strollers. EW's holograph note, "Evening
dresses on the street on colored girls for Sat. aft. may be a little
passé—but—." Kodak, 11 × 6, glossy, Standard Photo (Jackson,
Miss.)—09.08.1953.

Neg. #640, Untitled. Family home of Mary Moore Mitchell, EW's college roommate at MSCW. Grenada. EW's holograph note, "might

be basis of the Ponder house in country, with trimmings added. Right size & grounds." Kodak, 6 × 11, glossy, Standard Photo (Jackson, Miss.)—08.08.1953.

Neg. #727, Untitled. Girl in swing. EW's holograph note, "Though this girl is black, I believe Bonnie Dee might lie on the sofa or swing that way. Good Southern attitude." Kodak, 6 × 11, glossy, Standard Photo (Jackson, Miss.).

Neg. #985, Untitled. Sunday school child. Kodak, 11 × 6, glossy, Standard Photo (Jackson, Miss.).

Neg. #919, Untitled. Banana plant. EW's holograph note, "A banana plant might be in front yard of hotel, against the house, or at a corner." Kodak, 10 × 6, matte, original.

Neg. #731, Untitled. Canton street scene. EW's holograph note, "Saturday People on street usually about half divided, white & black. Judge Tip could have a sign like the little one that says 'Agents,' & 'upstairs' written below." Recomar, 10 × 8, glossy, Standard Photo (Jackson, Miss.).

Neg. #751, Untitled. Confederate veterans in a park. Recomar, 11 × 8, glossy, Standard Photo (Jackson, Miss.)—09.08.1953.

Neg. #974, Untitled. Confederate veterans in a park, another view. Recomar, 11 × 8, glossy, Standard Photo (Jackson, Miss.)—09.08.1953.

Neg. #68, Untitled. Confederate veterans in a park, a third view. EW's holograph note, "could be Grandpa's back. (R.)" Recomar, 10 × 8, glossy, Standard Photo (Jackson, Miss.).

Neg. #622, Untitled. Park bench gathering. Recomar, 11 × 8, Standard Photo (Jackson, Miss.)—09.08.1953.

Neg. #279, Untitled. Four boys leaning on a fence. EW's holograph note, "attitudes." Recomar, 11 × 8, glossy, Standard Photo (Jackson, Miss.)—09.08.1953.

Neg. #994, Untitled. Rides at the state fair. Recomar, 8 × 11, glossy, Standard Photo (Jackson, Miss.)—09.08.1953.

Neg. #975, "Politics—Pontotoc, Miss"—title in EW's hand. Watermelon on the grounds, Pontotoc. EW's holograph note: "Man seated (l) on ground might look like Old Man Gladney—elastic bands on shirtsleeves, etc. big black hat, suspenders, sharp-featured country face." Recomar, 20 × 24, matte, original.

Neg. #913, "Courthouse crowd"—title in EW's hand. Recomar, 8 × 11, glossy, Standard Photo (Jackson, Miss.)—09.08.1953.

Neg. #694, Untitled. Rankin County storekeeper. EW's holograph note: "A country storekeeper. The face & clothes are usual for people on the street (+ hat) (panama) & the telephone is good." Recomar, 25 × 20, matte, original.

Neg. #694, Untitled. Rankin County storekeeper. Recomar, 25 × 20, matte, original.

Neg. #694, Untitled. Rankin County storekeeper. Recomar, 25 × 20, matte, original.

Neg. #67, Untitled. Vicksburg street scene. Rolleiflex, 8 × 8, glossy, Standard Photo (Jackson, Miss.)—09.08.1953.

Neg. #745, Untitled. Vicksburg Courthouse. Rolleiflex, 8 × 8, glossy, Standard Photo (Jackson, Miss.)—09.09.1953.

Neg. #367, Untitled. Vicksburg boarding house. EW's holograph note, "This is too shabby & small for hotel, but the slatted shades are typical, & porches." Rolleiflex, 8 × 8, glossy, Standard Photo (Jackson, Miss.)—09.08.1953.

Neg. #339, Untitled. White frame house with metal fence. Holograph note, "Peacock-style, but too well-kept." 8 × 12, glossy, Standard Photo (Jackson, Miss.)—09.08.1953.

Neg. #364, Untitled. Nineteenth-century house. Holograph note, "Some touches that Grandpa might have added to his house-? (But this house far too run-down.)" 8 × 12, glossy, Standard Photo (Jackson, Miss.)—09.08.1953.

Neg. #430, Untitled. Two-story, white frame house with gallery. EW's holograph note, "Hotel-like." 8 × 12, glossy, Standard Photo (Jackson, Miss.)—09.08.1953.

Neg. #743, Untitled. Raymond Courthouse. 11 × 8, glossy, Standard Photo (Jackson, Miss.)—09.08.1953.

Neg. #744, Untitled. White frame house with porch rockers. EW's holograph note, "Peacock style, but this too nice." 8 × 12, glossy, Standard Photo (Jackson, Miss.)—09.08.1953.

Neg. #881, Untitled. Farmhouse with screen porch. EW's holograph note, "A situation like the Peacock house might have. Right size for house." 8 × 12, glossy, Standard Photo (Jackson, Miss.)— 09.08.1953.

Neg. #1010, Untitled. Elaborate, two-story, white frame house. EW's holograph note, "Grandpa Ponder touches on house. Or, for hotel." 8 × 12, glossy, Standard Photo (Jackson, Miss.)—09.08.1953.

Neg. #1042, Untitled. White frame house with plants in front. EW's holograph note, "I couldn't find verbena planted in an auto tire in a yard but this is the spirit of it. For Peacocks." 8 × 12, glossy, Standard Photo (Jackson, Miss.)—09.08.1953.

No Neg. Untitled. Interior of a once grand house. EW's holograph note, "This sofa & chair & the carpet & the angle of the pictures could be in Grandpa's house—not the rest!" 12 × 9, glossy, Standard Photo (Jackson, Miss.)—08.17.1939.

No Neg. Untitled. Farmhouse with tin roof and with chickens in the yard. EW's holograph note, "This is too poor a house even for Peacocks, but shows the foundation, the design, the roof, & the chickens that go under the house." 6 × 11, glossy, Standard Photo (Jackson, Miss.).

No Neg. Untitled. Carrying the ice for Sunday dinner. EW's holograph note, "road scene." 11 × 6, glossy, Standard Photo (Jackson, Miss.)—09.08.1953.

No Neg. Untitled. Carrying the ice for Sunday dinner. 10 × 6, matte.

No Neg. Untitled. Pampas grass. EW's holograph note, "Pampas grass might grow around hotel." 5 × 5, glossy, Standard Photo (Jackson, Miss.)—09.15.1939.

5.   Prints Made in 1963.

Neg. #342, Untitled. House near Raymond and Clinton. EW's holograph note, "Raymond." Rolleiflex, 8 × 8, glossy, July 1963.

Neg. #1052, Untitled. House near Raymond and Clinton. EW's holograph note, "Raymond." Rolleiflex, 8 × 8, glossy, July 1963.

Neg. #479, Untitled. Calf. EW's holograph note, in pencil, "Port Gibson" and in ink, "near Rocky Springs." Rolleiflex, 8 × 8, glossy, August 1963.

Neg. #664, Untitled. Ida M'Toy. Rolleiflex, 8 × 8, glossy, July 1963.

Neg. #667, Untitled. Ida M'Toy. Rolleiflex, 8 × 8, glossy, July 1963.

Neg. #39, Untitled. Vicksburg marker to Dr. Hugh Bodley, "Murdered by the Gamblers." Rolleiflex, 8 × 8, glossy, August 1963.

6.   Other Prints.

Eastman Kodak Camera

GRENADA

Neg. #196, Untitled. Ellen of Cindy's band. Kodak, 19 × 12, matte.

Neg. #1015, Untitled. Ellen's husband. Kodak, 19 × 12, matte, original.

Neg. #1015, Untitled. Ellen's husband. Kodak, 20 × 14, matte.

JACKSON

Neg. #717, Untitled. Elsewhere titled "Saturday off" or "Porch." Kodak, 20 × 12, matte.

Neg. #979, Untitled. Elsewhere titled "Coke." Kodak, 19 × 12, matte.

Neg. #979, Untitled. Elsewhere titled "Coke." Kodak, 20 × 12, glossy.

Neg. #264, Untitled. Mother and two children on porch swing. Kodak, 11 × 16, glossy.

Neg. #977, "Sunday School Teacher." Author and director of the Bird Pageant. Kodak, 24 × 14, matte, original.

Neg. #638, Untitled. Children in yard beneath hanging laundry. Kodak, 13 × 18, glossy.

Neg. #142, "Children and Maypoles"—title in EW's hand. Kodak, 10 × 20, glossy.

Neg. #142, Untitled. Elsewhere titled "Children and Maypoles." Kodak, 16 × 25, matte, original.

Neg. #452, Untitled. Pigeons. Kodak, 13 × 20, matte, original.

Neg. #452, Untitled. Pigeons. Kodak, 19 × 25, matte, original.

Neg. #435, Untitled. Fence, trees, wall—Jackson, Miss. Kodak, 25 × 20, matte, Standard Photo (Jackson, Miss.).

YALOBUSHA COUNTY

Neg. #963, Untitled. Washwomen. Kodak, 21 × 21, matte, original.

Recomar Camera

BIG BLACK RIVER

Neg. #551, Untitled. Big Black River. Recomar, 16 × 21, matte, original.

Neg. #548, Untitled. Big Black River. Recomar, 11 × 16, glossy.

JACKSON

Neg. #56, Untitled. Eagle on post, entrance to Confederate Park, intersection of State and Capitol Streets, Jackson, Miss. Recomar, 13 × 15, matte, original.

Neg. #149, Untitled. Two men on park bench, Confederate Park. Recomar, 20 × 13, matte.

Neg. #964, Untitled. Elsewhere titled "Schoolchildren meeting a visitor." Recomar, 20 × 26, glossy.

Neg. #460, Untitled. Pigs and laundry. Recomar, 24 × 18, matte, original.

Neg. #494, Untitled. Parade, cowboy on horseback with flag. Recomar, 25 × 20, matte, original.

Neg. #495, Untitled. Parade, horseback riders with plumed hats. Recomar, 25 × 20, matte, original.

Neg. #123, Untitled. Parade, man on circus wagon with trombone. Recomar, 21 × 12, glossy.

Neg. #123, Untitled. Reverse print of parade, man on circus wagon with trombone. Recomar, 23 × 16, glossy.

Neg. #488, Untitled. Lion. Recomar, 23 × 16, matte, original.

Neg. #121, Untitled. Circus wagon. Recomar, 21 × 11, glossy.

Neg. #686, Untitled. Sideshow hypnotist. Recomar, 24 × 16, glossy.

Neg. #122, "Sideshow"—title in EW's hand. Sideshow: "Mystifying Girl's." Recomar, 20 × 25, glossy.

Neg. #490, Untitled. Sideshow poster: "How Can She Live." Recomar, 14 × 20, glossy.

Neg. #490, "Sideshow Poster"—title in EW's hand. Sideshow poster: "How Can She Live." Recomar, 14 × 20, glossy, original.

Neg. #687, Untitled. Sideshow poster: "Junie|Cow with A Human Face." Recomar, 20 × 25, glossy.

Neg. #687, "Sideshow Poster"—title in EW's hand. Sideshow poster: "Junie|Cow with A Human Face." Recomar, 17 × 19, glossy.

Neg. #1044, "Sideshow Poster"—title in EW's hand. Sideshow poster: "Siamese Calves." Recomar, 23 × 20, glossy.

Neg. #978, "Fair"—title in EW's hand. Elsewhere titled "Beggar at the Fair gate." Recomar, 20 × 17, matte, original.

Neg. #493, Untitled. Sideshow: "MO . . . ." Recomar, 18 × 25, matte, original.

Neg. #789, Untitled. Cemetery monument, lady with wreath, side view. Recomar, 10 × 8, glossy, Standard Photo (Jackson, Miss.).

Neg. #784, Untitled. Cemetery monument, lady with wreath. Recomar, 10 × 8, glossy, Standard Photo (Jackson, Miss.).

Neg. #784, Untitled. Cemetery monument, lady with wreath. Recomar, 25 × 20, glossy.

Neg. #784, Untitled. Cemetery monument, lady with wreath. Recomar, 26 × 21, glossy.

Neg. #814, Untitled. Cemetery monument, robed, kneeling woman. Recomar, 10 × 8, glossy, Standard Photo (Jackson, Miss.).

Neg. #813, Untitled. Cemetery monument, mother and children beneath weeping willow. Recomar, 10 × 8, Standard Photo (Jackson, Miss.).

LEARNED

Neg. #310, Untitled. Erosion. Recomar, 12 × 20, matte, original.

NATCHEZ

Neg. #375, "Country Church"—title in EW's hand. Church Hill. Recomar, 25 × 20, glossy.

Neg. #375, Untitled. Church Hill. Recomar, 10 × 8, glossy, Standard Photo (Jackson, Miss.).

Neg. #637, Untitled. Church Hill. Recomar, 25 × 21, matte, original.

Neg. #14, Untitled. Dunleith, Natchez. Recomar, 20 × 13, glossy.

Neg. #14, Untitled. Dunleith, Natchez. Recomar, 19 × 12, glossy.

PEARL RIVER

Neg. #326, Untitled. Pearl River shantyboat. Recomar, 19 × 26, matte, original.

Neg. #484, Untitled. Father and child on Pearl River shantyboat. Recomar, 26 × 19, matte, original.

SMITH COUNTY

Neg. #83, Untitled. Cotton gin, Smith County. Recomar, 19 × 25, matte, original.

UTICA

Neg. #700, Untitled. Elsewhere titled "With a dog." Recomar, 19 × 26, glossy.

Neg. #700, Untitled. Elsewhere titled "With a dog." Recomar, 19 × 25, matte, original.

Neg. #815, Untitled. Cemetery angel, child. Recomar, 25 × 20, glossy.

CHARLESTON, SOUTH CAROLINA

Neg. #934, Untitled. Public market, Charleston, S.C. Recomar, 21 × 15, matte, original.

Neg. #934, Untitled. Public market, Charleston, S.C. Recomar, 22 × 16, matte, original.

Neg. #942, Untitled. Garden, Charleston, S.C. Recomar, 24 × 18, matte, original.

Neg. #946, Untitled. House, Charleston, S.C. Recomar, 25 × 18, matte, original.

No Neg. Untitled. Church, Charleston, S.C. 26 × 18, matte, original.

NEW YORK CITY

Neg. #953, Untitled. New York City. Recomar, 18 × 25, matte, original.

Neg. #957, "The Fence"—title in EW's hand. New York City park bench. Recomar, 18 × 14, matte, original.

Neg. #997, Untitled. New York City, Union Sq. Recomar, 15 × 18, glossy, original.

Neg. #997, Untitled. New York City, Union Sq. Recomar, 20 × 25, glossy, original.

Neg. #1000, Untitled. New York City, Union Sq. Recomar, 18 × 24, matte, original.

UNIDENTIFIED

Neg. #504, "Sideshow"—title in EW's hand. Sideshow: "Sex Mad." Recomar, 20 × 23, glossy.

Neg. #293, Untitled. Mare and foal. Recomar, 18 × 12, matte, original.

Neg. #792, Untitled. Two identical cemetery monuments, angels with fingers pointing heavenward. Recomar, 7 × 10, glossy, Standard Photo (Jackson, Miss.).

Rolleiflex Camera

CANTON

Neg. #74, Untitled. Store window with rifle, mailbox, bucket. Rolleiflex, 21 × 18, glossy.

COPIAH COUNTY

Neg. #737, "Hog Killing." Rolleiflex, 21 × 18, matte.

CRYSTAL SPRINGS

Neg. #855, Untitled. Cemetery monument, "Lily." Rolleiflex, 18 × 18, matte.

Neg. #811, Untitled. Cemetery monument, child with cross. Rolleiflex, 19 × 13, glossy.

Neg. #811, Untitled. Cemetery monument, child with cross. Rolleiflex, 19 × 13, glossy.

Neg. #811, Untitled. Cemetery monument, child with cross. Rolleiflex, 6 × 5, glossy, Standard Photo (Jackson, Miss.).

Neg. #779, Untitled. Cemetery monument, "Daisy." Rolleiflex, 6 × 5, glossy, Standard Photo (Jackson, Miss.).

Neg. #779, Untitled. Cemetery monument, "Daisy." Rolleiflex, 19 × 19, glossy.

Neg. #779, Untitled. Cemetery monument, "Daisy C." Rolleiflex, 15 × 18, glossy.

Neg. #779, Untitled. Cemetery monument, "Daisy C." Rolleiflex, 20 × 19, glossy.

Neg. #808, Untitled. Cemetery monument, "Daisy." Rolleiflex, 6 × 5, glossy, Standard Photo (Jackson, Miss.).

Neg. #808, Untitled. Cemetery monument, "Daisy." Rolleiflex, 18 × 18, glossy.

Neg. #808, Untitled. Cemetery monument, "Daisy C." Rolleiflex, 13 × 14, glossy.

Neg. #837, Untitled. Cemetery monument, "Daisy C." Rolleiflex, 14 × 16, glossy.

Neg. #837, Untitled. Cemetery monument, "Daisy C. " Rolleiflex, 18 × 20, glossy.

Neg. #810, Untitled. Cemetery monument, angel with cross. Rolleiflex, 13 × 19, glossy.

GRAND GULF

Neg. #706, Untitled. Elsewhere titled, "Fisherman and his boys." Rolleiflex, 8 × 8, glossy.

HERMANVILLE

Neg. #707, Untitled. Hermanville. EW's holograph note, "Port Gibson." Rolleiflex, 8 × 8, glossy.

Neg. #707, Untitled. Hermanville. Rolleiflex, 16 × 19, glossy.

JACKSON

Neg. #870, Untitled. Cemetery monument, man with cane. Rolleiflex, 21 × 13, glossy.

Neg. #797, Untitled. Cemetery monument, "True to the Public Trust." Rolleiflex, 21 × 19, glossy.

Neg. #859, Untitled. Cemetery monument, "Onslow Glenmore." Rolleiflex, 6 × 6, glossy, Standard Photo (Jackson, Miss.).

Neg. #859, Untitled. Cemetery monument, "Onslow Glenmore." Rolleiflex, 13 × 20, glossy.

Neg. #799, Untitled. Cemetery monument, "Onslow Glenmore." Rolleiflex, 15 × 12, glossy.

Neg. #799, Untitled. Cemetery monument, "Onslow Glenmore." Rolleiflex, 6 × 6, glossy, Standard Photo (Jackson, Miss.).

Neg. #817, Untitled. Cemetery monument, "Onslow Glenmore." Rolleiflex, 6 × 6, glossy, Standard Photo (Jackson, Miss.).

Neg. #824, Untitled. Cemetery angel seen from rear. Rolleiflex, 21 × 20, glossy.

Neg. #834, Untitled. Cemetery angel seen from rear. Rolleiflex, 6 × 6, glossy, Standard Photo (Jackson, Miss.).

Neg. #818, Untitled. Cemetery monument, mother and children beneath weeping willow. Rolleiflex, 13 × 20, glossy.

Neg. #818, Untitled. Cemetery monument, mother and children beneath weeping willow. Rolleiflex, 21 × 20, glossy.

Neg. #818, Untitled. Cemetery monument, mother and children beneath weeping willow. Rolleiflex, 20 × 13, glossy.

Neg. #818, Untitled. Cemetery monument, mother and children beneath weeping willow. Rolleiflex, 10 × 8, glossy, Standard Photo (Jackson, Miss.).

Neg. #757, Untitled. Cemetery monument, mother and children beneath weeping willow. Rolleiflex, 6 × 5, glossy, Standard Photo (Jackson, Miss.).

Neg. #757, Untitled. Cemetery monument, mother and children beneath weeping willow. Rolleiflex, 6×6, glossy, Standard Photo (Jackson, Miss.).

Neg. #757, Untitled. Cemetery monument, mother and children beneath weeping willow. Rolleiflex, 25×20, glossy.

Neg. #778, Untitled. Cemetery monument, dog on grave. Rolleiflex, 13×18, glossy.

Neg. #778, Untitled. Cemetery monument, dog on grave. Rolleiflex, 13×20, glossy.

MADISON COUNTY

Neg. #1020, Untitled. Making cane syrup. Rolleiflex, 21×19, matte, original.

PORT GIBSON

Neg. #434, Untitled. Port Gibson Presbyterian Church. Rolleiflex, 21×18, matte, original.

Neg. #860, Untitled. Decorative cemetery gate. Rolleiflex, 18×20, glossy.

Neg. #857, Untitled. Cemetery monument, "Graeme." Rolleiflex, 13×16, glossy.

ROCKY SPRINGS

Neg. #261, Untitled. Man on horse. EW's holograph note, "Port Gibson." Seems actually to be Rocky Springs. Rolleiflex, 8×8, glossy.

UTICA

Neg. #853, Untitled. Cemetery monument, "He was an honor to the earth on which he lived." Rolleiflex, 18×13, glossy.

Neg. #853, Untitled. Cemetery monument, "He was an honor to the earth on which he lived." Rolleiflex, 6×6, glossy, Standard Photo (Jackson, Miss.).

Neg. #842, Untitled. Cemetery monument, "Julia." Rolleiflex, 6×6, glossy, Standard Photo (Jackson, Miss.).

Neg. #842, Untitled. Cemetery monument, "Julia." Rolleiflex, 10×13, glossy.

Neg. #865, Untitled. Cemetery monument, "Come Ye Blessed." Rolleiflex, 13×13, glossy.

VICKSBURG

Neg. #35, "Garden Figure"—title in EW's hand. Statue of boy on a lamb. Rolleiflex, 18×15, glossy.

Neg. #827, Untitled. Cemetery angel. Rolleiflex, 20×19, glossy.

Neg. #827, Untitled. Cemetery angel. Rolleiflex, 21×20, glossy.

Neg. #771, Untitled. Cemetery angel, star in her crown. Rolleiflex, 6×6, glossy, Standard Photo (Jackson, Miss.).

Neg. #844, Untitled. Cemetery monument, "Shelton." Rolleiflex, 19×13, glossy.

UNIDENTIFIED LOCATIONS

Neg. #764, Untitled. Cemetery monument, "To our Nannie." Rolleiflex, 6×6, glossy, Standard Photo (Jackson, Miss.).

Neg. #765, Untitled. Cemetery monument, woman with hair in bun. Photo taken from rear of monument. Rolleiflex, 6×6, glossy, Standard Photo (Jackson, Miss.).

Neg. #838, Untitled. Cemetery monument, woman with hair in bun. Rolleiflex, 6×6, glossy, Standard Photo (Jackson, Miss.).

Neg. #838, Untitled. Cemetery monument, woman with hair in bun. Rolleiflex, 20×13, glossy.

Neg. #772, Untitled. Cemetery monument, overturned basket. Rolleiflex, 19×13, glossy.

Neg. #773, Untitled. Cemetery monument, woman and broken pillar. Rolleiflex, 19×13, glossy.

Neg. #773, Untitled. Cemetery monument, woman and broken pillar. Rolleiflex, 20×20, glossy.

Neg. #773, Untitled. Cemetery monument, woman and broken pillar. Rolleiflex, 18×13, glossy.

Neg. #776, Untitled. Cemetery monument, "Receive a crown that fadeth not." Rolleiflex, 21×13, glossy.

Neg. #777, Untitled. Cemetery monument with harp and wreath. Rolleiflex, 13×9, glossy, original.

Neg. #787, Untitled. Cemetery lamb. Rolleiflex, 12×18, glossy.

Neg. #807, Untitled. Cemetery monument, "Louise Eugenia." Rolleiflex, 18×18, matte.

Neg. #807, Untitled. Cemetery monument, "Louise Eugenia." Rolleiflex, 6×6, glossy, Standard Photo (Jackson, Miss.).

Neg. #807, Untitled. Cemetery monument, "Louise Eugenia." Rolleiflex, 19×13, glossy.

Neg. #874, Untitled. Cemetery monument, "Louise Eugenia." Rolleiflex, 20×13, glossy, original.

Neg. #812, Untitled. Cemetery monument, infant daughter of J.W. and H. M. Barber. Rolleiflex, 6×5, glossy, Standard Photo (Jackson, Miss.).

Neg. #812, Untitled. Enlargement of a portion of the negative, stone dove. Rolleiflex, 11×10, glossy.

Neg. #816, Untitled. Cemetery monument, "Simpson." Rolleiflex, 12 × 20, glossy.

Neg. #830, Untitled. Cemetery monument, handshake. Rolleiflex, 21 × 13, glossy.

Neg. #830, Untitled. Cemetery monument, handshake. Rolleiflex, 18 × 13, glossy.

Neg. #830, Untitled. Cemetery monument, handshake. Rolleiflex, 6 × 6, glossy, Standard Photo (Jackson, Miss.).

Neg. #841, Untitled. Cemetery monument, "Miller." Rolleiflex, 19 × 13, glossy.

Neg. #841, Untitled. Cemetery monument, "Miller." Rolleiflex, 13 × 14, glossy, original.

Neg. #845, Untitled. Cemetery lambs, "Willis." Rolleiflex, 14 × 17, glossy.

Neg. #850, Untitled. Cemetery monument, dove over gates of heaven. Figures in the print have been outlined in ink. Rolleiflex, 13 × 18, glossy.

Neg. #854, Untitled. Cemetery monument, "At Rest." Rolleiflex, 12 × 11, glossy.

Neg. #854, Untitled. Cemetery monument, "At Rest." Rolleiflex, 5 × 4, glossy, Standard Photo (Jackson, Miss.).

Neg. #862, Untitled. Cemetery monument, girl with finger to chin. Rolleiflex, 6 × 6, glossy, Standard Photo (Jackson, Miss.).

Neg. #872, Untitled. Cemetery monument, girl with finger to chin. Rolleiflex, 21 × 13, glossy.

Neg. #1048 or #832, Untitled. Cemetery monument, broken chain. Rolleiflex, 12 × 11, glossy.

Neg. #1048, Untitled. Cemetery monument, broken chain. Rolleiflex, 6 × 6, glossy, Standard Photo (Jackson, Miss.).

No Negatives Available

No Neg. Untitled. Cemetery monument, weeping willow. 17 × 12, glossy.

No Neg. Untitled. Cemetery monument, weeping willow. 18 × 13, glossy.

No Neg. Untitled. Cemetery monument, handshake. 19 × 13, glossy.

No Neg. Untitled. Cemetery monument, handshake. 18 × 13, glossy.

No Neg. Untitled. Grass fire. 13 × 19, matte.

No Neg. Untitled. Spanish moss. 20 × 12, matte.

No Neg. Untitled. Fruit in china bowl by a pillar, viewed from above. 14 × 24, matte.

No Neg. Untitled. Fruit in china bowl by a pillar. 14 × 24, matte.

No Neg. Untitled. Fruit in silver bowl on porch floor. 18 × 26, matte, Standard Photo (Jackson, Miss.).

No Neg. Untitled. Fruit, silver bowl, leaves, pillar. 25 × 14, matte.

No Neg. Untitled. Porcelain elephants in a meadow. 14 × 24, matte.

No Neg. Untitled. Coffee pot on window sill, flowers in juice glass. Holograph note on back: "(This is not one)." 16 × 20, matte.

No Neg. Untitled. Lilies of the valley. 20 × 25, matte.

No Neg. Untitled. Iris. 23 × 20, matte.

No Neg. Untitled. Wine bottle and flowers. 17 × 13, matte.

No Neg. Untitled. Champagne, apples, book. 17 × 11, matte.

No Neg. Untitled. Camellia blossom. 25 × 20, glossy.

No Neg. Untitled. Artichoke and celery. 24 × 18, matte.

No Neg. Untitled. Print of statue of Venus behind fruit and belt. 26 × 13, matte, Standard Photo (Jackson, Miss.).

No Neg. Untitled. Camellia blossom in wine glass. 20 × 12, matte.

No Neg. Untitled. Magnolia blossom and doll. 14 × 24, matte.

No Neg. Untitled. Sideshow poster: "Emile-Amelia,|Born Alive" and "Rose Marie|Born Alive No Sex." 19 × 16, glossy.

No Neg. Untitled. Dunleith, Natchez, First Pilgrimage. 9 × 16, glossy.

No Neg. Untitled. Portrait of a woman. 21 × 14, matte.

No Neg. Untitled. Grain or cement elevator. 20 × 13, matte.

No Neg. Untitled. Window display with FDR poster. 11 × 10, glossy.

No Neg. Untitled. Mexican street, palms and church bell. 13 × 15, matte.

No Neg. Untitled. Mexican street scene, another view. 13 × 15, matte.

No Neg. Untitled. Mexican scene, burro. 16 × 19, glossy.

No Neg. Untitled. Mexican church seen through archway. 20 × 19, glossy.

C. PUBLICATIONS

Twenty Photographs. Winston-Salem, N.C.: Palaemon Press, 1980. This is #3 in a signed, limited edition of 90 copies. (See Chapter 4, I.B.)

Neg. #740 (Recomar)—1. A Woman of the 'Thirties 1935

Neg. #1005 (Rolleiflex)—2. Old Midwife (Ida M'Toy) 1940

Neg. #987 (Recomar)—3. Mother and Child 1935

Neg. #691 (Rolleiflex)—4. Delegate 1938

Neg. #150 (Recomar)—5. Child on the Porch 1939

Neg. #693 (Recomar)—6. Preacher and Leaders of the Holiness
  Church 1939
Neg. #969 (Kodak)—7. Chopping in the Fields 1935
Neg. #960 (Recomar)—8. Tomato Packers' Recess 1936
Neg. #989 (Recomar)—9. Saturday Trip to Town 1939
Neg. #714 (Kodak)—10. Courthouse Town 1935
Neg. #703 (Kodak)—11. Saturday Strollers 1935
Neg. #44 (Rolleiflex)—12. Store Front 1940
Neg. #970 (Recomar)—13. Side Show, State Fair 1939
Neg. #983 (Recomar)—14. Houseboat Family, Pearl River 1939
Neg. #710 (Rolleiflex)—15. A House with Bottle Trees 1941
Neg. #1051 (Rolleiflex)—16. Ruins of Windsor 1942
Neg. #1055 (Rolleiflex)—17. Ghost River-Town 1942
No Neg.—18. Abandoned "Lunatic Asylum" 1940
No Neg. (Kodak)—19. Carrying Home the Ice 1936
Neg. #993 (Kodak)—20. Home by Dark 1936

D. Matted Prints Prepared for Exhibition by the Mississippi State Historical Museum

36 matted prints of pictures published in *One Time, One Place*.

III. FAMILY PHOTOGRAPH COLLECTION
(Archives Series 28)

RESTRICTED. The 594 negatives/contact prints collected here were
probably taken between 1903 and 1950. The principal photographer
was EW's father Christian Webb Welty, but EW took most of the post-
1931 and a few of the earlier photographs herself. Included are photographs of:

Eudora Alice Welty
Christian Webb Welty
Chestina Andrews Welty (EW's mother)
Edward Jefferson and Elinor Welty (EW's brother and sister-in-law)
Walter Andrews and Mittie Welty, Elizabeth and Mary Alice (EW's
  brother, sister-in-law, and their two children)

Jefferson Welty (EW's grandfather)
Ned Andrews (EW's grandfather)
Eudora Carden Andrews (EW's grandmother)

Stella Andrews Upshur and her daughters Mary Lee and Margaret (EW's aunt and cousins)

Grace Mary Welty and Arthur Welty (EW's aunt and uncle, her father's half-sister and half-brother)

Moses Andrews, John Andrews, Carl Andrews (EW's uncles, her mother's brothers)

Earluth and Valeria Epting, Elizabeth Heidelberg, William Hamilton, Joe Jeff Power, Jane Percy Slack, Ida Lemly Slack, Bessie Smith, Sara Virginia Thompson, and Sonny Withers (EW's childhood friends)

Mary Moore Mitchell (EW's roommate at the Mississippi State College for Women)

Harris Barksdale (a friend of Walter Welty)

Hubert Creekmore (EW's friend and the brother of Mittie Welty)

Henry Miller (on a trip through Jackson, Miss.)

Karnig Nalbandjian (an artist EW met at Yaddo in 1941)

Katherine Anne Porter (at Yaddo in 1941)

Although these photographs are not open for research, many of them are available in *Eudora*, selected and edited by Patti Carr Black and published by the Mississippi Department of Archives and History in 1984.

Correspondence

The correspondence in the Eudora Welty Collection is a mere fragment of Welty's total correspondence: the collection primarily includes professional correspondence—letters written to Welty by editors, writers, scholars, and theatrical people; only a few letters held at the Department of Archives and History were written by Welty. Yet despite the highly selective nature of the collected correspondence, it contains extremely valuable information about the course of Welty's career, about the literary communities to which she has belonged, about her views of her own fiction, and about the travel that has so enriched her fiction.

Most obviously the letters in this collection tell us about the course of Eudora Welty's career as a writer. From the time she began to submit stories to periodicals, Welty consistently received letters of acceptance from university quarterlies or little magazines, though stories we now regard highly often met with rejection before finding their way into print. Welty's career began in 1936 with John Rood's enthusiastic acceptance of "Death of a Traveling Salesman" and "Magic" for the journal *Manuscript*, which he and his wife published in Athens, Ohio. Rood praised "Death of a Traveling Salesman" as "one of the best stories we have ever read" (03.19.1936), but his enthusiasm was not always shared by editors. *Esquire* refused to print a story by a woman, rejecting "Petrified Man," though in 1975 Arnold Gingrich ruefully acknowledged his mistake and then printed "The Corner Store" in his magazine. The *Southern Review*, which printed seven of Welty's stories between 1937 and 1941, rejected "Flowers for Marjorie," "Acrobats in a Park," "Powerhouse," and "Petrified Man." Within a month of rejecting "Petrified Man," Robert Penn Warren wished to reconsider his decision, but unbeknownst to him, Welty had burned the manuscript; she reconstructed it from memory, and Warren went on to accept that story. Both "Keela, the Outcast Indian Maiden" and "Why I Live at the P.O." met with rejection before being accepted by periodicals. And some Welty stories never won publica-tion; today there is no trace of "Shape in Air," "Responsibility," "In the Station|The Visit," "Sister," or "The Death of Miss Belle." Welty may have revised and retitled these stories or she may have destroyed them; she certainly did not find publishers for them. Nevertheless, between 1936 and 1941, seventeen Welty stories found their way into print—a tribute to Welty's genius and her persistence.

Book publication did not come so readily. Welty sought to publish a book of her stories as early as 1936, but five years elapsed before she was able to do so. Repeatedly publishers rebuffed her efforts, but the steady stream of rejections was somewhat encouraging in nature. Whenever one of Welty's stories appeared in a small magazine or uni-versity review, editors at major publishing houses were quick to write their congratulations and to request a novel from the young writer. And when Welty asked that they consider a short story collection in-stead of a novel, they dismissed this notion, but also reiterated their desire that she write a longer work. Welty heard many a discour-aging word about the commercial viability of short story collections, but many an encouraging word about her own ability as a writer of fiction.

Harold Strauss of Covici-Friede Publishers was one of the first edi-tors to recognize Welty's genius and to solicit work from her. Soon after "Death of a Traveling Salesman" was published in 1936, Strauss urged Welty "to undertake a novel" (05.13.1936). And although origi-nally reluctant even to look at a volume of short stories, Strauss and Covici-Friede did later contemplate bringing out a collection of Welty's photographs and stories. The difficulty of marketing such a volume and the "acute but somewhat unfocused sensibility" of the stories themselves ultimately prompted Strauss and his colleagues to reject Welty's manuscript and to solicit a novel once again. Nevertheless, Strauss told Welty that she had occasioned the "most protracted" edi-torial discussion in his memory and that she clearly possessed "a very marked talent, both as a short story writer and a photographer" (11.01.1937).

Robert N. Linscott of Houghton Mifflin also greeted Welty's early work with praise. Although he rejected "The Cheated" as "the mate-rial for a novel rather than a novel itself" (09.17.1938), he encouraged Welty to revise and resubmit the manuscript, which he had read with "great interest and admiration." And when she failed to do so, he sent another letter, asking if she had revised "The Cheated" and say-ing that he remembered the book with "vividness and pleasure"

(04.18.1939). Welty now believes she may have thrown "The Cheated" into the trash, but this story of a woman artist living on the edge of a wilderness with its episode about a bootlegger who beats his daughter attracted the interest of a highly respected editor.

By 1940 Welty's rejection notices more emphatically called for a novel and more enthusiastically commended her talent. Stanley Young of Harcourt, Brace wrote Welty of the commercial difficulties posed by short story collections like her own, and he then went on to say that her stories would "have greater chances to see the light of day down through the years if a collection of them came in the wake of a novel or two" (02.26.1940). But Young, while reluctant to consider a volume of Welty's stories, paid her a fine compliment in begging, beseeching, and pleading with her to do a novel.

Another rejection and even more ardent praise came from G. P. Putnam's Sons. In a letter of April 16, 1940, Kennett L. Rawson, an editor at Putnam's, expressed interest in a novel or a collection of stories by Welty, though he cautioned that "the market for a volume of unrelated pieces is usually not a large one." And when he and his colleagues did see a collection of Welty's stories, they were unanimously impressed. Writing on behalf of the Putnam's editors, Rawson commented on Welty's ability "to convey the finest subtleties of meaning and emotion" and said that Putnam's had been moving toward a decision to offer her a contract until the war in Europe "darkened the publishing outlook" (06.10.1940). Clearly, G. P. Putnam's Sons had no worries about the artistic merits of Welty's stories, none of the slight reservations that troubled Covici-Friede and Houghton Mifflin. Commerical considerations alone, war or no war in Europe, blocked the publication of a volume of short stories by a writer who had not yet published a novel.

Welty's rejection notices thus demonstrated a widespread recognition of her talent and a widespread sentiment that she should write a novel. Still, Welty maintained her commitment to the short story. Her agent Diarmuid Russell has credited Welty's "iron purpose in writing" (16) for sustaining her during this five-year period of repeated rejection at major publishing houses, and Welty's entry into a literary community of which Russell was an important member was important in strengthening that iron purpose and in guaranteeing that she would be accepted on her own terms by the publishing industry. Welty's correspondence with Russell, not yet part of the Welty Collection, reveals a trust and concern that transcend the typical business relationship. Welty highly valued Russell's reactions to her work, and

Russell's guidance was crucial in obtaining book publication for her. It was Russell who insisted that Welty seek publication in national magazines, and without such publication Doubleday, Doran almost certainly would not have accepted her first book of stories.

Letters from Welty's first editor, John Woodburn, which are part of the Welty Collection, further show the personal in the professional. Woodburn was Welty's advocate at Doubleday, urging that house to publish her work. In November of 1939 Woodburn wrote to Welty, thanking her for the "unaffected hospitality" he had encountered on a trip to the South, reporting that her stories were being considered at Doubleday, and adding that he had falsely sworn she was at work on a novel. He then wryly asked Welty to save his "immortal soul" by actually beginning a novel (11.21.1939). A year later he wrote Welty to praise *The Robber Bridegroom* and to request "an entire book of Mississippi stories" (11.26.1940). "I am," he went on to say, "very anxious to get a book by you on our list." When, within a month, Welty had two stories accepted by the *Atlantic*, Woodburn wrote to express his great pleasure (12.13.1940). And well he might have been pleased, for on January 24, 1941, he was able to offer Welty a Doubleday, Doran contract for the story collection that was eventually titled *A Curtain of Green*. Woodburn's literary advice as well as his advocacy stood Welty in good stead. His call for a book of "Mississippi stories" (11.26.1940) seems to have been a call for the stories Welty would propose to write in her application for a 1942 Guggenheim Fellowship and would publish in *The Wide Net*. And that call is more explicit in a later letter announcing his desire to hold "Robber" out of *A Curtain of Green* and to save it for a future book on the Natchez Trace (01.24.1941).

Other letters from Woodburn deal with preparing the *Curtain of Green* manuscript for print, getting Welty to correct and promptly return her galleys, locating a photograph for publicity purposes, and organizing a cocktail party in honor of the book's publication. Later he would write Welty about the disappointing appearance of *The Robber Bridegroom* dust jacket and the need for minor revisions in *Delta Wedding*. But these business letters have a decidedly personal cast and suggest that Welty's career was being directed by a friend. In his letters to "Peaches," "Baby," "Eudora Bull Creecher," "Fate Malone," "Flora," and "Eu," Woodburn signs himself as "Your little friend and constant reader," "Your little friend and devoted Zombie, Toussaint L'Woodburn," "'Babe' McPheeters," and "your dream man, St. John the Woodburn." The whimsy and affection evident here are also evident in Woodburn's telegram congratulating "Eudora Welty the fairest flower of the Mississippi Delty" on her first Guggenheim (03.24.1942). Woodburn and Welty were both friends and business associates; small wonder then that Woodburn could write Welty about his disappointment at failing a 1942 army physical or that Welty would move to Harcourt, Brace and Company with Woodburn when he left Doubleday, Doran in 1942.

Woodburn's belief in Welty's work and his delight in her success were shared by many other members of the literary community. The correspondence in the collection reveals that even before they knew her well, Cleanth Brooks and Robert Penn Warren took an exceptional interest in Welty's work, accepting seven of her stories for the *Southern Review* and recommending her for a Houghton Mifflin prize and for a Guggenheim Fellowship. Katherine Anne Porter, when she was married to Albert Erskine of the *Southern Review*, met with Welty in Baton Rouge, perhaps in 1938, and went on to help her in many ways. Some of Woodburn's letters concern the introduction Porter generously wrote for *A Curtain of Green*, and Ford Madox Ford's letters to Welty came as a result of Porter's intercession on her behalf. Ford wrote Welty in November of 1938, proposing to find an English publisher for her because "Miss Porter speaks so highly" of her fiction. He wrote Welty again in January of 1939, praising her stories and anticipating great things for them, and later that month he wrote yet again asking that she send a copy of her stories to British publisher Stanley Unwin. In May 1939 Ford was still at work on Welty's behalf, having contacted Harold Strauss at Knopf. Ford died later that year without seeing Welty's stories published in book form. Although he never met Eudora Welty, he accepted her as a member of the literary community and expended great effort on her behalf.

Welty, of course, had long been part of a literary community, though not one based in New York City or even Baton Rouge. Small-town Jackson, Mississippi, and its citizens played an important role in Welty's development as a writer. When Welty seriously began to write, many talented individuals of her generation still called Jackson home. In the early 1930s Frank Lyell, Lehman Engel, and Hubert Creekmore, all of whom receive mention in the Correspondence Calendar, joined with Welty to form the "Night-Blooming Cereus Club," which met at "Eudora's." The close friendships and regular encounters with these bright, talented young men must have provided Welty with a stimulating atmosphere in which to write, and her continuing relationships with these men after they left Jackson must have sustained and enriched her career. Frank Lyell, whom Woodburn mentions in his letters of July 28, 1941, and August 20, 1941, and whose 1956 postcard praises the Broadway production of *The Ponder Heart*, was a lifelong friend of Welty's. He received a Ph.D. in English from Princeton University, went on to teach at the University of Texas, and published a study of the novels of John Galt. Lehman Engel, another Jacksonian Welty had known from childhood, became a composer of concert music and of incidental music for the stage, a choral conductor, and the preeminent musical director on Broadway. Engel, like Welty, believed that his childhood in Jackson was a spur to creativity. In his autobiography he wrote,

> I saw whatever shows came to town. Al G. Fields's Minstrels was an annual event. Fritz Leiber brought us tattered grandeur in Shakespearean repertoire. There were Walker Whiteside, *Maytime*, *Blossom Time*, *The Student Prince*, *Chu Chin Chow*, the St. Louis Symphony Orchestra, Paderewski, John McCormack, Galli-Curci, and Sousa's Band, and the Redpath Chautauqua, which brought smiling culture in a large tent for five full days each spring.
>
> But my most profound experiences were in the Majestic Theatre, the local moviehouse: the Griffith pictures, Gish, Nazimova, and Chaplin. A small orchestra presided over by Sara B. McLean at an upright piano accompanied the pictures. Mrs. McLean would lean far back in her swivel chair peering at the screen over the top of her nose-glasses. The "score" consisted of bits and pieces taken from movie-music albums: "hurries," romantic melodies, marches—primitive music whose dramatic intentions were clear to all. The music changed as abruptly as the film frames, and Mrs. McLean would indicate these changes with a sudden jerk of the head, cutting off the orchestra often after she had already plunged ahead. (18)

Welty did not meet Hubert Creekmore until he was a young man, but he became a close friend and a family member—his sister married Welty's brother Walter. The youthful Creekmore was an amateur photographer (Welty recommended his photographs to Samuel Robbins, who mounted both of her New York photographic exhibits) and an aspiring writer, who early on wrote a play performed by a little theater group in Jackson. He also established the short-lived *Southern Review* in Jackson. When it became obvious that the project was a failure and would have to be abandoned after one issue, Creekmore and his staff members (including Welty) threw most of the issues into the Pearl River. If their magazine could not succeed, Creekmore reasoned, it could at least be rare. Later Creekmore's efforts would meet greater success. After moving to New York City, he would publish three novels and several volumes of poetry, write a book on gardening, and translate Latin poetry.

Another close Jackson friend who left home and with whom Welty has ever since corresponded is John Fraiser Robinson, the man to whom "The Wide Net" and *Delta Wedding* are dedicated and the man who told Welty of actual events on which these works are based. Robinson, a Delta native, lived for a time in Jackson, moved on to New Orleans, served in Italy during World War II, returned to earn an M.A. in English at the University of California at Berkeley, and ultimatedly settled in Italy. Wherever he lived, Robinson corresponded with Welty, and she sent him copies of her stories as they came from her typewriter; Robinson saved these early typescripts and in 1985 returned them to Welty, who in turn gave them to the Department of Archives and History. Robinson wrote stories of his own and saw three of them published—in *Harper's*, the *New Yorker*, and the British periodical *Horizon*. Of special interest in the correspondence collection are Welty's 1948–1949 letters to Robinson concerning the dramatization of *The Robber Bridegroom*. Welty and Robinson corresponded at length about their collaboration on this script, and Welty's letters provide an interesting commentary on an aspect of the novel that has proved troubling to some readers. When Robinson suggested eliminating Little Harp's rape of an Indian maiden, Welty replied:

> About the Indian girl scene, I'm not sure. I feel in one way that the murder or rape should stand—because in that scene we have detached Jamie from it, as hero, and yet all that bandit scene with girl who might have been Rosamond if she weren't herself really pertains to him and is the black half of his deeds—and is a reality of the times—and I feel that the actual horror should be given—simply and quickly, but no mistake—I feel this element should be in it. ([1948], dated only Tues.)

Welty attempted to help Lehman Engel, Hubert Creekmore, and John Robinson, putting them in touch with Diarmuid Russell, her agent, recommending their work, collaborating with them. They had little to do with shaping her career, though Engel's advice was indispensable when dramatizations of Welty's plays were done. These men were more important in providing Welty with an easy, good-humored, intellectually stimulating environment in which to begin writing and in providing advice, encouragement, and friendship throughout her career.

In addition to reflecting the course of Welty's career and indicating the friendships that were crucial to it, the letters in the Welty Collection reveal how well traveled an individual Eudora Welty is. Although Welty has lived most of her life in Jackson, Mississippi, she has led a cosmopolitan existence. Her correspondence shows what we have long known but seldom focused upon: the early travels described in *One Writer's Beginnings* did not cease when Welty's father died and she decided she must settle in Jackson. An April 1935 letter finds Welty in New York City in quest of a publisher for a book of photographs. In a July 1937 letter, Dale Mullen of *River* magazine envies Welty her recent trip to Mexico, a trip she made with three friends by car over primitive roads. An April 1940 letter informs Welty that she has been awarded a fellowship to the Bread Loaf Writers' Conference in Vermont. In the summer of 1941 John Woodburn wrote several letters to her at Yaddo in Saratoga Springs, New York. And in May 1943 Woodburn, then at Harcourt, Brace, lamented Welty's departure from New York City after a visit. In 1947 Lambert Davis, who succeeded Woodburn as Welty's editor at Harcourt, made note of her "Far West" trip and of her upcoming participation in Seattle's Northwest Writers Conference. And in the fall of 1947 Davis twice wrote to Welty in San Francisco, where she spent three months or so. In June 1949 Donald Brace of Harcourt, Brace wrote to Welty at the Hotel Irving in New York to say he had delivered her note to E. M. Forster. And in June 1951 A. M. Heath and Company of London forwarded a letter to Welty in care of Mrs. Alan Cameron [Elizabeth Bowen], Bowen's Court, Ireland. In 1954 Welty was again receiving mail in New York City, and in the summer of 1954 mail reached her in London and Cambridge; during this time in England, Welty not only lectured at Cambridge University, but also managed to visit with Elizabeth Bowen, Elizabeth Spencer, and Stephen Spender. The correspondence includes only bits and pieces of Welty's professional correspondence after 1954, but those bits and pieces indicate that her travels did not cease. Her regular trips to New York City continue to the present day, and trips elsewhere around the country or abroad still take place.

This lifetime of journeying has proven exceedingly important to Welty's fiction. It has inspired the settings of many stories, stories like "Flowers for Marjorie," "Music from Spain," "No Place for You, My Love," and "Going to Naples." And travel has also had a less direct, but more pervasive impact upon Welty's work. "Through travel," Welty has stated, "I first became aware of the outside world; it was through travel that I found my own introspective way into becoming a part of it" (*One Writer's Beginnings* 76). Travel helped Welty to discover that the outside world was "the vital component" of her "inner life," that her imagination took its strength and direction from what she could "see and hear and learn and feel and remember of [the] living world," that the outside world could stand as an emblem for her stories' most profound concerns.

The correspondence in the Eudora Welty Collection thus tells us a good deal about the course of Welty's career as a writer, about the friendships that sustained her as an artist and as an individual, and about the travel that enriched her life and her fiction. The collected correspondence, in fact, provides the best available account of Welty's professional life. It tells us of the struggles and triumphs, of the cosmopolitan yet rooted existence that emerged from Eudora Welty's "sheltered" beginnings.

Perhaps this all sounds like over-praise. But believe me, we are quite sincere. Mary Lawhead came to your stories last evening after having read through a dozen or so very dull and worthless stories. She told me about it at the dinner table today -- yes, she is Mrs. Rood. "After reading those stories," I stopped," she said. "Everything else read like nothing on earth. You must read them before you go back to the office." So I sat down and read both of them, and I can only agree with her.

And now, before you begin to have qualms, perhaps thinking, "There must be a flaw somewhere," let us assure you that there is not. Before this, we have been asked by authors, whose work we liked, "Why are you so interested?" Probably they think we're some sort of correspondence course teachers, or agents. Well, we aren't. We just happen to be two young people who are interested in writing, and a hobby with us, since we have our own printing press, if we didn't have, the expense would be prohibitive. We have "discovered" a dozen or so really gifted young writers, and have encouraged them. For we know how difficult it is at first to get any sort of recognition. In the beginning we said, "If we can find even one new young writer a year, and make him feel that it is important to write honestly, sincerely, we shall be simply repaid for the time and the money spent." We have had no reason to charge our idea. It has not been too easy; we have received many disappointments; at times it seemed that we could no go on bearing the expense of the publication, but we have gone ahead - and after nearly three years, we are gratified with the reception our magazine has received. Just recently a national publication listed us as the most important literary magazine in the United States. That was some reward.

Our rule is to publish stories, as nearly as possible, in the order they are received. In your case, we are going to make an exception. For by the usual method, it would be a year before you were published. We hope to publish one of the stories in either the June or August issue. So please let us have the material about yourself, your work, and the photograph, as soon as possible.

Sincerely,

MANUSCRIPT A bi-monthly magazine

Published at 17 West Washington Street, Athens, Ohio

EDITORS:
MARY LAWHEAD
JOHN ROOD

March 19, 1936.

Dear Miss Welty:

We are very much impressed with both of the stories you send. And we should like to have both of them for MANUSCRIPT, providing, of course, that you know we do not pay for material - can't, rather, being like most literary magazines "in the red" all the time.

Without any hesitation, we can say that DEATH OF A TRAVELING SALESMAN is one of the best stories that has come to our attention - and one of the best stories we have ever read. It is superbly done. And MAGIC is only slightly short of it in quality. Needless to say we are excited over the stories, and over you - since you say these are the first two stories you have submitted.

Will you please let us have a photograph of yourself, for publication; also a full and detailed sketch about yourself. If you only realised how much utterly worthless material came to us for consideration, you would know how excited we are to have found these stories, and a new author who shows a great deal more than promise.

We should also like to know what else you have written; whether you are working on a novel, or whether you have written many short stories which you consider to be as fine as these two. The reason we ask this is that we feel sure the various publishers will be interested as soon as we publish one of the stories. Incidentally, all of the more important publishers watch our pages closely, for enough talent, and should you have either a novel, or enough short stories to make a volume, whose quality was comparable with these two stories, we should not hesitate at all to insist that they be published; you might be interested in knowing that we never have approached a publisher with any of our author's work before, but the quality of your work is really amazing.

A Letter from John Rood to Eudora Welty. Reprinted with the permission of Mrs. John Rood.

HARCOURT, BRACE AND COMPANY, INC.

PUBLISHERS

383 MADISON AVENUE, NEW YORK

June 7, 1943

Miss Eudora Welty
1119 Pinehurst
Jackson, Miss.

Dear Ek:

The galleys. We want them. We want to make a book out of them. We want to make a narrow margin of profit out of THE WIDE NET. We gotta have galleys, gal. What has tooken you so long? Was you tryin' to memorize them in case they got lost comin' back? Was you showin' them around to folks in Jackson and lettin' folks read 'em so that they won't have to buy the book?

I was in Washington a week ago and it was hot. I came back to New York and it was hot. I was over-exposed in the solar rays yesterday and I am bolnt. I was also bitten by green flies and today I am all covered with painful, itching welties.

I'd like to hear from that articulate crow. I suppose if he ever says anything he has to take back he turns cannibalistic. (That's a deep one.) If you get a chance to talk with him I'd like to hear him on the Crow-Magnon period. Also whether they always fly in a straight line. And see if he didn't write a book under the pen name of Aldous Huxley called CROW-M-m YELLOW.

I hear Katherine Anne Porter's writing a novel.

Get those galleys up here, gal. We tuns wants 'em.

Here's a poetry for you:

Life is thrilling. Life is nice.
I would like to live mine twice.
Twice as thrilling, twice as funny,
And, of course, twice as much money.

Another poetry, called "My Impressions of Washington":

Washington, D. C. is very pretty.
Of the United States it is the capital city.

The President resides on Capitol Hill
If he isn't defeated in the next election he'll
be residing there still.

Miss Eudora Welty   - 2 -   June 7, 1943

(continued)

His wife, Eleanor, is a ubiquitous woman.
She's not without faults, but like everyone
else, she's human.

and one I saw somewhere, sometime -

I think that I shall never see
A Party like the G.O.P.
. . . .

A P. whose hungry mouth is pressed
Against the Treasury's flowing breast.
. . . .

Poems are wrote by fools like me;
I did not make the G.O.P.

That's the end. I forget the rest. That's the way it is in life, you remember the fatigue and forget the rest. I found another Southern gal that can write. That makes, let me see, how many? I feel another poem coming on!

Down in Jackson, in the State of Mississippi,
Lived a young woman, centuries after Fra Lippo Lippi.

There in Jackson she practices her art,
And the literary Yankees have taken her to their heart.

She writes beautiful stories, each one a jewel.
It's the opinion of the critics she can write like a fool.

The Bronte of the South, of the Black Belt she
Is the one and only, incomparable, Eudora Welty.

Some of that doesn't seem to go as smoothly as it might, but it tells a story and it sings the praise. In other hands, say T. S. Eliot's, you would have had an entirely different poem, but it wouldn't have been this one. No matter what you want to say about it, this one is. There's quite a good deal to be said for a thing's being itself, and this is. Who knows whether or not a poem is good poem - or not? I can answer that, I do. And you will too, when you read it.

I have to leave you now.

John

A letter from John Woodburn to Eudora Welty. Reprinted with the permission of Mr. Charles R. Woodburn.

The following abbreviations have been used in the Correspondence Calendar (Archives Series 29):

EW = Eudora Welty
s.l. = *sine loco*, without place
s.n. = *sine nomine*, without name
ts. = typescript
tss. = typescript signed
al. = autograph letter
als. = autograph letter signed

Commentary on the correspondence appears in parentheses within individual entries.

08.29.1921. J.H. W_____, Mackie Pine Oil Specialty Co., Covington, La., to EW, Jackson.

Tss. letterhead, informing EW that she has won the "Jackie Mackie Jingles contest" and enclosing a check for $25.00; offers congratulations and the hope that EW "will improve in poetry to such an extent as to win fame."

04.02.1935. Harrison Smith, Harrison Smith and Robert Haas, Publishers, New York, to EW, New York.

Tss. letterhead, rejecting a book of photographs called "Black Saturday"; praises the photographs, but feels publishing them would not be profitable; says he will hold the manuscript for EW; addressed to EW, c/o Miss Gallagher, 253 West 16th Street, New York. (Miss Gallagher was a friend of EW's from her Columbia School of Business days.)

03.19.1936. John Rood, *Manuscript*, Athens, Ohio, to EW, s.l.

Tss. letterhead, accepting both "Death of a Traveling Salesman" and "Magic"; praises "Death of a Traveling Salesman" as "one of the best stories we have ever read"; asks for a photo and a biographical sketch; will forego the usual year-long wait and publish one of the stories in June or August. 2 pages.

04.14.1936. John Rood, *Manuscript*, Athens, Ohio, to EW, s.l.

Tss. letterhead, saying that "Death of a Traveling Salesman" will be in the June issue and inviting EW to visit in Athens, Ohio.

04.30.1936. John Rood, *Manuscript*, Athens, Ohio, to EW, s.l.

Tss. letterhead, asking for a photo of EW to use in his magazine and regretting that *Manuscript* can't purchase some of her photographs.

05.13.1936. Harold Strauss, Covici-Friede, Inc. Publishers, New York, to EW, Jackson.

Tss. letterhead, telling how much he enjoyed "Death of a Traveling Salesman," which he had just read in *Manuscript*; believes it contains "the seeds of a broad social perspective"and asks EW to"undertake a novel."

05.27.1936. Harold Strauss, Covici-Friede, Inc., Publishers, New York, to EW, Jackson.

Tss. letterhead, saying it is "impossible to publish a volume of stories by a relatively unknown author," although the collected stories of well-known writers are occasionally published; encourages her to write a novel and to submit the manuscript to him.

06.05.1936. John Rood, *Manuscript*, Athens, Ohio, to EW, s.l.

Tss. letterhead, telling EW that he liked the rhymes she had sent him and asking her to send some more for the notes section of *Manuscript*.

07.18.1936. Samuel A. Robbins, The Camera House, Inc., New York, to EW, Jackson.

Tss. letterhead, informing EW that he has left Lugene Inc. and has established his own business; fills her film order; hopes to arrange a fall exhibit of her photographs, with an emphasis upon "poor white photos"; writes that he can do nothing for Hubert Creekmore until he sees "an assortment of his work." (Mississippian, poet, novelist, and translator, Hubert Creekmore was EW's long-time friend; he eventually left Jackson, Miss., to live and work in New York City; his sister married EW's brother Walter.)

08.17.1936. John Rood, *Manuscript*, Athens, Ohio, to EW, s.l.

Tss. letterhead, praising a story from EW, but saying it is both "too long and too short" and encouraging revision; believes "There is material here for a novel . . . "; EW's holograph note at top reads, "(Shape in the Air)."

09.23.1936. Robert Penn Warren, *The Southern Review*, Baton Rouge, La., to EW, Jackson.

Tss. letterhead, rejecting Welty's "verse."

11.02.1936. S.R.M. [S. Robert Morse], *Literary America*, New York, to EW, s.l.

Ts. letterhead notecard, rejecting "the enclosed"; EW's holograph note reads, "Shape in Air|Flowers for Marjorie|Responsibility [?] |Petrified Man."

11.09.1936. S.A. Robbins, The Camera House, Inc. New York, to EW, Jackson.

Tss. letterhead, asking if it would be possible "to arrange for an exhibition early in January"; EW's holograph note at bottom of page reads, "Ans. Nov 19. also paying bills Oct. $4.24 & ordering 6 pkg 8 × 10 defender singleweight, glossy, contr.& med hard & 1 bottle Quinal developer."

11.21.1936. S.A. Robbins, The Camera House, Inc., New York, to EW, Jackson.

Tss. letterhead, reporting that EW's prints will be on exhibition from 21–30 of Jan.; is pleased that she now owns a Rolleiflex camera because it should enable her "to make better photographs than ever."

12.14.1936. S.A. Robbins, The Camera House, Inc., New York, to EW, Jackson.

Tss. letterhead, dealing with technical problems EW is having preparing her photos—choice of paper to use for developing, control of lighting in the photos themselves. 2 pages.

———.———.[1936/7?] s.n. s.l.

Undated interoffice communication on a piece of *Esquire* notepaper: "m" praises EW's portrait of a beauty parlor and asks if *Esquire* should make "an exception"; "AG" declines to do so and finds the plot to be improbable at times. ("AG" is Arnold Gingrich, the editor. "m" is Meyer Levin. Gingrich later wrote in *Esquire* that he had rejected EW's story because *Esquire* at that time printed only pieces by men. Gingrich makes this admission and recants his early position in *Esquire*'s Dec. 1975 issue, which contains pieces by Grace Paley, Nora Ephron, Jean Stafford, Joan Didion, and EW.)

———.———.[1937?] S. Robert Morse, *Literary America*, New York, to EW, s.l.

Tss. post card, announcing that *Literary America* has suspended publication and returning EW's submission.

01.13.1937. Robert Penn Warren, *The Southern Review*, Baton Rouge, La., to EW, Jackson.

Tss. letterhead, rejecting "Flowers for Marjorie" and "Petrified Man," but praising EW and encouraging her to submit other work to *The Southern Review*; has reservations about the structure of "Petrified Man" and thinks "Flowers for Marjorie" is perhaps too "conventional in subject matter."

01.29.1937. Frank Hall Fraysur, *Life*, New York, to EW, Jackson.

Tss. letterhead, thanking EW for her tombstone prints and asking to hold them for a while; rejects her "Valentine collection," though it is a "'true vintage' bit of Americana"; expresses interest in the

Negro Holiness Church story; suggests she consider *Life*'s "Speaking of Pictures" and "Pictures to the Editors" departments. With envelope.

02.04.1937. Robert Penn Warren, *The Southern Review*, Baton Rouge, La., to EW, Jackson.

Tss. letterhead, rejecting an unnamed story but expressing regret that he had previously rejected "Petrified Man."

03.11.1937. Dale Mullen, *River*, Oxford, Miss., to EW, s.l.

Tss. letterhead, stating that EW's copies of *River* have been shipped; encourages her to send more of her work; hopes to visit EW and [Nash] Burger in Jackson in April. (Nash Burger was a high school classmate of EW's; he taught English at Central High School in Jackson and went on to become an editor at the *New York Times Book Review*. *River* printed EW's story "Retreat" in the March 1937 issue, which also included stories by Burger, Hubert Creekmore, and Peter Taylor.) With envelope.

03.18.1937. Samuel A. Robbins, The Camera House, Inc., New York, to EW, Jackson.

Tss. letterhead, informing EW that her prints are now on exhibition. (The exhibition began March 6 and lasted until the end of the month.)

05.17.1937. Robert Penn Warren, *The Southern Review*, Baton Rouge, La., to EW, Jackson.

Tss. letterhead, accepting "A Piece of News" and returning an unnamed story.

06.01.1937. Dale [Mullen], s.l., to EW, s.l.

Tss., returning an unidentified manuscript; asks EW to send photographs and more stories; writes that he hopes to be meeting in Memphis with Marion [George Marion O'Donnell], Peter Taylor, and others on a monthly basis; hopes EW will join them sometime.

[Summer 1937]. [Dale Mullen], s.l., to EW, s.l.

Ts., discussing publication of EW's photographs; reports on correspondence with August Derleth about EW's recent story in *Prairie Schooner* ["Lily Daw and the Three Ladies"]; refers to EW's visit to Oxford, Miss.

07.22.1937. Frances Broene, Covici-Friede, Inc., Publishers, New York, to EW, Jackson.

Tss. letterhead, replying to Welty's inquiry about the status of a manuscript and promising that a decision will soon be forthcoming.

07.29.1937. Dale Mullen, *River*, Oxford, Miss., to EW, Jackson.

Tss. letterhead, reports that *River* has suspended publication and regrets that he therefore will not be able to publish her photographs; envies EW's having been to Mexico; praises story recently in the *Southern Review* [probably "A Piece of News"]; reports that Weldon Kees, an editor of *Midwest*, had expressed interest in EW's stories. (In 1937 EW and three friends vacationed in Mexico. See Welty Photograph Collection for pictures from that trip.) With envelope.

08.17.1937. Cleanth Brooks, *The Southern Review*, Baton Rouge, La., to EW, Jackson.

Tss. letterhead, returning two stories, although praising them; likes "In the Station" and suggests that its ending might be revised; EW's holograph note at top of letter reads, "In the Station|The Visit."

09.23.1937. Robert Penn Warren, *The Southern Review*, Baton Rouge, La., to EW, Jackson.

Tss. letterhead, accepting "A Memory."

10.25.1937. Eleanor Clark, W. W. Norton & Company, Inc., Publishers, New York, to EW, c/o *The Southern Review*, Baton Rouge, La.

Tss. letterhead, saying that she liked "A Piece of News" in *The Southern Review* and that Norton would like to see any longer work EW has underway or in mind and would be glad to consider her shorter work for *New Letters in America*.

11.01.1937. Harold Strauss, Covici-Friede, Inc., Publishers, New York, to EW, Jackson.

Tss. letterhead, saying that EW has occasioned the "most protracted" editorial discussion he can remember, but that Covici-Friede has decided to reject her book of stories and photos combined; feels it wouldn't sell; reports that he likes the stories but thinks their architecture is "at war with the content"; believes a novel would force EW to solve both her "commercial and artistic problems." 2 pages.

11.03.1937. Frank Hall Fraysur, *Life*, New York, to EW, Jackson.

Tss. letterhead, thanking EW for a "splendid job" of covering "the Mount Olive elixir story"; says that the story will run on 11.08.1937 and that a $75 check is forthcoming. (It seems that EW did the research and someone else wrote the article, "Life on the American Newsfront: Bad Medicine Leaves Trail of Dead Patients," *Life*, 8 November 1937: 33. The story concerns a doctor in Mt. Olive, Mississippi, who prescribed the drug sulfanilamide in its new liquid form only to discover that this form of the drug was deadly. Six of his patients died despite his courageous efforts to warn them. Elsewhere in the country, the drug took 35 more lives. The story includes six Welty photographs. EW was especially concerned that *Life* not vilify the doctor who was himself a victim.) With envelope.

12.28.1937. Frank Hall Fraysur, *Life*, New York, to EW, Jackson.

Tss. letterhead, providing "hearty thanks" for the "Logan H. McLean pictures" and promising a check for $20; reports that "one of the prints is scheduled for a promotion page in a forthcoming issue." (The picture appeared in *Life*, 17 January 1938: 57. *Life* ran a promotional page about itself, its series on medicine, and its recent essay on tuberculosis. The promo included pictures of doctors who had praised that recent essay, and it quoted from their letters of praise. Logan H. McLean, Executive Secretary of the Mississippi Tuberculosis Association, was one of the authorities cited.) With envelope.

01.03.1938. Edward O'Brien, London, to EW, c/o *Prairie Schooner*, Lincoln, Neb.

Tss., requests right to reprint "Lily Daw and the Three Ladies" in *The Best Short Stories*.

02.16.1938. Harriet Colby, Reynal and Hitchcock, Inc., to EW, Jackson.

Tss. letterhead, asking EW to send anything of book length; has read "Lily Daw" and has received a recommendation of EW from Dr. Lowry Wimberly of *Prairie Schooner*.

02.22.1938. Robert Penn Warren, *The Southern Review*, Baton Rouge, La., to EW, Jackson.

Tss. letterhead, accepting "Old Mr. Grenada" and saying that it is "very brilliantly done."

02.24.1938. Whit Burnett, *Story* and The Story Press, New York, to EW, s.l.

Tss. letterhead, rejecting photographs because the cost of producing such a book would be prohibitive; recommends that EW submit her photographs to documentary magazines.

03.23.1938. Robert Penn Warren, *The Southern Review*, to EW, Jackson.

Tss. letterhead, telling EW about a fiction competition at Houghton Mifflin and saying that *The Southern Review* will push her case; says to list Cleanth Brooks, Katherine Anne Porter, and himself as sponsors; reports that "Old Mr. Grenada" will be in the spring issue and asks to see "Petrified Man" again.

04.05.1938. Robert Penn Warren, *The Southern Review*, Baton Rouge, La., to EW, Jackson.

Tss. letterhead, discussing the Houghton Mifflin contest and the need to submit an application as soon as possible.

04.27.1938. Harriet Colby, Reynal and Hitchcock, Inc., New York, to EW, Jackson.

Tss. letterhead, following-up on a letter of 02.16.1938, again asking EW to send a novel.

05.25.1938. Harriet Colby, Reynal and Hitchcock, Inc., New York, to EW, Jackson.

Tss. letterhead, thanking EW for her letter and expressing interest in the novel or novelette EW has underway; not interested in a book of photographs and feels that publication of short stories is unlikely for a writer who is "not widely known."

05.28.1938. R.N. Linscott, Houghton Mifflin Company, Boston, to EW, Jackson.

Tss. letterhead, informing EW that her novel received an "A" rating in the Houghton Mifflin fellowship competition but that the final award went "to a girl in Idaho for a novel dealing with the Mormon migration." (According to Michael Kreyling, EW's novel was an approximately 90-page version of "The Key.")

07.14.1938. Whit Burnett, *Story* and The Story Press, New York, to EW, s.l.

Tss. letterhead, saying that he liked a story but that other editors could not agree; returns it, but inquires about the status of a novel; EW's holograph note at the top of the letter reads, "Keela."

07.19.1938. Harriet Colby, Reynal and Hitchcock, Inc., New York, to EW, Jackson.

Tss. letterhead, concerning the status of the novel about which EW had written Reynal and Hitchcock.

08.08.1938. L.C. Wimberly, University of Nebraska, Lincoln, Neb., to EW, s.l.

Als., thanks EW for "The Whistle" and promises to try to run it in the next issue. (Wimberly edited *Prairie Schooner*.) With envelope.

09.13.1938. R. N. Linscott, Houghton Mifflin Co., Boston, to EW, Jackson.

Tss. letterhead, thanks her for a manuscript and asks her to visit if she's in Boston next month.

09.17.1938. R. N. Linscott, Houghton Mifflin Co., Boston, to EW, Jackson.

Tss. letterhead, discussing a novel called "The Cheated"; likes the writing and characterization but thinks the architecture is weak. (According to Linscott, the novel concerns a woman artist who comes to a small village on the edge of a wilderness and includes an episode about a bootlegger who beats his daughter. EW believes she may have thrown this novel away.) 2 pages.

09.28.1938. Robert Penn Warren, *The Southern Review*, Baton Rouge, to EW, Jackson.

Tss. letterhead, asking EW to air-mail the revised "A Curtain of Green"; reports great interest in it for the fall issue; also asks to see "Keela" and "Petrified Man"; expresses disappointment about the "Houghton Mifflin business" but assures EW that "if it isn't that, it will be something else, and soon."

10.17.1938. Whit Burnett, *Story* and The Story Press, New York, to EW, s.l.

Tss. letterhead, praising "atmosphere" in a story but returning the story because there is not complete editorial agreement about it.

10.20.1938. Whit Burnett, *Story* and The Story Press, New York, to EW, s.l.

Tss. letterhead, begins "I think 'Why I Live at the P.O.' is the closest yet"; rejects the story but encourages EW to submit the short novel on which she is working.

11.03.1938. Ford Madox Ford, New York, to EW, Jackson.

Tss. letterhead, proposing to find an English publisher for EW's stories because "Miss Porter [Katherine Anne Porter] speaks so highly" of them. With envelope.

01.06.1939. Edward J. O'Brien, London, to EW, c/o *Southern Review*, Baton Rouge, La.

Tss., requesting permission to reprint "A Curtain of Green" in *The Best Short Stories*.

01.07.1939. Ford Madox Ford, New York, to EW, Jackson.

Tss. letterhead, saying that he has read her stories, likes them, and anticipates great things; offers to recommend a book of her stories to publishers, including his English publisher. With envelope.

01.17.1939. Robert Penn Warren, *The Southern Review*, Baton Rouge, La., to EW, Jackson.

Tss. letterhead, rejecting an unnamed story.

01.19.1939. Ford Madox Ford, New York, to EW, Jackson.

Tss. letterhead, thanking EW for her reply to his earlier letter; asks her to send a copy of her stories to Stanley Unwin in London; Ford will use his copy to try to find a New York publisher. With envelope.

03.23.1939. Stanley Unwin, George Allen and Unwin Ltd., London, to EW, Jackson.

Tss. letterhead, saying that he is impressed by and interested in EW's stories but that there is no market for short stories. 2 pages. With envelope.

04.14.1939. Harold Strauss, Alfred A. Knopf, Inc., New York, to EW, c/o *Southern Review*, New York.
Tss. letterhead, inquires whether EW feels "ready to write a novel"; is interested if she does.

04.18.1939. R. N. Linscott, Houghton Mifflin Co., Boston, to EW, Jackson.
Tss. letterhead, inquiring if EW has ever revised "The Cheated" or if she is working on any other novel Houghton Mifflin could consider.

04.22.1939. Robert Penn Warren, *The Southern Review*, Baton Rouge, La., to EW, Jackson.
Tss. letterhead, returning "Sister" but holding another story for consideration.

05.03.1939. Harold Strauss, Alfred A. Knopf, Inc., New York, to EW, Jackson.
Tss. letterhead, thanking EW for a note of April 20 and promising to get in touch with Ford Madox Ford regarding her short stories; is particularly interested in "the story of 100 pages."

05.25.1939. Ford Madox Ford, New York, to EW, Jackson.
Tss. letterhead, reporting that Stokes has rejected her short story collection but that the collection is now with Strauss at Knopf; encourages EW to write a novel. With envelope.

06.05.1939. Harry Hansen, *New York World-Telegram*, s.l., to EW, s.l.
Tss. letterhead, requesting permission to reprint "Petrified Man" in the "O. Henry Prize Stories of 1939."

07.06.1939. Harold Strauss, Alfred A. Knopf, Inc., New York, to EW, Jackson.
Tss. letterhead, lamenting the death of Ford Madox Ford, but also rejecting the collection of EW's stories that Ford had sent to him; praises EW's writing but says that market considerations prevent publication of short stories.

07.25.1939. Barry Benefield, Reynal and Hitchcock, Inc., New York, to EW, Jackson.
Tss. letterhead, answering an inquiry from EW; says that he is interested in seeing her novelette and stories, but that he feels the publication of shorter works is unlikely.

08.11.1939. Cleanth Brooks, *The Southern Review*, University, La., to EW, Jackson.

Tss. letterhead, replying to a letter from EW; reports that Robert Penn Warren is en route to Italy; accepts "The Hitch-Hikers," but suggests dropping the last sentence. (Welty did indeed drop the last sentence. In an early typescript of the story EW has lined out the sentence, "He knew he would have to come back later to testify, but he got out of Clearwater a little before noon, and drove toward Memphis." See Chapter 1, I.A4.) Brooks tells EW that it was good to meet her a few weeks ago and regrets not having the chance to talk more. (In William Ferris's *Images of the South* (23), EW says that she met Cleanth Brooks in Baton Rouge when she went there to see Katherine Anne Porter.)

——.——.[1939]. Robert Penn Warren, *The Southern Review*, Lago di Garda, Italy, to EW, s.l.

Tss. letterhead, saying that he will be "more than happy" to recommend EW for a Guggenheim; thinks chances are good "with Miss Porter's support." (Charlotte Capers suggests 1939 as the probable date of this letter.)

09.22.1939. Cleanth Brooks, *The Southern Review*, University, La., to EW, s.l.

Tss. letterhead, rejecting "The Death of Miss Belle" and inviting EW to visit in Baton Rouge.

11.07.1939. Albert Erskine, *The Southern Review*, University, La., to EW, s.l.

Tss. letterhead, returning an unnamed novelette (possibly "The Cheated").

11.21.1939. John M. McK. Woodburn, Doubleday, Doran, and Co., New York, to EW, Jackson.

Tss. letterhead, thanking EW for some pictures and for her hospitality; says her stories are being read at Doubleday.

01.18.1940. James Laughlin, *New Directions*, Norfolk, Conn., to EW, s.l.

Tss. letterhead, accepting a story for *New Directions 1940*, though he anticipates objections to its Caldwell-like quality and to the debased view of the South it might encourage in Northerners. (*New Directions* went on to print "Keela the Outcast Indian Maiden" in its 1940 issue.)

01.27.1940. Edward J. O'Brien, London, to EW, c/o *Southern Review*, Baton Rouge, La.

Tss., requesting permission to reprint "The Hitch-Hikers" in *The Best Short Stories*.

02.09.1940. Stanley Young, Harcourt, Brace and Company, Inc., New

York, to EW, c/o *The Southern Review*, Baton Rouge, La.

Tss. letterhead, hopes that EW is working on a novel.

02.24.1940. Theodore Morrison, Bread Loaf Writers' Conference, Middlebury, Vt., to EW, s.l.

Tss. letterhead, informing EW that she has been recommended for a fellowship at the Bread Loaf Writers' Conference in August; asks if she wants to come, if she wants to be considered for a fellowship, if she can come *only* if granted a fellowship.

02.26.1940. Stanley Young, Harcourt, Brace and Company, Inc., New York, to EW, Jackson.

Tss. letterhead, replies to EW's letter asking if Harcourt, Brace wants "a novel or nothing"; doesn't absolutely say no to the idea of a story collection, but begs, beseeches, and pleads with EW to do a novel.

03.25.1940. Henry Allen Moe, John Simon Guggenheim Memorial Foundation, New York, to EW, Jackson.

Tss. letterhead, informing EW that she has not been granted a Guggenheim Fellowship.

04.01.1940. Theodore Morrison, Bread Loaf Writers' Conference, Middlebury, Vt., to EW, Jackson.

Tss. letterhead, granting EW a fully paying fellowship to attend the Bread Loaf Writers' Conference in the summer.

04.16.1940. Kennett L. Rawson, G. P. Putnam's Sons, New York, to EW, Mississippi Advertising Commission, Jackson.

Tss. letterhead, inquiring whether Welty has a novel "in train" and saying he would consider the possibility of a story collection.

04.29.1940. R. N. Linscott, Houghton Mifflin Company, Boston, to EW, Jackson.

Tss. letterhead, asking about a novel from EW.

06.10.1940. Kennett L. Rawson, G. P. Putnam's Sons, New York, to EW, Jackson.

Tss. letterhead, praising all of the stories in EW's collection; says Putnam's was "rapidly approaching a decision" to accept the collection when "ominous developments of the last several weeks darkened the publishing outlook"; regrets that they cannot publish her book. (The war in Europe, Rawson has since stated, was not Putnam's major reason for rejecting EW's manuscript; the difficulty of marketing short stories was.)

06.27.1940. John Woodburn, Doubleday, Doran and Company, Inc., New York, to EW, Jackson.

Tss. letterhead, asking EW to meet him in New York en route to

Bread Loaf; closes with a p.s. asking her to write a novel. 2 pages. With envelope.

07.01.1940. Cleanth Brooks, *The Southern Review*, University, La., to EW, Jackson.

Tss. letterhead, returning "Acrobats in a Park"; says that a decision on "Powerhouse" is forthcoming; reports that Warren has safely returned from Italy; invites EW to Baton Rouge.

09.18.1940. Robert Penn Warren, *The Southern Review*, University, La., to EW, s.l.

Tss. letterhead, returning "Powerhouse."

11.26.1940. John [Woodburn], Doubleday, Doran and Company, Inc., New York, to EW, Jackson.

Tss. letterhead, praising "The Robber Bridegroom" and suggesting "an entire book of Mississippi stories"; holograph p.s. saying that "Diarmuid has shown me your letter, which is exactly what I wanted." (Diarmuid Russell of Russell and Volkening was EW's agent.) With envelope.

12.13.1940. John [Woodburn], Doubleday, Doran and Company, Inc., to EW, Jackson.

Tss. letterhead, saying he is pleased about *Atlantic* accepting the stories; wishes EW a Merry Christmas. With envelope.

12.30.1940. Frances Phillips, William Morrow & Co., Inc., New York, to EW, Jackson.

Tss. letterhead, saying she has just spent the weekend with Caroline and Allen Tate and has just read "The Hitch-Hikers"; inquires about a novel from EW. With envelope.

01.24.1941. John [Woodburn], Doubleday, Doran and Company, Inc., New York, to EW, Jackson.

Tss. letterhead, saying that Doubleday wants to offer a contract and to publish a collection of her stories; will hold out "The Robber Bridegroom" for a future book on the Natchez Trace; will use revised version of "Clytie." (A typescript entitled *Stories* and prepared before Feb. 1941 contains a version of "Clytie" which varies from the *Curtain of Green* and *Southern Review* texts of the story. See Chapter 1, I.A4.) With envelope.

02.07.1941. Cleanth Brooks, *The Southern Review*, University, La., to EW, Jackson.

Tss. letterhead, replying to Welty's letter about the forthcoming publication of her short story collection; gives permission for reprinting stories from the *Southern Review*; asks her to keep the *Southern Review* "in mind for the new short story and for the long story"; holograph note that a missed letter may have gone to Warren who is at Iowa for the semester. With envelope.

02.11.1941. John [Woodburn], Doubleday, Doran and Company, Inc., to EW, Jackson.

Tss. letterhead, asks for "a better title for the book"; sends along some humorous items. (Doubleday wanted a story title for the title of the book, and "A Curtain of Green" was the only title that did not provoke serious objections.) With envelope.

06.18.1941. John [Woodburn], Doubleday, Doran and Company, Inc., New York, to EW, Yaddo, Saratoga Springs, N.Y.

Tss. letterhead, reporting that he has mailed the manuscript and reader's galleys to EW and has mailed a set of galleys to Katherine Anne Porter for use in writing the introduction to *A Curtain of Green*; says he wants EW in New York City for a party around publication date; asks when he should come up to Yaddo and how long he can stay there. With envelope.

07.28.1941. John [Woodburn], Doubleday, Doran and Company, Inc., New York, to EW, Yaddo, Saratoga Springs, N.Y.

Tss. letterhead, thanking EW for his good visit at Yaddo; reports that Frank read "Asphodel" aloud on way back in car. (Frank is Frank Lyell, EW's friend from Jackson who went on to become a professor of English at the University of Texas.) With envelope.

07.31.1941. John [Woodburn], Doubleday, Doran and Company, Inc., New York, to EW, Yaddo, Saratoga Springs, N.Y.

Telegram, reporting that the publication of *A Curtain of Green* has been postponed until September 19 and may have to be indefinitely postponed unless Katherine Anne Porter immediately sends him her introduction to the volume.

08.13.1941. John [Woodburn], Doubleday, Doran and Company, Inc., New York, to EW, Jackson.

Telegram, requesting an eight by eight enlargement of a picture of EW that had appeared in *Harper's Bazaar*; says that *A Curtain of Green* will be published November 7. (EW reports that her mother took this picture in front of a camellia house. The picture was used in a separate publication of "The Key," advertising the forthcoming publication of *A Curtain of Green*.)

08.20.1941. John [Woodburn], Doubleday, Doran and Company, Inc., New York, to EW, Jackson.

Tss., begins "Hello Peaches"; reports that Porter's introduction is in the mail to him; mentions a cocktail party scheduled for Nov. 7, 1941, in honor of the publication of *A Curtain of Green*; says

Frank Lyell will attend and adds "You better too." 2 pages. With envelope.

08.22.1941. [John] Woodburn, Doubleday, Doran and Company, Inc., New York, to EW, Jackson.
Tss. letterhead, begins "Baby"; sends her proof of "title page and the page opposite." With envelope.

08.27.1941. J [ohn Woodburn], Doubleday, Doran and Company, Inc., New York, to EW, Jackson.
Tss. letterhead, begins "Baby" and closes "Yours-in-the-Faith"; sends Porter's introduction, "unproof-read"; signed "J." With envelope.

09.09.1941. J [ohn Woodburn], Doubleday, Doran and Company, Inc., New York, to EW, Jackson.
Tss. letterhead, begins "Dear Little Friend" and closes "Your little friend and constant reader"; signed "J"; sends EW a questionnaire from Doubleday's publicity department.

09.24.1941. [John Woodburn], Doubleday, Doran, and Company, Inc., New York, to EW, Jackson.
Tss. letterhead, reports that "indirect reference to Bread Loaf" which was originally in Porter's introduction to *A Curtain of Green* has been deleted; mentions cocktail party of Nov. 7, 1941; closes "Your little friend and devoted Zombie, Toussaint L'Woodburn." With envelope.

01.19.1942. John [Woodburn], New York, to EW, Jackson.
Telegram, sending enigmatic greetings.

03.17.1942. John [Woodburn], New York, to EW, Jackson.
Telegram, inquiring about EW's well-being and reporting "tribulations of the heart." (Perhaps this concerns the Guggenheim Fellowship which Welty would receive on 03.24.1942 according to a Woodburn telegram cited below.)

03.24.1942. John [Woodburn], New York, to EW, Jackson.
Telegram, sending verse congratulations to "the finest writer of our time" on her selection for a Guggenheim Fellowship.

04.22.1942. John [Woodburn], Doubleday, Doran and Company, Inc., New York, to EW, Jackson.
Tss. letterhead, grants Robert Penn Warren permission to print two EW stories "for the price of one" and grants Alan Swallow a free reprint; Woodburn also states that Henry [Volkening of Russell and Volkening] has said EW will be coming to New York in May, and Woodburn hopes that is the case. (Warren and Cleanth Brooks printed "Old Mr. Marblehall" and "A Piece of News" in *Understanding Fiction*, 1943. Swallow printed "A Visit of Charity" in 1942

and "A Still Moment" in 1943, both in *American Writing*.) With envelope.

06.04.1942. John [Woodburn], Doubleday, Doran and Company, Inc., New York, to EW, Jackson.
Tss. letterhead, wants a Nalbandjian sketch for the dust jacket of *The Robber Bridegroom*; if not a sketch, would like one of his snapshots. (Karnig Nalbandjian was an Armenian artist EW met at Yaddo.) With envelope.

07.23.1942. John [Woodburn], Doubleday, Doran and Company, Inc., New York, to EW, Jackson.
Tss. letterhead, discusses inappropriate sketches Karnig has sent for the dust jacket; probably no picture on jacket as a result; reports that the dedication of *The Robber Bridegroom* to Katherine Anne Porter has been arranged; says he has heard EW will be coming north soon; holograph p.s. discouraging EW from using the subtitle "A Tale" for *The Robber Bridegroom* (Published text does not include subtitle.) 2 pages. With envelope.

08.03.1942. John [Woodburn], Doubleday, Doran and Company, Inc., New York, to EW, Jackson.
Tss. letterhead, discusses disappointing appearance of the dust jacket for *The Robber Bridegroom*; says that Doubleday has paid Karnig even though they did not use his sketches; reports a correction to the "dummy description of the book." With envelope.

09.26.1942. Charles Shattuck, *Accent*, Urbana, Illinois, to EW, Jackson.
Als. on *Accent* notepaper, thanking EW for sending him a letter from Ida M'Toy and for sending pictures of Ida. (*Accent* published EW's essay "Ida M'Toy." The tablet to which Shattuck refers contained Ida's letter to him. "Mama's Death" is Ida's watch, named after the anniversary on which she purchased the watch. The book edition of Welty's essay [Urbana, Chicago, London: Univ. of Illinois Press, 1979] contains Ida's letter, the pictures EW took of her, and EW's letter to which Shattuck replies in this note.) With envelope.

11.07.[1942]. John [Woodburn], Doubleday, Doran, and Company, Inc., New York, to EW, s.l.
Tss. letterhead, reporting his distress at not being accepted to serve in the army.

11.16.[1942]. John [Woodburn], Doubleday, Doran and Company, Inc., New York, to EW, Jackson.
Tss. letterhead, begins "Eudora Bull Creecher"; again discusses rejection by the army; signed "'Babe' McPheeters"; holograph p.s. "I sent your 16 R.B.'s." With envelope.

[11.26.1942]. John [Woodburn], Doubleday, Doran, and Company, Inc., New York, to EW, Jackson.

Als. letterhead, dated Thanksgiving Day; deals with Woodburn's move to Harcourt Brace; tells EW why he is pleased to be making the move and asks EW to move to Harcourt with him. 4 pages with text on recto and verso of each page. With envelope.

11.30.1942. Ken McCormick, Doubleday, Doran and Company, Inc., New York, to EW, Jackson.

Tss. letterhead, tells EW how much he likes "The Wide Net"; says that John [Woodburn] has been offered a better job at Harcourt, but hopes that she will continue at Doubleday with Bucklin Moon as editor.

[12.02.1942]. John [Woodburn], Doubleday, Doran and Company, Inc., New York, to EW, Jackson.

Tss. letterhead, begins "Dear, dear Fate Malone"; expresses gratitude that she has decided to move to Harcourt with him. With envelope.

12.03.1942. [John Woodburn], Doubleday, Doran and Company, Inc., New York, to EW, Jackson.

Tss. letterhead, begins "Fate Malone, Baby" and is signed "Babe McPheeters"; asks EW to put in a good word for Bucklin Moon at Doubleday; thanks EW for agreeing to move to Harcourt. With envelope.

12.08.1942. Ken McCormick, Doubleday, Doran and Company, Inc., New York, to EW, Jackson.

Tss. letterhead, discusses EW's request to move to Harcourt and tries to dissuade her. With envelope.

12.11.1942. EW, Jackson, to Ken McCormick, Doubleday, Doran and Company, Inc., New York.

Carbon ts., discusses her reasons for moving to Harcourt with Woodburn.

12.15.1942. Ken McCormick, Doubleday, Doran and Company, Inc., New York, to EW, Jackson.

Tss. letterhead, reporting that "a formal option canceller" is attached so that EW may move to another house. With envelope.

01.04.[1943]. John [Woodburn], Harcourt, Brace and Company, Inc., to EW, Jackson.

Tss. letterhead; misdated as 1942; primarily writes about personal matters; mentions that financial arrangements with Russell and Volkening have been completed. With envelope.

01.18.1943. John [Woodburn], Harcourt, Brace and Company, Inc., to EW, Jackson.

Tss. letterhead, thanks EW for a letter and picture; says he has two large portfolios of her photos; asks for the negative of a picture she took of him with Katherine Anne Porter at Saratoga. With envelope.

03.20.1943. [John Woodburn], Harcourt, Brace and Company, Inc., to EW, Jackson.

Tss. letterhead, begins "Eudora Bull Creecher" and is signed "I remain, as ever, your dream man, St. John the Woodburn"; sends along a tract for the Church of Aphrodite. With tract.

05.15.1943. John [Woodburn], Harcourt, Brace and Company, Inc., to EW, Jackson.

Tss. letterhead, begins "Dear Flora"; regrets EW's departure from New York City and wishes he could have seen more of her during her visit; reports that "The Wide Net" galleys are in the mail. With envelope.

06.07.1943. John [Woodburn], Harcourt, Brace and Company, Inc., to EW, Jackson.

Tss. letterhead, begins "Dear Eu" and asks her to return the galleys of "The Wide Net." 2 pages. With envelope.

06.11.1943. John [Woodburn], Harcourt, Brace and Company, Inc., to EW, Jackson.

Tss. letterhead, writes to assure a worried EW that "The Wide Net" galleys have arrived; says that the dust jacket for this book is beautiful. With envelope.

08.23.1943. John [Woodburn], Harcourt, Brace and Company, Inc., to EW, Jackson.

Tss. letterhead, tells EW she is first person to win "two O. Henry firsts in succession"; reports that letter "putting Diarmuid in the clear" has been passed on to "proper authorities." 2 pages. With envelope.

11.10.1943. John [Woodburn], Harcourt, Brace and Company, Inc., to EW, Jackson.

Tss. letterhead, sending EW a "sackful of reactions" to *The Wide Net* and enclosing Katherine Anne Porter's address.

08.22.1945. John Woodburn, Harcourt, Brace and Company, Inc., to EW, Jackson.

Tss. letterhead, saying he is excited about EW's forthcoming novel, which is going to Ted Weeks, editor of the *Atlantic*; hasn't seen the manuscript yet but eagerly anticipates it; mentions that Harvey Breit (*New York Times Book Review*) asked to be remembered to EW. (Ted Weeks cut "Delta Wedding" to its periodical length.) With envelope.

11.13.1945. John Woodburn, Harcourt, Brace and Company, Inc., to EW, Jackson.

Tss. letterhead, reports that the copy editor has discovered that 09.11.1923 was a Tuesday; suggests that EW change her carbon of "Delta Wedding" accordingly; conveys other suggested detail revisions for her consideration; encloses carbon ts. of copy editor's tracing of the "Delta Wedding" chronology. (The only changes necessary were the change of Monday to 9.10.1923 and of Tuesday to 9.11.1923.) 2 pages. With envelope.

[01.29.1946]. Mary Elizabeth Russell, [Los Angeles, Calif.], to EW, c/o *The Atlantic*, Boston, Mass.

Als., praising the first installment of *Delta Wedding* in *The Atlantic*; especially pleased by the reference to Port Gibson, Miss., her home town; writes about her brother, poet Irwin Russell. With envelope.

03.20.1946. John Woodburn, Harcourt, Brace and Company, Inc., to EW, Jackson.

Tss. letterhead, asking EW to sign copies of *Delta Wedding* at Lowenstein's Department Store in Memphis and asking for a list of people who should receive advance copies of the book. (EW does not recall signing books in Memphis.) With envelope.

03.21.1946. John Woodburn, Harcourt, Brace and Company, Inc., New York, to EW, Jackson.

Tss. letterhead, reports that a "mystery" about the text of "Delta Wedding" has been solved and that EW should not be upset about the incident; refers to EW's "reworking of Troy's character."

10.29.1946. Lambert Davis, Harcourt, Brace and Company, Inc., New York, to EW, Jackson.

Tss. letterhead, reports plan "to bring out a new edition of *A Curtain of Green*" and to bring *The Wide Net* back into print; further reports that he has found EW a copy of *Georgia Scenes* and that he is searching for the Baldwin book [*Flush Times of Alabama and Mississippi*]; says he finds EW to be in the tradition of these works. 2 pages.

11.20.1946. Lambert Davis, Harcourt, Brace and Company, Inc., New York, to EW, Jackson.

Tss. letterhead, thanks EW for sacrificing British copy of *A Curtain of Green*; may need to use it to set new edition; is glad EW has no plans to change text; says he sent the Baldwin [*Flush Times*] to EW last week; holograph p.s. saying he just learned she'll be in New York City tomorrow; plans for lunch on Friday.

04.18.1947. Lambert Davis, Harcourt, Brace and Company, Inc., New York, to EW, Jackson.

Tss. letterhead, reporting on his travels for Harcourt; says he is glad that EW's short story writing "continues in the alien corn." (Davis seems to refer to a visit EW had made to the "Far West" and to writing she had done during that visit. This letter predates EW's extended stay in San Francisco, a stay that came later in 1947.) With envelope.

05.01.1947. Lambert Davis, New York, to EW, Jackson.

Telegram, in verse. (Probably announcing publication of *The Wide Net* and *A Curtain of Green* by Harcourt. *A Curtain of Green* was republished May 1, 1947. *The Wide Net* was reissued at same time.)

06.13.1947. Lambert Davis, New York, to EW, Jackson.

Telegram, inviting EW to a June 16 cocktail party for E.M. Forster.

06.23.1947. Lambert Davis, Harcourt, Brace and Company, Inc., New York, to EW, Jackson.

Tss. letterhead, reporting Forster's enthusiasm for *The Wide Net*; Davis has sent him copies of *A Curtain of Green* and *The Robber Bridegroom*; asks EW to do a signing in Seattle during her visit to the Northwest Writers' Conference (Aug. 4–10, 1947); sends news about John Woodburn's new wife and new job. 2 pages. With envelope.

07.18.1947. Lambert Davis, Harcourt, Brace and Company, Inc., New York, to EW, Jackson.

Tss. letterhead, saying he does not know "whether to be pleased or sorry" about EW changing her mind and agreeing to sign books in Seattle; holograph p.s. about John Woodburn. With envelope.

08.28.1947. Lambert Davis, Harcourt, Brace and Company, Inc., New York, to EW, Victoria Hotel, San Francisco, Calif.

Tss. letterhead, saying he is disappointed that EW has no new short story collection just now; has heard "wonderful reports" on her Washington speech. With envelope. (EW's holograph note on reverse of envelope reads, "Past-Time Antiques—Haight St.|Beaver Hat Works|Mutual Cleaners—Clement St.|Mutual Furniture Spraying Co.—Folsom St.|Darling Abrasive & Tool Co.|Los Angeles Sex Offense Bureau.")

10.01.1947. Lambert Davis, Harcourt, Brace and Company, Inc., New York, to EW, c/o Olson, San Francisco, Calif.

Tss. letterhead, telling EW that he is eager to see the essay on the short story that she read in Seattle; thinks it might serve as the introduction to an anthology which EW could compile (an idea EW had previously suggested). With envelope.

12.19.1947. Lambert Davis, Harcourt, Brace and Company, Inc., New York, to EW, Jackson.

Tss. letterhead, praising EW's essay on the short story; expresses delight that it will be published in part in the *Atlantic*; although he and EW had thought it could be the introduction to an anthology of stories, Davis now thinks this won't work; is interested in an anthology of essays on contemporary fiction. 2 pages. With envelope.

02.09.1948. Ben Wasson, The Levee Press, Greenville, Miss., to EW, Jackson.

Tss. letterhead, sending EW the manuscript of "Music from Spain" and asking to have it back as soon as possible because he wants to start printing; suggests dropping the "Danny Kaye motif" but leaves it up to EW; EW's holograph note on the back of page: "8 P [paragraph sign] end p. 2—3?|Miss Dimdummie ~~Dinwiddie~~ Dumdiddie." (That name is used in "Music from Spain." See page 396 of *Collected Stories*.)

02.16.1948. Lambert Davis, Harcourt, Brace and Company, Inc., New York, to EW, Jackson.

Tss. letterhead, discussing Harcourt's acquistion of Reynal and Hitchcock; comments on *Atlantic*'s use of EW's essay and on Harcourt's desire to see the periodical version of the essay before making its own plans; hopes EW's "spring expedition" to NYC "becomes a reality"; wants to discuss publication of the "Short Story" essay. (*Atlantic* published parts of the essay in February and March 1949. Harcourt published the complete essay under the title *Short Stories* in December 1949.) Sends a collection of Peter Taylor's stories to EW; holograph p.s. reads, "We [sic] planning definitely on bringing out *The Robber Bridegroom* in the Fall. Details later." (Harcourt did indeed bring out *The Robber Bridegroom* in 1948.) 2 pages. With envelope.

02.21.1948. Herschel [Brickell], Ridgefield, Conn., to EW, Jackson.

Als., text on recto and verso of the page, expressing pleasure that EW wants to dedicate "Music from Spain" to him; discusses Capote's new novel and Brickell's own "J.P. Bishop piece." (Mississippian Brickell was literary editor of the *New York Evening Post* (1934–38) and later became editor of the *O. Henry Memorial Prize Stories*.) With envelope.

04.02.1948. R. K. Haxton, The Levee Press, Greenville, Miss., to EW, s.l.

Tss. letterhead, sending EW the galleys of "Music from Spain" and suggesting minor revisions.

[11.____.1948]. EW, [Jackson], to John [Robinson], [Berkeley, Calif.].

Tss. with holograph p.s., dated only Friday; discusses Robinson's

idea for a screenplay of *The Robber Bridegroom* to be written in collaboration by EW and Robinson; also discusses EW's recent letter
to the *New Yorker*, the fiction of William Faulkner, literary criticism
in general, Truman's election victory over Dewey, and camellia
growing; signed "E." 4 pages. (See Chapter 1, IV.B3, for a description of the screenplay.)

[12.____.1948]. EW, [Jackson], to J [John Robinson], [Berkeley, Calif.].
Tss., typing on recto and verso of each page; praises dialogue Robinson has written for the script of "The Robber Bridegroom"; discusses Robinson's upcoming exams; comments on Joyce's fiction;
discusses the movie *Red River* and possible casting for "The Robber
Bridegroom"; EW is to write scenes 17–22 of the script; mentions
the recent Jackson Opera production of *Il Trovatore* [Dec. 6 and 7,
1948]; holograph p.s. 2 pages.

[12.____.1948]. EW, [Jackson], to J [John Robinson], [Berkeley, Calif.].
Tss., dated only Tues.; discusses "The Robber Bridegroom" script,
arguing that the scene with the Indian girl should remain part of
the text; discusses script of "Things to Come" by H. G. Tono Wells;
mentions that Clarence Brown will be directing *Intruder in the Dust*
in Oxford, Miss., in the spring. 2 pages, with typing on recto and
verso of each page.

[12.____.1948?] EW, [Jackson], to J [John Robinson], [Berkeley, Calif.].
Tss., dated only Wed. A.M.; sends some notes on "The Robber
Bridegroom" which she had made the night before; discusses two
graphs for the play's action.

____.____.[1949]. EW, [Jackson], to John [Robinson], [Berkeley, Calif.].
Tss., dated only Thursday; typed on recto and verso of the page;
sends her attempts at an opening scene and a scene to go between
scenes 26 and 27; reports on cold weather in Mississippi; holograph p.s.

____.____.[1949?] EW, [Jackson], to John [Robinson], [Berkeley, Calif.].
Tss., dated only Sunday; sends synopsis of 22 pages. (See Chapter
1, IV.B3.)

____.____.[1949?] EW, [Jackson], to John [Robinson], [Berkeley, Calif.].
Tss., dated only Saturday, typing on recto and verso of the page;
discusses work on the "The Robber Bridegroom" script; considers
possible financing for their work; reports on cold weather in Mississippi and on completing *The Golden Apples*; thanks Robinson for
retyping a story for her; mentions having seen the movie *San Francisco* [*San Francisco* played in Jackson Jan. 27–29, 1949.].

____.____.[1949?] Harkins the Florist, Jackson, to EW, Jackson.

Ts., sending orchids and listing EW's achievements; holograph note on two small slips of paper details accomplishments not listed in the letter. (The letter itself could have been written in 1947, for it mentions EW's recent return from the West Coast. However, the slips of paper mention the publication of *The Golden Apples*, EW's 2nd Guggenheim, and her travel in Europe, suggesting 1949 as the date.) 3 pages.

01.03.1949. Maurice Evans, New York, to EW, c/o The Levee Press, Greenville, Miss.

Als. letterhead, saying he has just read a review of "Music from Spain" and is excited by the prospect of a dramatization; asks EW "to delay any action" on an adaptation until he can evaluate the possibilities. With envelope.

01.14.1949. Eddie Dowling, New York, to EW, s.l.

Als. letterhead, praises "Music from Spain"; says he is awaiting a copy of *The Robber Bridegroom*; hopes it won't present problems of dramatization that "Music from Spain" does; asks if EW has done any work on a dramatization. (Eddie Dowling was a Broadway producer, playwright, and actor.) 2 pages.

02.05.1949. Eddie Dowling, New York, to EW, Jackson.

Als. letterhead, praises *The Robber Bridegroom*; thinks it would make a "grand operetta"; says he is anxious to read what EW has "written on the scenario or dramatization"; suggests that she try breaking the story down into dramatic [tableaux]; advises her not to worry about the number of scenes; he can handle that in production; would be happy to work with her and awaits further word. 3 pages. With envelope.

02.14.1949. [EW], Jackson, to [Eddie Dowling], s.l.

Carbon ts., saying she is very pleased by his interest in staging *The Robber Bridegroom*; reports that she and John Robinson have collaborated on a movie play and promises to send it to Dowling; he can then suggest whether the movie version could be adapted or whether they might start fresh on a stage version; describes Rodney for Dowling; feels structure of the movie script is an improvement over that of the novel which was written spontaneously; sends him some pictures of the Rodney country where the story is set.

06.13.1949. Donald Brace, Harcourt, Brace and Company, Inc., New York, to EW, Hotel Irving, New York.

Tss. letterhead, reports that he delivered EW's note to E.M. Forster; hopes she enjoyed the reception for Forster after the Institute of Arts and Letters meeting.

06.15.1951. John Woodburn, Little, Brown & Co., New York, to EW, c/o A. M. Heath & Co., London.

Tss. letterhead, says he had hoped EW "would remember about *A Bonfire of Weeds*," though he was "willing to forgive" her if she had not; tells EW to "say hello to DeValera" for him. (*A Bonfire of Weeds* by John Morton, also known as the Beachcomber, was a book to which Woodburn had introduced EW. He probably wanted her to find him a copy of this out-of-print book. Letter forwarded to EW, c/o Mrs. Alan Cameron [Elizabeth Bowen], Bowen's Court, Kildorrery, Co. Cork, Eire.) With envelope.

04.22.1952. Mrs. Matthew Josephson, American Academy of Arts & Letters, New York, to EW, Jackson.

Tss. letterhead, thanking EW for sending typescript of *A Curtain of Green* for manuscript show at the American Academy of Arts and Letters; suggests insuring typescript for $500–750; signed "In Charge of the Library."

04.23.1952. Bill Archibald, Setauket, Long Island, N. Y., to EW, Jackson.

Als., reports that he and Baldwin Bergersen have done quite a bit of work on a musical version of *The Robber Bridegroom*, but that he has to set project aside for two or three months; states that a good producer (unnamed) is very interested in the show. (Archibald died before he could complete "The Robber Bridegroom" script. While working on it, he encountered financial difficulties, especially after an unsuccessful production at the Edinburgh Festival. Archibald is the playwright who dramatized *The Turn of the Screw*. EW visited him in Nyack when he was working on the "The Robber Bridegroom" script.) 2 pages. With envelope.

07.17.1953. Robert Giroux, Harcourt, Brace, and Company, New York, to EW, Jackson.

Tss. letterhead, praising "The Ponder Heart" manuscript; in a p.s. Giroux notes that Diarmuid [Russell] has told him the good news about the *New Yorker*'s forthcoming publication of "The Ponder Heart." (Giroux became EW's editor after Lambert Davis moved to the University of North Carolina Press.) With envelope.

07.22.1953. Eugene Reynal, Harcourt, Brace and Company, New York, to EW, Jackson.

Tss. letterhead, praising "The Ponder Heart" manuscript; reports that he will send mimeographed copies to the Book-of-Month-Club which has already accepted it as an A book. With envelope.

4 sheets of yellow typing paper. Heading on sheet 1 is "Notes on 'The

Ponder Heart'—Eudora Welty." These seem to be an editor's notes and are keyed to the galleys of the novella. EW has written holograph comments by some of the notes. Someone has dated this item as 1953.

09.29.1953. Robert Giroux, Harcourt, Brace and Company, New York, to EW, Jackson.

Tss. letterhead, sending a set of corrected galleys for "The Ponder Heart"; says she needn't return the galleys unless there are additional changes to be made; reports that Joe Krush was impressed with the photographs EW sent and that he found them helpful in doing illustrations for *The Ponder Heart*; hopes *The Hill of Devi* has arrived. (The photographs Joe Krush used are part of the Welty Photograph Collection, and many of them have EW's holograph comments on the reverse side; see Chapter 2, II.B4.)

11.02.1953. Robert Giroux, Harcourt, Brace and Company, to EW, Jackson.

Tss. letterhead, sending photostats of 8 "double-page illustrations by Joseph Krush for *The Ponder Heart*"; recommends rephrasing of acknowledgement note to the *New Yorker*. With envelope.

12.11.1953. Robert Giroux, Harcourt, Brace and Company, New York, to EW, Jackson.

Tss. letterhead, sending EW a set of advance sheets of *The Ponder Heart*; bound books due on Friday; says he can send some copies before Christmas if she wishes; asks for names and addresses of those to receive books. With envelope.

12.17.1953. Eugene Reynal, Harcourt, Brace and Company, New York, to EW, Jackson.

Tss. letterhead, sending air-mail the first copy of *The Ponder Heart*.

12.17.1953. Robert Giroux, Harcourt, Brace and Company, New York, to EW, Jackson.

Tss. letterhead, reporting that the first copy of *The Ponder Heart* received from the bindery has been air-mailed to EW, that nine additional author's copies are being shipped, and that 25 copies EW had ordered will arrive soon after that; says that the publication date is January 7; notes that the photos EW mailed to Joe Krush are being shown to the press and will be used in book store window displays; a p.s. reports that Mary Louise Aswell (EW's friend and the fiction editor at *Harper's Bazaar* in the forties and fifties) likes the illustrations. (See Chapter 2, II.B4, for a description of the photographs.) With envelope.

12.26.1953. Lehman Engel, New York City, to EW, Jackson.

Telegram, telling EW not to stop her contract with Herman Levin;

reports that Levin plans a dramatization by John Patrick or by the Goetzes. (Jacksonian Lehman Engel, EW's long-time friend, had a successful New York career as a composer, conductor, and writer. John Patrick is the playwright of *Teahouse of the August Moon* and screenwriter of *Three Coins in a Fountain*; Herman Levin is a Broadway producer who was interested in *The Ponder Heart*.)

01.08.1954. Robert Giroux, Harcourt, Brace and Company, New York, to EW, Jackson.

Tss. letterhead, sending EW reviews of *The Ponder Heart* from *Newsweek* and *Saturday Review* and reporting that "It's a wonderful press."

01.11.1954. Herman Levin, New York, to EW, Jackson.

Telegram, thanking EW for the opportunity to bring her "book to the stage" and promising to keep her "advised of important developments"; hopes to meet her when she comes to New York.

01.22.1954. Bob [Giroux], New York, to EW, Jackson.

Telegram, reporting that *The Ponder Heart* has been accepted as the May Book-of-the-Month and that the author is guaranteed $2000.

01.23.1954. Robert Giroux, Harcourt, Brace and Company, New York, to EW, Jackson.

Tss. letterhead, explaining the telegram cited above; says that *The Ponder Heart* will be the alternate selection as May Book-of-Month and that the Club will send out 600,000 circulars advertising the book; congratulates EW on dramatic contract for *The Ponder Heart*.

02.16.1954. Herman Levin, New York, to EW, Jackson.

Tss. letterhead, discusses dramatization of *The Ponder Heart*; says that no playwright has yet been selected; reports that he has spoken with Josh Logan about dramatizing and directing and that Logan is considering the matter. With envelope.

03.05.1954. Bill [Archibald], to EW, Jackson.

Tss., apologizing for the fact that he and Bergersen have not been able to work on a dramatization of *The Robber Bridegroom*; says they still want to do it and hope to do so soon. With envelope.

03.06.1954. Katherine Hinds, Durham, N.C., to EW, Jackson.

Als., sending a checklist of EW's fiction and non-fiction to that date. (See Chapter 5, II.B)

03.16.1954. Katherine Hinds, Durham, N.C., to EW, Jackson.

Als., post card suggesting that EW add the title "Retreat" to the checklist of EW's fiction that Hinds had recently mailed her.

04.14.1954. Herman Levin, New York, to EW, Jackson.

Tss. letterhead, saying he is looking forward to EW's arrival in New York; plans to take her to *Ondine* on May 10; has discussed *The*

Ponder Heart with Moss Hart and wants EW to meet with them both on May 11 or 12. With envelope.

07.04.[1954?] Hamish Hamilton, London, to EW, Green Park Hotel, London.

Als. letterhead, sending flowers to EW and apologizing that the flowers were not at the hotel on her London arrival; explains that Green Park Hotel had originally said there was no reservation for EW; says he will see her at lunch on Tuesday. With envelope. On reverse of envelope EW has written, in pencil, her schedule for several days: "Wed.| 1:30 Elizabeth|White Tower|8:00 S. Spender,| Etoile, Charlotte St.| Thurs. AM collect money|lunch, Palie [illegible] & Eliz.|Eva, Elizabeth S.|Danny Kaye & dinner|Sat. 5:15 matinee &|dinner, Elizabeth." (Elizabeth is writer Elizabeth Bowen; Elizabeth S. is writer and Mississippian Elizabeth Spencer; Etoile and White Tower are London restaurants; Eva is Eva Boros Brandt, a young Hungarian writer who was living in London at the time.)

07.08.[1954?] Jamie [Hamish Hamilton], London, to EW, Green Park Hotel, London.

Als. letterhead, saying that he enjoyed seeing EW last evening and regretting that they couldn't dine together. With envelope.

07.18.1954. EW, Cambridge, England, to Danny Kaye.

Carbon ts., asking Danny Kaye to consider doing *The Ponder Heart* if anything comes of theatrical negotiations; says she will be in Cambridge until Aug. 15, 1954.

08.11.1954. Russell & Volkening, New York, to EW, Cambridge, England.

Envelope, with EW's holograph note on reverse: "Proctorial Notice, Trinity For repeatedly using bicycles without consent of the owners a member of the University *in statu pupillari* has been severely fined by the Proctors & gated by his College for a substantial period" (*in statu pupillari* = in the position of a ward or orphan).

10.01.1954. Jamie [Hamish Hamilton], Hamish Hamilton, Ltd., London, to EW, Hotel 33, New York.

Als. letterhead, thanking EW for an inscribed copy of *The Ponder Heart*; promises to send notices when they appear. (Hamish Hamilton, Ltd., published *The Ponder Heart* in England.) With envelope.

10.08.1954. Danny Kaye, Santa Monica, Calif., to EW, Jackson.

Tss. letterhead, thanking EW for offering him the role of Uncle Daniel Ponder but declining because of other commitments; praises her fiction. With envelope.

10.09.1954. EW, Hotel Thirty-Three, to Mrs. C. W. Welty, Jackson.

Als. hotel letterhead, describing her stay in New York City and her eagerness to get home; says she has seen Mary Lou [Aswell], Bill Maxwell [a novelist and, from 1936 to 1976, a fiction editor at the *New Yorker*], the Smiths [poet William Jay Smith and his wife], Diarmuid [Russell], Hubert [Creekmore], Hildy [Hildegard Dolson], and is to see Jack Fischer [the editor of *Harper's*]; reports that she will be spending Saturday evening at Diarmuid's in Katorah; notes that she saw [Robert] Giroux yesterday and went to a play that night with Hubert (*By the Beautiful Sea* with Shirley Booth); writes that Jimmie [Wooldridge of Jackson] is on his way home and had offered her a ride. With envelope.

10.20.1954. Jamie [Hamish Hamilton], Hamish Hamilton, Ltd., London, to EW, Jackson.
Tss. letterhead, sending mixed first reviews of the English edition of *The Ponder Heart*. With envelope.

11.03.1954. Jamie [Hamish Hamilton], Hamish Hamilton, Ltd., London, to EW, Jackson.
Tss. letterhead, enclosing reviews of *The Ponder Heart*, one good, two bad; reports that sales are slow; holograph p.s. says that "Punch" review is enclosed as well. With envelope.

12.01.1954. Jamie [Hamish Hamilton], Hamish Hamilton, Ltd., London, to EW, Jackson.
Tss., sending specially bound copy of *The Ponder Heart* for Christmas.

12.28.1954. Joseph Fields and Jerome Chodorov, Famous Artists Corporation, New York, to EW, Jackson.
Tss., saying that they are pleased to be doing *The Ponder Heart* dramatization; hope to send EW a first draft in a few months and to get her comments and suggestions; Lehman [Engel] has told them about EW, and they are anxious to meet her. With envelope.

02.18.1955. Jerry Chodorov and Joe Fields, Famous Artists Corporation, New York, to EW, Jackson.
Tss. letterhead, saying that they plan to come to Jackson for a week or ten days; will leave New York on February 27; want to spend time in locales EW mentions; ask her to reserve hotel room for them. With envelope.

02.23.1955. Jerry Chodorov and Joe Fields, Famous Artists Corporation, New York, to EW, Jackson.
Tss. letterhead, saying that they plan to come to Jackson but that EW (whose mother is to undergo an operation) should not worry about meeting with them; they hope for an hour or so with EW if

she's back in Jackson by March 1; Lehman [Engel], they note, has told them of people and places to visit. With envelope.

03.28.1955. EW, Jackson, to Joe [Fields] and Jerry [Chodorov], s. l.
Carbon ts., concerning the Chodorov and Fields script of *The Ponder Heart*; praises the "construction" and "dramatic manipulation" required to turn the story into a play, but offers three reservations about the script: 1) Uncle Daniel's innocence needs to be "more carefully established"; 2) a point of view for the community needs to be established; 3) the "texture" of play is too "thin"—this is lost when Edna Earle is no longer the narrator; recommends "making more of community feeling"—"Family, friends, stories, gossip, the town reaction in general—which is peculiarly southern"; recommends establishing a sense of community and of community affection for Uncle Daniel; recommends establishing the importance of family and community to Daniel himself; "Uncle Daniel's world cherishes him, protects him, enjoys him, and is *responsible* for him—the attitude as embodied whole in Edna Earle." 5 pages. (See Chapter 5, V.A1, for description of the final script.)

03.29.1955. Joe [Fields] and Jerry [Chodorov], Famous Artists Corporation, New York, to EW, Jackson.
Tss. letterhead, thanking EW for her long letter about their script; report that Tom Ewell "is anxious to play Uncle Daniel" and that Ewell suggested Danny Mann as director; no producer will be selected until the director is set. With envelope.

04.07.1955. Denver Lindley, New York, to EW, Jackson.
Telegram, sending congratulations on the publication of *The Bride of the Innisfallen* and reporting that the "reviews are ecstatic"; hopes to see EW before the end of April. (Lindley was an editor at Harcourt, Brace and World.)

04.12.1955. Warren Beck, Lawrence College, Appleton, Wis., to EW, s.l.
Tss. letterhead, sending complete text of his review of *The Bride of the Innisfallen* and praising her "beautiful and wonderful" book. 2 pages.

07.25.1955. Joe [Fields] and Jerry [Chodorov], Savoy Hotel, London, to EW, Jackson.
Als. letterhead, written by Fields for himself and Chodorov; envelope of this date was posted from New York City, but Fields has written "Savoy Hotel|London" in the upper right-hand corner of the stationery; Fields reports that he will be in London for a month;

says there has been a change in plans about the producer—it will be David Merrick; favors David Wayne as lead; hopes for Josh Logan as director. (*The Ponder Heart* was produced by the Playwrights' Company and opened on February 16, 1956. Written by Jerome Chodorov and Joseph Fields; starring David Wayne, Una Merkel, Don Hanmer, Will Geer, and Sarah Marshall; directed by Robert Douglas. See Chapter 5, VII.B1, for citation of ephemeral materials related to this production.) With envelope.

[08.26.1955]. Joe [Fields], Claridge's, London, to EW, Jackson.

Als., reports that "David Wayne is all set" for *The Ponder Heart* and that Dorothy Gish will be Edna Earle. With envelope.

[09.15.1955]. Joe [Fields], Midland Hotel, Manchester, England, to EW, Jackson.

Als., reports that his show opened successfully there, that Roger Stevens has been signed to produce *The Ponder Heart*, and that David Wayne is likely as the lead; no director yet signed. With envelope.

02.16.1956. Una Merkel, New York, to EW, Music Box Theatre, New York.

Telegram, expressing delight with the role of Edna Earle in EW's "enchanting story." (This is an opening night telegram.)

03.26.1956. Una Merkel, New York, to EW, Jackson.

Easter card with holograph note. With envelope.

04.02.1956. D. [Dolly Wells?], New York, to EW, Jackson.

Autograph post card, signed, reporting that she has just seen the TONY presentations on TV and was pleased that Edna Earle won best supporting actress; says she is looking forward to EW's visit next month. (Dolly Wells, EW's friend from Jackson, went on to work in New York City.)

04.15.1956. _____, New York, to EW, Jackson.

Autograph post card, signed, signature illegible; praises the production of *The Ponder Heart*.

04.23.1956. Bill [Archibald], Nyack, New York, to EW, Jackson.

Tss., wants to arrange a meeting while EW is in New York; since she will be seeing *The King and I* on May 4, he suggests they meet on May 5; promises to phone her at the Algonquin to check on arrangements. With envelope.

06.05.1956. Sarah [Marshall], New York, to EW, Jackson.

Als., thanking EW for a silver bell; regrets that she missed seeing EW the previous night; asks EW to return to New York soon. (Sarah

Marshall, the daughter of actor Herbert Marshall, played Bonnie Dee Ponder in *The Ponder Heart*.) With envelope.

06.09.1956. Una Merkel, New York, to EW, Jackson.

Tss., regretting that she must leave play [*The Ponder Heart*] and thanking EW for a gift; sends her father's [Arno Merkel's] regards as well; encloses a newspaper clipping about EW. 2 pages. With envelope.

06.18.1956. F. [Frank Lyell], New York, to EW, Jackson.

Autograph post card, signed, describing how much he enjoyed a performance of *The Ponder Heart*; return address: c/o H. Creekmore|124 East 72 Street|New York City. (H. is Hubert Creekmore.)

12.01.1956. Louis _____, Los Angeles, to EW, s. l.

Als., on Los Angeles Athletic Club stationery, sending EW a playbill from the Players Ring Gallery Theatre production of *The Ponder Heart*; says he was delighted by the production; informs EW that he is in the steel brokerage business.

[12._____.1956?] Una Merkel, s. l., to EW, Hotel Algonquin, [New York].

Gift card, with holograph note saying how nice it was to see EW again and to meet her mother; asks if gift reminds EW of her story.

[12._____.1956?] Sarah Marshall, s.l., to EW, s.l.

Christmas card with holograph question, "and how's your play coming?"

[12._____.1956?] Una Merkel, s. l., to EW and her mother, s. l.

Christmas card with holograph greetings. With envelope.

01.09.1957. Arno Merkel, New York, to EW, Jackson.

Tss. letterhead, reports that he wanted to do a film version of *The Ponder Heart*; says he had interested several Chicago friends in the prospect but in New York was told "it would not go." (Arno Merkel is Una Merkel's father.) With envelope.

[08._____.1958]. Leona Jordan, s. l., to EW, s. l.

Als., sending EW a copy of her Mississippi State University Master's Thesis "Humor in the Work of Eudora Welty"; thesis is dated August, 1958. (See Chapter 5, IV.D.)

04.13.1965. Emily Helen Evans, Dept. of Dramatic Arts, Western Reserve University, Cleveland, Ohio, to EW, s. l.

Tss., sending prompt book for dramatized versions of "A Piece of News" and "Petrified Man"; discusses changes she has made in stories for dramatic purposes. 2 pages. (See Chapter 5, V.B1)

05.13.1966. Margaret Benitez, Children's Book Department, Harcourt, Brace and World, New York, to EW, Jackson.

Tss. letterhead, returning manuscript of *The Shoe Bird*. (See Chapter 1, I.G4.)

06.30.1966. DMA, *New Yorker*, Fiction Department, New York, to EW, Jackson.

Tss., letterhead, returning typescript of *"Where is the Voice Coming From?"* (See Chapter 1, I.K3.a.)

01.14.1967. John Schaffner, New York, to EW, s. l.

Tss. letterhead, photocopy, informing EW of a memorial evening in New York City for Hubert Creekmore; tells EW who will be speaking and hopes she will attend; if not, asks her to write a brief letter to be read at the gathering. EW's holograph note at bottom of letter reads, "Dear Jimmy, I gave Mittie the original of this—E." (Jimmy is probably Jacksonian James Wooldridge, an old friend of EW's and an archivist at the Mississippi Department of Archives and History. Mittie is EW's sister-in-law and Hubert Creekmore's sister.)

09.04.1974. Alfred Uhry, New York, to EW, s. l.

Tss., telling EW that the script and most of the lyrics of *The Robber Bridegroom* are complete, that Robert Waldman has composed the music, and that the play will be performed at St. Clement's Church in New York City as a workshop production; hopes she can attend. (Alfred Uhry is the playwright who wrote the script for *The Robber Bridegroom*.)

10.15.1974. Stephanie W. Copeland, St. Clement's, New York, to EW, s.l.

Tss. letterhead, mimeographed, inviting recipients to buy tickets to St. Clement's production of *The Robber Bridegroom*; Alfred Uhry has written "Dear Miss Welty-" at the head of the letter; in a holograph note at its close, Uhry tells EW that the company would be honored if she could attend their production, and he notes that her book has been read aloud to the cast.

11.04.1974. St. Clement's, New York, to EW, Jackson.

Mimeographed post card, announcing the 11/4-11/9 production of *The Robber Bridegroom*.

11.05.1974. Lehman Engel, New York, to EW, s. l.

Tss. letterhead, begins "Dear Princess" and reports that he has seen the dress rehearsal of St. Clement's production of *The Robber Bridegroom*; details limitations of that workshop production; regrets that he and EW will miss connections in New York City in November and in Jackson in January. (See Chapter 5, VII.B5.a, for a listing of ephemeral materials concerning this production of *The Robber Bridegroom*.)

[___.___.1975]. John Houseman, City Center Acting Company, New York, to EW, s. l.

Als. letterhead, telling EW "how happy" his Acting Company "is to be doing the musical version of *The Robber Bridegroom*"; says he looks forward to meeting her; encloses reviews of the company, a description of company, and a schedule of its performances. (See Chapter 5, VII.B5.b.)

08.11.1975. Alred Uhry, Waldman and Uhry, New York, to EW, s. l.

Tss. letterhead, reporting that John Houseman has told him that EW will see *The Robber Bridegroom* in Ravinia; asks her to do so on August 26 or 27 while he [Uhry] is there.

09.30.1975. Margot Harley, The Acting Company, New York, to EW, Algonquin Hotel, New York.

Tss. letterhead, thanking EW for agreeing to sign copies of *The Robber Bridegroom* for the cast; says she looks forward to seeing EW opening night and at the cast party following.

10.03.1975. Marilynn M. Smith, The Acting Company, New York, to EW, Algonquin Hotel, New York.

Tss. letterhead, enclosing EW's tickets to the opening of *The Robber Bridegroom*. With envelope.

10.03.1975. Margot Harley, The Acting Company, New York, to EW, Algonquin Hotel, New York.

Tss. letterhead, telling EW when copies of *The Robber Bridegroom* will arrive and enclosing a list of actors to whom autographed books will be given. 2 pages.

10.06.1975. Geraldine Fitzgerald, New York, to EW, Algonquin Hotel, New York.

Telegram, sending regrets that she cannot attend the opening of *The Robber Bridegroom* and sending good wishes for its success.

[10.___.1975]. Jean Dalrymple, New York, to EW, s. l.

Tss. letterhead, praising the Broadway production of *The Robber Bridegrom*; sends a 10.07.1975 review of the production; regrets not seeing EW in New York; says she thinks often of their good time together on the Council [National Council on the Arts]. (Jean Dalrymple is a theatrical producer and publicist. See Chapter 5, VII.B5.b, for a listing of ephemeral materials about the Broadway production of *The Robber Bridegroom*.)

10.30.1975. Louis Rubin, University of North Carolina, Chapel Hill, to EW, s. l.

Tss. letterhead, sending EW a chapter from Lucinda MacKethan's book *A Dream of Arcady*. (See Chapter 5, III.A5.)

08.30.1977. Matthew J. Bruccoli, *First Printings of American Authors*, Columbia, S.C., to EW, Jackson.

Tss. letterhead, sending EW an offprint of her entry in *First Printings of American Authors*. (See Chapter 5, II.A.)

02.28.1978. Seymour Gross, University of Detroit, Detroit, Mich., to EW, s. l.

Tss. letterhead, enclosing an article he has written on *Losing Battles* and asking EW for any comments she may have; EW's holograph note on envelope reads, "*Essay on Losing Battles*|(a good one)|for Archives." (See Chapter 5, III.A3.)

07.14.1978. Tom Cutrer, University of Texas, Austin, Tex., to EW, s. l.

Tss. letterhead, thanking EW for her help with his book about the *Southern Review* and for her hospitality while he and his wife were in Jackson. 2 pages.

05.17.1979. Linda Peterson, Brigham Young University, Provo, Utah, to EW, Jackson.

Tss. letterhead, sending EW her Brigham Young University Master's Thesis. (See Chapter 5, IV.E.)

03.25.1980. Deborah Yarrow, Roanoke, Va., to EW, s. l.

Als., sending EW a story and part of a novel to read. (See Chapter 5, VI.A & B.)

10.12.1980. Lowry Pei, Cambridge, Mass., to EW, s. l.

Tss., sending an essay he has written on *The Golden Apples*. (See Chapter 5, III.A9.)

05.04.1981. Nancy Clarke Williams, Santa Cruz, Calif., to EW, s. l.

Tss., sending a paper she has written on *The Golden Apples* at the University of California, Santa Cruz, and sending her proposal for a major program there; invites EW to comment if she wishes. 2 pages. (See Chapter 5, III.B3.)

04.02.1986. Joyce Backman, Harvard University Press, Cambridge, Mass., to EW, s. l.

Tss. letterhead, sending EW the typescript setting copy and the master proof of *One Writer's Beginnings*. (See Chapter 1, II.E5.a and E6.a.)

05.12.1980. EW, s. l., to Stuart Wright, s. l.

Ts., photocopy, discussing selection of photographs to be published by Wright; warns that "The Store" is not well exposed and votes against "Confederate Veterans"; recommends "Saturday Off," "Staying Home," "The Rides or Sideshow," "Mother and Child," "Carrying the Ice," "Preacher and Leaders of Holiness Church,"

"Crossing the Pavement," "Coke," "With a Dog," and "Bottle Trees"; holograph note at head of letter reads, "Dear Patti, I sent this answer to Stuart Wright. I wonder if we'll ever get together! I feel we can do it when we meet. Many thanks for all your patience & help. Love, Eudora." (Wright published a collection of Welty photographs entitled *In Black and White* [Northridge, Calif.: Lord John Press, 1985]; Patti is Patti Carr Black, Director of the Mississippi State Historical Museum.)

Publications and Memorabilia

(Items within each category are listed chronologically
by publication date.)

I. BOOKS
(Archives Series 37)

A.   *The Ponder Heart.* New York: Harcourt, Brace, 1953, 1954. First
copy printed. With dust jacket. Without side boards.
B.   *Twenty Photographs.* Winston-Salem, N.C.: Palaemon Press, 1980.
Also listed in Chapter 2, II.C.

II. CONTRIBUTIONS TO BOOKS AND PERIODICALS

A. Fiction
(Archives Series 22)
(Collection includes complete issues of all periodicals cited.)

A1.   "Death of a Traveling Salesman." *Manuscript* III.3 (1936): 21–29.
A2.   "Retreat." *River* I.1 (1937): 10–12.
A3.   "A Memory." *Southern Review* 3 (1937): 317–22.
A4.   "The Hitch-Hikers." *Southern Review* 5 (1939): 293–307.
A5.   "A Worn Path." *Atlantic* February 1941: 215–19. EW's signature
on cover. Plus duplicate copy.
A6.   "Why I Live at the P.O." *Atlantic* April 1941: 443–450. EW's sig-
nature on front cover.
A7.   "Powerhouse." *Atlantic* June 1941: 707–13.
A8.   "Clytie." *Southern Review* 7 (1941): 52–64.
A9.   "The Key." *Harper's Bazaar* August 1941: 71, 132–34.
A10.   "The Purple Hat." *Harper's Bazaar* Nov. 1941: 68–69, 115. Illus-
trated by George Grosz.

A11. "First Love." *Harper's Bazaar* Feb. 1942: 52–53, 110, 112, 115–16, 118. Illustrated by Richard Erdoes.

A12. "A Still Moment." *American Prefaces* 7 (1942): 226–40.

A13. "The Wide Net." *Harper's Magazine* May 1942: 582–94.

A14. "The Petrified Man." *Horizon* 6.31 (1942): [57]–70. British publication.

A15. "The Winds." *Harper's Bazaar* August 1942: 92–93, 121–25.

A16. "Asphodel." *Yale Review* 32.1 (1942): [146]–157.

A17. "Livvie is Back." *Atlantic* Nov. 1942: 57–64.

A18. "The Robber Bridegroom." *Philadelphia Inquirer* 11 April 1943: 2–17, 19 Gold Seal Novel Section. With cover and envelope. Some holograph notations on manila envelope in which this publication is stored.

A19. "A Sketching Trip." *Atlantic* June 1945: 62–70.

A20.a. "Delta Wedding." *Atlantic* March 1946: 121–34.

A20.b. "Delta Wedding." *Atlantic* April 1946: 179–94.

A21. "Hello and Good-Bye." *Atlantic* July 1947: 37–40.

A22. "The Burning." *Harper's Bazaar* March 1951: 184, 238, 241, 243, 244, 247; cover of magazine is missing.

A23. "The Bride of the Innisfallen." *New Yorker* 1 Dec. 1951: 53–56, 58, 60–62, 64–68, 71–78.

A24. "Kin." *New Yorker* 15 Nov. 1952: 39–48, 50, 52–54, 56, 58–60, 62, 64–67.

A25.a. "The Ponder Heart." *New Yorker* 5 Dec. 1953: 47–58, 60, 62, 64–65, 68–70, 72, 74–76, 78, 80–84, 86, 89–91, 94–96, 99–100, 102, 104–06, 109–10, 112, 114–16, 121–24, 126–28, 131–38. Rough Copy. Stored in gray *New Yorker* envelope with EW's holograph identification on the envelope.

A25.b. "The Ponder Heart." *New Yorker* 5 Dec. 1953: 47–58, 60, 62, 64–65, 68–70, 72, 74–76, 78, 80–84, 86, 89–91, 94–96, 99–100, 102, 104–06, 109–10, 112, 114–16, 121–24, 126–28, 131–38. Finished issue. Stored in a *New Yorker* envelope with EW's holograph identification on the envelope.

A26. "Going to Naples." *Harper's Bazaar* July 1954: 54–58, 100–103, 108, 111–13.

A27. "Lily Daw and the Three Ladies." *Prairie Schooner* 30.4 (1956): 387–94. (Rpt.)

A28. "Where is the Voice Coming From?" *New Yorker* 6 July 1963: 24–25.

A29. "The Demonstrators." *New Yorker* 26 Nov. 1966: 56–63.

A30.a. "The Optimist's Daughter." *New Yorker* 15 March 1969: 37–

46, 48, 50, 53–54, 56, 61–62, 64, 67–68, 70, 75–76, 78, 81–82, 84, 86, 88, 93–95, 98, 100, 103–06, 111–14, 117–20, 125–28. Rough Copy.

A30.b. "The Optimist's Daughter." *New Yorker* 15 March 1969: 37–46, 48, 50, 53–54, 56, 61–62, 64, 67–68, 70, 75–76, 78, 81–82, 84, 86, 88, 93–95, 98, 100, 103–06, 111–14, 117–20, 125–28.

A30.c. "The Optimist's Daughter." *New Yorker* 15 March 1969: 37–46, 48, 50, 53–54, 56, 61–62, 64, 67–68, 70, 75–76, 78, 81–82, 84, 86, 88, 93–95, 98, 100, 103–06, 111–14, 117–20, 125–28.

A31. "Death of a Traveling Salesman." *The Georgia Review* 33 (1979): 756–69.

Text of story as first published in 1936; this issue also includes EW's essay, "Looking Back at the First Story" (751–55)—see II.C.18 below.

B. Reviews
(Archives Series 23)
(Unless otherwise noted, Collection contains
the pages cited, not complete issues of periodicals.)

B1. "Mirrors for Reality." Rev. of *A Haunted House, and Other Short Stories*. By Virginia Woolf. *NYTBR* 16 April 1944: 3. Photocopy.

B2. "Strictly Perelman." Rev. of *Crazy like a Fox*. By S. J. Perelman. *NYTBR* 2 July 1944: 6. Photocopy.

B3. "Ghoulies, Ghosties and Jumbees." Rev. of *Sleep No More*. Ed. August Derleth and *Jumbee and Other Uncanny Tales*. By Henry S. Whitehead. *NYTBR* 24 Sept. 1944: 5, 21. Photocopy.

B4. "Hand-Picked Spooks." Rev. of *Six Novels of the Supernatural*. Ed. Edward Wagenknecht. *NYTBR* 10 December 1944: 6. Photocopy.

B5. "Salem and Its Founding Father." Rev. of *Roger Conant, A Founder of Massachusetts*. By Clifford K. Shipton. *NYTBR* 25 Feb. 1945: 4. Photocopy.

B6. "Creole Get-Together." Rev. of *Gumbo Ya-Ya, A Collection of Louisiana Folk Tales*. By Lyle Saxon, Edward Dreyer, and Robert Tallent. *NYTBR* 20 Jan. 1946: 5, 14. Photocopy.

B7. "High Jinks Travelogue." Rev. of *Westward Ha! Around the World in 80 Cliches*. By S. J. Perelman. *NYTBR* 8 August 1948: 5. Photocopy.

B8. "Somnolence and Sunlight, Sound of Bells, The Pacific Surf." 1948. Rev. of *Our Gifted Son*. By Dorothy Baker. *NYTBR* 15 August 1948: 5. Plus photocopy.

B9. "Vets' Mental Hospital is Site of Moving Novel." Rev. of *The World Next Door*. By Fritz Peters. *NY Post* 18 Sept. 1949: M. Photocopy.

B10. "In Yoknapatawpha." Rev. of *Intruder in the Dust*. By William

Faulkner. *Hudson Review* 1 (1949): 596–98. Complete issue and photocopy of review.

B11. "Wise, Witty Novel of Europe Now." Rev. of *The World My Wilderness*. By Rose Macauley. *NY Post* 12 Nov. 1950. Photocopy.

B12. "A Search, Maddening and Infectious." Rev. of *The Witch Diggers*. By Jessamyn West. *NYTBR* 14 Jan. 1951: 5. Photocopy.

B13. "A Collection of Colette." 1951. Rev. of *Short Novels of Colette*. *New York Post* 30 Dec. 1951: 12M. Plus photocopy.

B14. "The Seeds of Evil." Rev. of *The West Pier*. By Patrick Hamilton. *NYTBR* 5 Oct. 1952: 5. Photocopy.

B15. "The Thorntons Sit for a Family Portrait." Rev. of *Marianne Thornton: A Domestic Biography*. By E. M. Forster. *NYTBR* 27 May 1956: 5. Three originals.

B16. "Hollingsworth Show Is 'Superlative Exhibit.'" 1958. Rev. of paintings by William Hollingsworth on exhibit at Art Gallery in Jackson. Jackson *Clarion-Ledger* 14 Sept. 1958, sec. C: 1, 4.

B17. "Uncommon Reader." 1958. Rev. of *Granite and Rainbow. Essays by Virginia Woolf*. *NYTBR* 21 Sept. 1958: 6.

B18. "All Is Grist for His Mill." Rev. of *The Most of S. J. Perelman*. *NYTBR* 12 Oct. 1958: 4, 14. Photocopy.

B19. "The Acceptance of Life is a Defense of the Story." Rev. of *The World of Isak Dinesen*. By Eric O. Johannesson. *NYTBR* 17 Dec. 1961: 6. Holograph addition to text.

B20. "Time and Place—and Suspense." Rev. of *The Stories of William Sansom*. *NYTBR* 30 June 1963: 5, 27. Plus photocopy.

B21. "S. J. Perelman Should Be Declared a Living National Treasure." Rev. of *Baby, It's Cold Inside*. By S. J. Perelman. *NYTBR* 30 Aug. 1970: 1, 25. Photocopy.

B22. "Everything writers and composers of musicals need to know." Rev. of *Words with Music*. By Lehman Engel. *NYTBR* 28 May 1972: 7, 10.

EW's holograph note to an unidentified person reads, "This might amuse you. Nash Burger, also of Jackson High School, asked me (J.H.S.) to review the book by Lehman (J.H.S.)." [Nash Burger, EW's Jackson High School classmate, was an editor at the *NYTBR*; Lehman Engel, another old Jackson friend, was a noted musical conductor in New York City.]

B23. "Africa and Paris and Russia." 1974. Rev. of *The Last of the Nuba*. By Leni Riefenstahl. *J'Aime Paris*. By Andre Kertesz. *About Russia*. By Henri Cartier-Bresson. *NYTBR* 1 December 1974: 5, 22, 28. Two sets of original pages.

B24. "As If She Had Been Invited into the World." Rev. of *Pictures and Conversations*. By Elizabeth Bowen. *NYTBR* 5 Jan. 1975: 4, 20.

B25. "Life's possibilities are those very things once felt as dangers." Rev. of *The Cockatoos*. By Patrick White. *NYTBR* 19 Jan. 1975: 4, 37. Plus photocopy; holograph correction to original.

B26. "Virginia Woolf." Rev. of *The Letters of Virginia Woolf*, Vol. II: 1912–1922. *NYTBR* 14 Nov. 1976: 1, 10, 12, 14, 16, 18, 20.

B28. "Post Mortem." Rev. of *The Never-Ending Wrong*. By Katherine Anne Porter. *NYTBR* 21 Aug. 1977: 9, 29.

B29. "Dateless Virtues." Rev. of *Essays of E.B. White*. *NYTBR* 25 Sept. 1977: 7, 43.

C. Essays
(Archives Series 24)

C1. "Women!! Make Turban in Own Home!" *Junior League Magazine* Nov. 1941: 20–21, 62. Complete issue.

C2. "Ida M'Toy." *Accent* 2.4 (1942): 214 22. Complete issue.

C3. "Pageant of Birds." *New Republic* 25 Oct. 1943: 565–67. Complete issue plus photocopy of essay only.

C4. "Some Notes on River Country." *Harper's Bazaar* Feb. 1944: 86–87, 150–56. Complete issue.

C5. "Jose de Creeft." *Magazine of Art* Feb. 1944: 43–46. Complete issue. Photographs of de Creeft's work are on pages 42 and 47.

C6.a. "Place in Fiction." *The Archive* 67 (1955): 5–7, 9–11, 13–14. Complete issue.

A Duke Univ. publication edited by Reynolds Price; issue includes three Welty photographs on pages 4, 8, and 12.

C6.b. "Place in Fiction." *The Archive* 67 (1955): 5–7, 9–11, 13–14. Complete issue.

C7. "Place in Fiction." *South Atlantic Quarterly* LV.1 (1956): 57–72. Complete issue.

C8. "A Sweet Devouring." *Mademoiselle* Dec. 1957: 49, 114–16. Complete issue.

C9. "A Sweet Devouring." *That Eager Zest*. Ed. Frances Walsh. Philadelphia: Lippincott, 1961. 212–218. Photocopy.

Final lines of the essay were typed onto essay and photocopied here; originally published in *Mademoiselle* Dec. 1957: 49, 114–16—see II.C8 immediately above.

C10. "The Short Story." *Three Papers on Fiction*. Northhampton, Mass: Smith College, 1962. 26–46. Photocopy.

C11. "And They All Lived Happily Ever After." *NYTBR* 10 Nov. 1963: 3.

C12. "Must the Novelist Crusade?" *Atlantic* Oct. 1965: 104–08. Complete issue.

C13. "Words into Fiction." *Southern Review* ns 1 (1965): 543–53. Complete issue.

Holograph revisions to essay; brackets around some passages, other passages marked for deletion.

C14. "The Eye of the Story." *Yale Review* LV.2 (1965–66): 265–74. Complete issue.

C15. "The Feast Itself." *NY Times* 5 Dec. 1974: C47. Photocopy.

C16. "The Point of the Story." *NYTBR* 5 March 1978: 3, 32–33. Photocopy.

C17. "For Allen Tate." *Quarterly Journal of the Library of Congress* 36.4 (1979): 354. Complete issue.

EW's tribute to Allen Tate.

C18. "Looking Back at the First Story." *The Georgia Review* 33 (1979): 751–55. Complete issue.

This issue includes the text of "Death of a Traveling Salesman" as it was published in 1936 (pp. 756–69)—see II.A.31 in this chapter.

D. MISCELLANEOUS
(Archives Series 25)

D1. *Lamar Life Radio News* 24–30 Jan. 1932: 1–4.

EW notes that this newsletter "contains editorial and a news story I wrote on a flood in the studio."

D2. *Lamar Life Radio News* 18–24 Sept. 1932: 1–4.

Written in part by EW.

D3. *Mississippi Women's War Bond News Letter* 13 May 1944: 1–9.

Edited by EW.

D4. "Department of Amplification." *New Yorker* 1 Jan. 1949: 50–51.

EW's letter, responding to Edmund Wilson's criticism of William Faulkner's fiction.

D5. "Eudora Welty Blames Lack of Reading for Lack of Creative Ability in Child." *Jackson Daily News* 17 Nov. 1955, sec. 2: 4.

D6. "A Salute from One of the Family." *A Tower of Strength in the Deep South: 50th Anniversary, Lamar Life Insurance Company.* [Montgomery, Alabama: Paragon Press, 1956]. 3–5.

D7. "A Flock of Guinea Hens Seen from a Car." *New Yorker* 20 April 1957: 35. Complete issue.

D8. Press release of 13 April 1961, calling for books for Mississippi hospitals and institutions (4 pages).

Holograph corrections; accompanying letter from William E. Keith, Chairman, Publicity Committee, National Library Week.

D9. TCG Reprint. Feb. 1975. Excerpts from "a speech delivered at the opening of the Governor's Conference on the Arts, Jackson, Mississippi, last fall by Eudora Welty, Pulitzer Prize-winning novelist and a member of the National Council on the Arts" (1 page).

The speech was the basis for a 5 Dec. 1974 *NY Times* article entitled "The Feast Itself"—see Chapter 4, II.C15.

III. MEMORABILIA
(Archives Series 36)

A. Dust jacket of *A Curtain of Green*, First Edition. 1941.

B. Gift card, reading "Love and Congratulations|Book Department of The Office Supply Co." [1949].

C. Check stub from the American Library Association, Chicago, Illinois, for foreign language condensation rights to "Livvie is Back." [1953].

D. A card for the St. Regis Maisonette in New York City with the address of Moss Hart on reverse. [1954].

E. A slip of paper with the address of Julie Harris Guriau. [1956].

F. A slip of paper with the address of David Wayne. [1956].

G. A program of the 60th Annual Commencement Convocation at Southern Methodist University; EW received an honorary degree at the Convocation. 1975.

H. EW's Columbia University Doctor of Letters honorary degree. 1982.

Secondary Materials

I. REVIEWS OF WELTY'S WORK
(Archives Series 30)

Welty's works are listed chronologically by publication date; reviews of each work are listed alphabetically. Citations that include information I have not personally verified are marked with an asterisk. When I have not been able to provide complete citations, I have listed all information available at the Mississippi Department of Archives and History or in previously published bibliographies. I am indebted to the work of Noel Polk, Victor Thompson, and Pearl McHaney.

A. REVIEWS OF A CURTAIN OF GREEN (1941)

A1.   Hartley, L. P. "New Stories." *Time and Tide* 4 Oct. 1947: 1068.

B. REVIEWS OF THE WIDE NET (1943)

B1.   "Briefly Noted." *New Yorker* 25 Sept. 1943: 80.

B2.   Engle, Paul. "3 Volumes Stress Vitality of American Short Story." *Chicago Tribune* 10 Oct. 1943: 17.*

B3.   Rosenfeld, Isaac. "Consolations of Poetry." *New Republic* 18 Oct. 1943: 525–26.

B4.   Shattuck, Charles. Rev. of *The Wide Net*. *Accent* Autumn 1943: 124.*

B5.   Trilling, Diana. "Fiction in Review." *Nation* 2 October 1943: 386–87. Galleys of 22 Sept. 1943, 23–24.

B6.   Woods, Katherine. Rev. of *The Wide Net*. *Tomorrow* Nov. 1943: 54.*

C. Reviews of Delta Wedding (1946)

C1. Anderson, Barbara Tunnell. "A Delta Wedding and a 9-Year-Old." Louisville *Courier-Journal* 19 May 1946, sec. III: 10.*

C2. Appel, David. "Mississippi Delta Nuptials." *Chicago Daily News* 17 April 1946.*

C3. Balakian, Nona. "New Fiction in Review." *Tomorrow* [April? 1946]: 74. Two copies.*

C4. Basso, Hamilton. "Look Away, Look Away, Look Away." *New Yorker* 11 May 1946: 86, 88–89.

C5. B.C.C. Rev. of *Delta Wedding*. *Providence Journal* 14 April 1946, sec. VI: 8.*

C6. Boatner, Maxine Tull. "Color of Mississippi Lives." *Hartford Courant* 21 April 1946, Magazine: 14.

C7. Bookhart, Mary Alice. "Eudora Welty." Jackson *Clarion-Ledger* 28 April 1946: 8.

C8. Bowen, Elizabeth. "Book Shelf." *The Tatler and Bystander* 6 August 1947: 183.

C9. Bullock, Florence Haxton. "A Southern Family Sliding Downhill." *Chicago Sun* 14 April 1946, sec. 5: 1. Two copies.

C10. Canfield, Dorothy. Rev. of *Delta Wedding*. *Book-of-the-Month Club News* May 1946: 7.

C11. Church, Richard. "A Tale for Laughter." *John O'London's Weekly* 11 July 1947: 483.

C12. Cournos, John. "The Reviews." *NY Sun* 15 April 1946: 21.*

C13. Dangerfield, George. "A Family Rarely in Repose." *Saturday Review* 20 April 1946: 12.

C14. Daniel, Frank. "Delta Flavor Aptly Caught." Memphis *Commercial Appeal* 7 April 1946: IV 12.

C15. Dexter, Ethel Hathaway. "Delta Wedding." *The Republican* [Springfield] [19 or 27] May 1946: D4.*

C16. Engle, Paul. "Miss Welty's Full Charm in First Novel." *Chicago Sunday Tribune* 14 April 1946, Part 4: 3, 12. Three copies.

C17. Gannett, Lewis. "Books and Things." *NY Herald Tribune* 15 April 1946: 19. Two copies.*

C18. Gray, James. "Family Life is Theme of Eudora Welty's Novel." *St. Paul Sunday Pioneer Press* 14 April 1946, Magazine: 11.*

C19. Hieronymus, Clara W. "Eudora Welty's First Novel Called Writing at Its Best." *Tulsa Daily World* 7 July 1946.

C20. Kane, Harnett T. "Eudora Welty's Authentic and Vital Talent." *NY Herald Tribune Weekly Book Review* 14 April 1946: VII 3. Five copies.

C21.   K.H. "Su'th'n Family in Full Array." *Philadelphia Inquirer* 12 May 1946: 15.*

C22.   McGrath, Thomas. "Life in Mississippi." *New Masses* 4 June 1946: 23.*

C23.   Meador, Frank. "A Different Group of Southerners." *Boston Daily Globe* 17 April 1946: 12.*

C24.   North, Sterling. "Delta Alpha, Omega?" *NY Post* 18 April 1946: 30.

C25.   Poore, Charles. "A Fine Novel of the Deep South." *NYTBR* 14 April 1946: 1, 41. Uncorrected Rough Proof of entire issue plus 4 copies of p. 1.

C26.   Prescott, Orville. "Books of the Times." *NY Times* 17 April 1946: 23. Five copies.

C27.   Ricketts, Leone. "Eudora Welty Achieves Rare Mood in her 'Delta Wedding.'" *Jackson Daily News* 14 April 1946, sec. 2: 1. Four copies.

C28.   Robinson, Ted. "Van Paassen Carries on his Life Story Through War Era." *Cleveland Plain Dealer Pictorial Magazine* 28 April 1946: 16.
Review of *DW* included with reviews of several new books.

C29.   Rosenfeld, Isaac. "Double Standard." *New Republic* 29 April 1946: 633–34. Two copies.

C30.   Steele, Mary Q. "Little Plot, Enormity of Detail Make Fine Book on Delta Folk." *Chattanooga Times* 28 April 1946.*

C31.   Rev. of *Delta Wedding*. *TLS* 19 July 1947: 361.

C32.   Trilling, Diana. "Fiction in Review." *Nation* 11 May 1946: 578. Two copies.

C33.   Weeks, Edward. "Southern Weddings." *Atlantic* May 1946: 154, 156.

C34.   Williamson, Margaret. "Essence of the Deep South." *Christian Science Monitor* 15 April 1946: 16. Two copies.*

C35.   Wilson, Kathleen. "Rare Portrait of the South in Eudora Welty's Novel." *Milwaukee Journal* 14 April 1946, sec. V.*

D. REVIEWS OF THE GOLDEN APPLES (1949)

D1.   Bailey, Mary. Rev. of *The Golden Apples*. *Book-of-the-Month Club News* August 1949: 9.*

D2.   Basso, Hamilton. "Morgana, Mississippi." *New Yorker* 3 Sept. 1949: 56.

D3. Bookhart, Mary Alice. "Eudora Welty Writes Another Magic Story." Jackson *Clarion-Ledger* 22 Aug. 1949, sec. 1.

D4. Bowen, Elizabeth. "Elizabeth Bowen Reviews *The Golden Apples*." *Books of Today* Sept. 1950: 2–3.

D5. Breit, Harvey. "Books of the Times." *NY Times* 18 Aug. 1949: 19.

D6. Brickell, Herschel. "Dragons in Mississippi." *Saturday Review* 27 Aug. 1949: 9. Two copies, one is untitled page proof.

D7. Beauchamp, Elise. "Literature and Less." New Orleans *Times-Picayune* 28 Aug. 1949, sec. II: 15.*

D8. Cowley, Malcolm. "Seven New Stories by Eudora Welty." 1949. 1 p. A newspaper review.

D9. Guilfoil, Kelsey. "Eudora Welty Spins Her Magic Spell." *Chicago Sunday Tribune* 14 August 1949, sec. 4: 3. Two copies.

D10. Haxton, Kenneth. "Collection of Short Stories Keeps Welty's Name at the Top." *Delta Democrat-Times* [Greenville, MS] 21 Aug. 1949: 18.

D11. Hobgood, Burnett. "Miss Welty Paints Series of Portraits for Fine Example of Superior Artistry." *Lexington Herald Leader.**

D12. Hutchens, John K. "Books and Things." *NY Herald Tribune* 18 Aug. 1949: 13.*

D13. Marshall, Margaret. "Notes by the Way." *Nation* 10 Sept. 1949: 256.

D14. M.M. "Small Town Dreamers Made Vivid." *Los Angeles Times* 28 Aug. 1949, sec. IV: 9.

D15. Rosenberger, Coleman. "Miss Welty's Trance-like Mississippi." *NY Herald Tribune Book Review* 21 Aug. 1949: 6. Plus Table of Contents.*

D16. Sheffield, Martha. "Eudora Welty Adds Statue [sic] to Reputation with Latest Stories, 'Golden Apples.'" *Jackson Daily News* 18 Sept. 1949, sec. IV: 3.

D17. Steegmuller, Francis. "Small-Town Life." *NYTBR* 21 Aug. 1949: 5. Five Copies.

D18. Thesmar, Sarah. "Living People Grace Pages of Eudora Welty's New Tale." Memphis *Commercial Appeal*, sec. IV: 12. Two copies.

D19. Rev. of *The Golden Apples*. *TLS* 8 Sept. 1950: 561.

D20. Weeks, Edward. "Eudora Welty of the Delta." *Atlantic* Sept. 1949: 80.

D21. Wyndham, Francis. "New Novels." *The Observer* 27 Aug. 1950.*

E. Reviews of The Ponder Heart (1954)

E1.   Hieronymus, Clara. "Mississippi Magic." *Nashville Tennessean* 10 Jan. 1954: 18C.

E2.   Lane, Robert R. "Off the Fiction Shelf." October 1954. 1 p.

E3.   Little, Carl Victor. "New Books." *Houston Press* 8 Jan. 1954.

E4.   MacGregor, Martha. "Eudora Welty Excels In Brief, Comic Novel." [1954?]. 1 p.*

E5.   Poore, Charles. "Books of the Times." *NY Times* 7 Jan. 1954: 29.

E6.   Pritchett, V.S. "Bossy Edna Earle Had a Word for Everything." *NYTBR* 10 Jan. 1954: 5.

E7.   Roberts, Albert. "Ponder Heart is Eudora Welty's Finest Achievement." Jackson *Clarion-Ledger* 3 Jan. 1954, sec. I: 3.

E8.   Rosenberger, Coleman. "Eudora Welty Tells a Wise and Comic Story of a Mississippi Town." *NY Herald Tribune Book Review* 10 Jan. 1954: 1.

E9.   J.V.d.S. "The Ponder Heart." *Gazet Van Antwerpen* 4 May 1954.

E10.   Sampson, Paul. "The Ponders of Clay, Miss.: A Richly Comic Character Study." *Washington Post* 10 Jan. 1954, sec. B: 6.*
Ts of review, pages [1]–3.

E11.   Smith, Harrison. "Lead Review of the Week." *Book Service for Newspapers* 9 Jan. 1954: [1]–3.
Press release, mimeographed ts.

E12.   "Southern Legend." *Newsweek* 11 Jan. 1954: 82–83.

E13.   Tunstall, Caroline H. "A Small Comic Masterpiece about a Mississippi Family." 24 Jan. 1954.

F. Reviews of The Bride of the Innisfallen (1955)

F1.   Arp, Thomas. "Welty's New Book of Short Stories." *San Francisco Chronicle* 3 April 1955, This World: 16. Two copies.*

F2.   Barkham, John. "Prismatic Observations." *Saturday Review* Syndicate.
Press release, mimeographed ts.

F3.   Beck, Warren. "The Realization of Sheer Genius." *Chicago Tribune* 10 April 1955, sec. IV: 3.*

F4.   Benet, Rosemary. Rev. of *The Bride of the Innisfallen*. *Book-of-the-Month Club News*.

F5.   "Collector's Items." *Newsweek* 11 April 1955: 114–15. Two copies.

F6. Davenport, John. "Micrologophily." *The Observer* 16 Oct. 1955: 12.*

F7. Frye, Harriet. "Miss Welty's Private World of Whimsey." *Columbus Dispatch* 17 April 1955: 12.*

F8. Gaither, Frances. "Of the South and Beyond." *NYTBR* 10 April 1955: 4. Two copies.

F9. Gannett, Lewis. "Book Review." *NY Herald Tribune* 7 April 1955: 19.

F10. Hains, Frank. "Miss Welty Magnificent in Newest Short Pieces." 1955. *Clarion-Ledger and Jackson Daily News* 10 April 1955, sec. IV: 6.

F11. Hutchens, John K. "Miss Welty's Somewhat Puzzling Art." *NY Herald Tribune Book Review* 10 April 1955: 2. Two copies.

F12. J.M.-R. Rev. of *The Bride of the Innisfallen. Punch* 9 Nov. 1955.

F13. Peden, William. "The Incomparable Welty." *Saturday Review* 9 April 1955: 18.

F14. Prescott, Orville. "Books of the Times." *NY Times* 8 April 1955: 19. Two copies.

F15. Shay, Arthur. "Seven Slices of Life Served with Perfection." *Chicago Sun-Times* 10 April 1955, sec. 3: 4.

F16. Spearman, Walter. "Eudora Welty Describes Own Success." *Sunday Star-News* [Wilmington, N.C.] 17 April 1955.*

F17. Steggert, Frank X. "Variety of Stories by Eudora Welty." *Books on Trial* May 1955.*

F18. Swan, Michael. "New Fiction." [1955?]. 1 p.

F19. Tunstall, Caroline. "Eudora Welty's Tales Waver like Images in an Old Mirror." *Virginian-Pilot* 10 April 1955, sec. III: 6.*

F20. Weeks, Edward. "Miss Welty's World." *Atlantic* May 1955: 76, 78.

F21. White, Milton C. "Sensuous Imagery, Vivid Impressions in Welty's New Collection of Stories." *State Times* [Jackson, MS] 10 April 1955: 3D.

G. Reviews of Losing Battles (1970)

G1. Aldridge, John W. "Eudora Welty: Metamorphosis of a Southern Lady Writer." *Saturday Review* 11 April 1970: 21–23, 35–36.

G2. Bitker, Marjorie M. "Reunion in Mississippi: A Matriarch Turns 90." *Milwaukee Journal* 26 April 1970, sec. V: 4.*

G3. Boardman, Anne Cawley. "Eudora Welty's new novel of South worth the wait." *Minneapolis Star* 29 April 1970, sec. B: 4. Two copies.

G4. Boatwright, James. Rev. of *Losing Battles*. *NYTBR* 12 April 1970: 1, 32–34. Three complete issues, two originals of review, one photocopy of review.

G5. Bradley, Van Allen. "Eudora Welty's new novel a triumph." *Chicago Daily News* 11 April 1970, Panorama: 8*, and *Philadelphia Inquirer* 19 April 1970, Book News: 7. Three copies, one from *Daily News* and two from *Inquirer*.

G6. Burton, Marda. "Welty Wins the Battle." *The Sun Herald* [Biloxi, MS].

G7. Caldwell, David S. "Sad Old Clan Loses All, With a Shiny Exception." *Pittsburgh Press* 12 April 1970, sec. VI: 6.*

G8. Cheney, Frances Neel. "Life Seen Through Eyes of Great Artist." *Nashville Banner* 17 April 1970: 28. One original (2 pp.) and one photocopy.

G9. Coppel, Alfred. "The Keenly Reasoned Welty Prose." *San Francisco Sunday Examiner & Chronicle*, This World: 30. Original and photocopy.

G10. Davenport, Guy. "Mozartean music in Mississippi." *Life* 17 April 1970: 10. Three originals and one photocopy.

G11. "Deep South Hoedown." *Newsday* 11 April 1970. Photocopy.*

G12. Dollarhide, Louis. "Eudora Welty's 'Losing Battles' Is Magnificent Feast." *Mississippi Library News* June 1970: 96–98.

G13. Dollarhide, Louis. "Eudora Welty's 'Losing Battles': A Major Work by a Major Writer." Jackson *Clarion-Ledger* 12 April 1970, sec. E: 6. Three originals, one photocopy.

G14. Donnelly, Tom. "Delicious things to be enjoyed by all." *Washington News* 17 April 1970: 26. Photocopy.*

G15. Duhamel, Albert. "Meet the Vaughns!" *Boston Herald-Traveler* 13 April 1970. Photocopy.*

G16. Elder, Paul. "Birth of a Classic Novel." *San Francisco Examiner* 8 May 1970: 37. Photocopy.*

G17. "Books in Brief." *Orlando Sentinel* 21 June 1970, sec. F: 18–19.

G18. Fuller, Edmund. "Goings-On in the Rural South." *Wall Street Journal* 13 April 1970: 16. Three originals, one photocopy.

G19. Gaines, Ervin J. "16 Years Later . . . Eudora Welty is Still a Master." *Minneapolis Tribune* 26 April 1970, sec. E: 9. Photocopy.*

G20. Gilreath, Emily. "Miss Welty Loses the Battle of Words." *Cleveland Press* 17 April 1970, Showtime: 23.*

G21. Gossett, Louise Y. "Eudora Welty's New Novel: The Comedy of Loss." *SLJ* 3.1 (1970): 122–37.

G22. Govan, Christine. "Masterpiece of a Family Reunion." *Chatta-nooga Times* 28 June 1970, sec. B: 4.

G23. VPH. "Tobacco Road Types, Talk, and Din Abound in Eudora Welty's New Book." *Omaha Morning World-Herald* 26 April 1970. Photocopy.*

G24. Hall, Wade. "Welty Novel a Dazzling Linguistic Tour de Force." Louisville *Courier-Journal* 10 May 1970: F4. Original and photocopy.

G25. Hamlin, William C. "The Multitudes Arrive and the Talk Goes On." *Kansas City Star* 10 May 1970, sec. H: 10. Photocopy.*

G26. Hartley, Lodwick. "Intricate Folk Comedy." *News and Observer* [Raleigh, N.C.] 10 May 1970, sec. IV: 6.*

G27. Hobby, Diana. "Get behind a barefoot boy and push." *Houston Post* 10 May 1970, Spotlight: 14. Photocopy.*

G28. Hopper, Lynn. "Miss Welty's Southern Scene More Cheerful." *Indianapolis Star* 10 May 1970. Photocopy.*

G29. Hutsell, James K. "Eudora Welty." *Huntsville Times* 17 April 1970.

G30. Idema, James. "Backwoods America Comes Alive in 'Losing Battles.'" *Denver Post* 19 April 1970, Roundup: 16. Photocopy.*

G31. Janeway, Elizabeth. "Comic novel with epic characters and un-predictable action." *Chicago Sun Times Book Week* 12 April 1970: 3. One original, one photocopy.

G32. Kroll, Jack. "The Lesson of the Master." *Newsweek* 13 April 1970: 90–91. Two copies.

G33. Kuehl, Linda. "Books." *Commonweal* 42 (18 Sept. 1970): 465–66.

G34. Lehmann-Haupt, Christopher. "Books of the Times." *NY Times* 10 April 1970: 37. Three copies.

G35. Leighton, Betty. "Granny Vaughn's Clan." *Winston-Salem Journal and Sentinel* 19 April 1970, sec. D: 4. Original and photocopy.

G36. Macneil, Alan. "Dialogue so true." *Connecticut Valley Times Reporter.* 1970.

G37. Maxwell, Allen. "Strong Fiction for Spring." *Dallas News* 5 April 1970, sec. F: 10. Photocopy.*

G38. Moody, Minnie Hite. "Mississippi Kinfolk Posed for a Portrait." *Columbus Dispatch* 3 May 1970. Photocopy.*

G39. Morton, Kathryn. "The Reunion." *Virginian-Pilot* 3 May 1970, sec. C: 6. Three originals, one photocopy.

G40. Moss, Howard. "The Lonesomeness and Hilarity of Survival." *New Yorker* 4 July 1970: 73–75.

G41.   Murray, Michele. "Talk is Art in Miss Welty's 'Losing Battles.'" *National Observer* 27 April 1970: 19. Three originals, one photocopy.

G42.   Oates, Joyce Carol. "Eudora's Web." *Atlantic* April 1970: 118–20, 122. Photocopy.

G43.   Parrill, William. "Unique Imagination Earmark of Durrell." *Nashville Tennessean* 19 April 1970.

G44.   Price, Reynolds. "'Frightening Gift.'" *Washington Post* 17 April 1970, sec. C: 1, 4. Three originals, one photocopy.

G45.   Rev. of *Losing Battles*. *Publisher's Weekly* 23 February 1970: 149. Two copies.

G46.   Rhodes, Richard. "The family way." *Washington Post Book World* 12 April 1970: 3, and *Chicago Tribune Book World* 12 April 1970: 3. Three originals, two photocopies.*

G47.   Robbins, J. Albert. "Voices of a Mighty Family." *St. Louis Post-Dispatch* 19 April 1970, sec. B: 4.*

G48.   Rogers, W. G. Rev. of *Losing Battles*. *NY Post* 13 April 1970: 50*, *North Carolina Leader* 15 April 1970: 5, *Waukegan News-Sun* 11 April 1970*, *Youngstown Vindicator* 12 April 1970*, two unidentified newspapers. Variously titled. Five originals, two photocopies.*

G49.   Rose, Jeanne. "Land of Laughter, But with a Catch." Baltimore *Evening Sun* 26 April 1970, sec. D: 5. Photocopy.*

G50.   Rubin, Louis D. "Books: Delight Ending in Wisdom in Welty Novel." *Washington Star* 26 April 1970, sec. D: 10. Photocopy.*

G51.   Rubin, Louis D. "Everything Brought Out in the Open: Eudora Welty's Losing Battles." *Hollins Critic* VII.3 (1970): 1–7, 9–12. Complete issue.

G52.   Ruffin, Carolyn. "Sensitivity runs a poor second." *Christian Science Monitor* 11 June 1970: 17. Three copies.

G53.   Shaffner, Claire. "For Those Who Like Downright Good Story-Telling . . . ." *Charlotte Observer* 12 April 1970, sec. F: 5.*

G54.   "Shangri-la South." *Time* 4 May 1970: 100–101. Two copies of p. 100, one copy of p. 101.

G55.   Short, Kathryn S. "Beautiful Writing of Eudora Welty Apparent in Novel." *Baton Rouge Advocate* 3 May 1970. Photocopy.*

G56.   Simmons, Mabel C. "Long Wait is Rewarded—New Welty Novel is Here." New Orleans *Times-Picayune* 26 April 1970, sec. II: 2. Photocopy.*

G57.   Spacks, Patricia Meyer. "Losing Battles—A view of life in Mississippi." *Boston Morning Globe*, 2 May 1970: 12. Photocopy.*

G58. Sparrow, Bonita. "New Welty Novel Written to Endure." Memphis *Commercial Appeal* 19 April 1970, sec. 6: 6. One original, three photocopies.

G59. Spearman, Walter. "Eudora Welty is Alive—And How." *Chapel Hill Weekly*, 19 April 1970: 4. Two originals, one photocopy.

G60. Stuart, Reece. "The Family Resembles a Breughel Painting." *Des Moines Register* 17 May 1970.*

G61. Thornton, Eugenia. "The Vital Eudora Welty." Cleveland *Plain Dealer* 19 April 1970, sec. H: 7. Original, two photocopies.

G62. Torgerson, Margaret. "Major Literary Event." *Worcester Telegram*. 26 April 1970.*

G63. Vande Kieft, Ruth. "'Granny's' big reunion." *Boston Herald-Traveler* 26 April 1970, Book Guide: 3–4. Photocopy.

G64. Walsh, Anne C. "Roots and Relationships—The Supporting Mesh." *Phoenix Gazettte* 18 April 1970, Marquee: 22. Photocopy.

G65. Wasson, Ben. "The Time has come . . . . " *Delta Democrat-Times* [Greenville, MS] 19 April 1970: 23. Original and photocopy.

G66. Wellejus, Ed. "The Book Shelf." *Erie Times-News* 7 June 1970, sec. E: 14.

G67. Wharton, Will. "Kin Turns Out for Granny, 100." *St. Louis Globe-Democrat* 19 April 1970. Photocopy.*

G68. White, Edward. "'Battles' Lifts Novelist to Major Rank." *Los Angeles Times* 10 May 1970. Photocopy.*

G69. Wilson, W. Emerson. "Books in the News." *Wilmington News* [DE] 29 April 1970. Photocopy.*

G70. Winfrey, Lee. "'Losing Battles'—an Author's Triumph." *Detroit Free Press* 19 April 1970, sec. B: 5. Four originals, photocopy.

G71. Woestendiek, Jo. "Eudora Welty Emerges as 'Very Important' American Writer." *Houston Chronicle* 12 April 1970. Two originals, two photocopies.*

G72. Yardley, Jonathan. "The Last Good One?" *New Republic* 9 May 1970: 33–36. Photocopy.

G73. Yardley, Jonathan. "'Losing Battles': Farewell to the 'Southern Novel'?" *Greensboro News* 12 April 1970. Photocopy.

H. Reviews of One Time, One Place (1971)

H1. Avant, John Alfred. Rev. of *One Time, One Place*. *Library Journal* 15 Dec. 1971: 4086.

H2.   Boozer, William. "Capturing a Time, Place." Memphis *Commercial Appeal* 14 Nov. 1971. Photocopy.*

H3.   Cockshutt, Rod. "Of Welty, Wine and a Welshman." *News and Observer* [Raleigh, N.C.] 21 Nov. 1971, sec. IV: 6.

H4.   Gill, Brendan. "The Inconstant Past." *New Yorker* 25 Dec. 1971: 66–68. Two copies.

H5.   Govan, Christine. "True Understanding." *Chattanooga Times* 5 Dec. 1971, sec. B: 4. Photocopy.*

H6.   Hains, Frank. "'One Time, One Place': Photographs of Her Mississippi by Eudora Welty." Jackson *Clarion-Ledger* 31 Oct. 1971, sec. C: 8. Three copies.

H7.   "In Brief." *New Republic* 12 Feb. 1972: 30–31.

H8.   Jones, Madison. Rev. of *One Time, One Place*. *NYTBR* 21 Nov. 1971: 60, 62, 64. Two originals, one photocopy.

H9.   "Kafka and other writers featured in new biographies." Portland *Oregonian* 14 Nov. 1971. Photocopy.*

H10.   Putney, Michael. "Gift Books: Land, Sea, and the Faces of Man." *National Observer* 4 Dec. 1971: 22.

H11.   Rathborne, Tina. Rev. of *One Time, One Place*. *Harvard Crimson* 1 Dec. 1971. Photocopy.

H12.   Spearman, Walter. "A Mississippi Scrapbook." *Chapel Hill Weekly* 21 Nov. 1971: 4. Photocopy.

H13.   Wasson, Ben. "Welty hits again." *Delta Democrat-Times* [Greenville, MS] 31 Oct. 1971: 25. Two copies.

I. Reviews of The Optimist's Daughter (1972)

I1.   "After the Funeral." *Philadelphia Inquirer* 21 May 1972. Photocopy. *

I2.   Alexander, Holmes. "The Dimension of Character." *Tampa Tribune-Times* 21 May 1972. Photocopy.

I3.   Arp, Tom. "From Eudora Welty, Patient, Calm Love." *Dallas Morning News* 28 May 1972, sec. E: 8. Three copies.

I4.   "Bittersweet family story told in new Welty novel." *Sunday Oregonian* 21 May 1972, sec. F: 4.

I5.   Boatwright, James. "The Continuity of Love." *New Republic* 10 June 1972: 24–25. One complete issue, three photocopies.
EW's holograph note on one of the photocopies reads: "Dear Bill and Emmy, I was so happy over this review I wanted you to see it—Love,

E." (Bill and Emmy are Mr. and Mrs. William Maxwell; Maxwell, a novelist and short story writer, was also a fiction editor at the *New Yorker* from 1936 to 1976.)

I6. Boozer, William. "'Optimist's Daughter' Is Vintage Welty." Memphis *Commercial Appeal* 11 June 1972.*

I7. Braverman, Millicent. "KABC's Book of the Day." Press release from KABC Radio (Los Angeles). Ts, photocopy.

I8. Buitenhuis, Peter. "When gossamer becomes a brittle network." *The Globe and Mail* 10 June 1972. Photocopy.*

I9. Burton, Hal. "'Small work of genius.'" *Newsday* 16 May 1972.*

I10. Cabau, Jacques. "Texas contre Mississippi." Unidentified French magazine, p. 108. Photocopy.

I11. Chalon, Jean. "La grand-mere gourmande de la litterature americaine." *Le Figaro* 20 July 1974, Litteraire: 11. Original and photocopy.

I12. Cheney, Frances Neel. "Profound Novel of Love, Death, Old Age." *Nashville Banner* 19 May 1972: 58. Two copies.

I13. Clemons, Walter. "Chorale of Blunderers." *Newsweek* 22 May 1972: 100–101. Two originals, one photocopy.

I14. Conklin, Richard W. "Novel That Relives Memories." *South Bend Tribune* 2 July 1972: 9.*

I15. M.D. "The Limits of Love." *Time* 5 June 1972: 88, 90, 92. Three copies.

I16. Davenport, Guy. "Primal Visions." *National Review* 23 June 1972: 697–98.

I17. Davies, Russell. "Californians at play." *The Observer* [London] 18 March 1973.*

I18. Donovan, Laurence. "Gentle Artistry of Simple Story Hard to Analyze." *Miami Herald* 21 May 1972.*

I19. Evett, Robert. "Surprising Novel from Welty." *Washington Star* 14 May 1972, sec. C: 5.*

I20. Frazer, Jan. "Radio Script Welty-Optimist's Daughter." Review broadcast on WNOG Radio, Naples, FL, and WDEA Radio, Ellsworth, ME. Carbon ts. with holograph revisions. 2 pp.

I21. Freshwater, Philip. "Of Life and Living." *Leisure* 18 June 1972: 14. (Newspaper not identified.)

I22. Fuller, Edmund. "Miss Welty, Mississippi and Meaning." *Wall Street Journal* 1 June 1972: 16. Three originals.

I23. Gaines, Ervin J. "A master at work." *Minneapolis Tribune* 21 May 1972, sec. D: 8.

I24.   Geismar, Maxwell. "Woman of culture and feeling." *Chicago Sun-Times* 28 May 1972, sec. Five: 22. Photocopy.

I25.   Govan, Christine. "High Point of a Career." *Chattanooga Times* 9 July 1972, sec. B: 2.*

I26.   Halliday, Mark. "The craft and wisdom of Eudora Welty." *Providence Sunday Journal* 9 July 1972, sec. H: 15.

I27.   Hartley, Lodwick. "Eudora Welty's 'The Optimist's Daughter.'" *News and Observer* [Raleigh, N.C.] 4 June 1972, sec. IV: 6.

I28.   Hicks, Granville. "Universal Regionalist." *New Leader* 7 August 1972: 19.

I29.   Hill, William B. Rev. of *The Optimist's Daughter*. *Best Sellers* 15 May 1972: 95–96.

I30.   Holliday, Barbara. "Some Weltian Insights on Life, Dying and Love." *Detroit Free Press* 21 May 1972, sec. C: 5. Two originals.

I31.   Holloway, David. "Recent Fiction." London *Daily Telegraph* 22 March 1973.*

I32.   "In Mourning." *TLS* 30 March 1973: 341.

I33.   Jackson, Marni. "Eudora Welty's latest book says life is really worthwhile." *Toronto Star*. Photocopy.

I34.   Janeway, Elizabeth. Rev. of *The Optimist's Daughter*. *Saturday Review* 1 July 1972: 60.

I35.   Kennedy, Monsignor John S. "Cultural Clashes." Unidentified periodical. Photocopy.

I36.   King, Francis. "All systems go." London *Sunday Telegraph* 18 March 1973.*

I37.   Rev. of *The Optimist's Daughter*. *The Kirkus Reviews* 18 May 1972: 351.*

I38.   Kirsch, Robert. "Trying to Track Down the Respite Novels." *Los Angeles Times* 25 June 1972, Calendar: 48, 50.

I39.   Lane, George. "Chinaberry Trees and Garden Party Chat." *Patriot Ledger* 16 May 1972: 28.

I40.   Lashley, Jim. "Eudora Welty Has 'Literary Treat.'" *Durham Morning Herald* 18 June 1972, sec. D: 5.

I41.   Lawson, Anna. "Precise Parts of an Art that Entertains, Explains." *Roanoke Times* 21 May 1972, sec. B: 13. Four originals.

I42.   Lindau, Betsy. "Some Looks at Books." *The Pilot* [N.C.] 26 April 1972, sec. B: 2.

I43.   Lucid, Robert F. "What We Flee." *Philadelphia Sunday Bulletin* 4 June 1972, sec. 7: 1. Original and photocopy.

I44.   Manning, Margaret. "Survival—strangest fantasy of all." *Boston Globe* 22 May 1972: 19. Two copies.

I45. Morton, Kathryn. "Eudora's Best." *Virginian-Pilot* 25 June 1972, sec. C: 6.

I46. Moss, Howard. "Eudora Welty's new novel about death and class." *NYTBR* 21 May 1972: 1, 18. Three complete issues, one copy of review (with advertisement on p. 9 attached), one set of galleys.

I47. Murray, Michele. "Eudora Welty Traces a Circle of Empty Lives." *National Observer* 10 June 1972: 22. Original and photocopy.*

I48. Pryce-Jones, Alan. "Viewpoint." *TLS* 14 July 1972: 800.

I49. Rev. of *The Optimist's Daughter*. *Publisher's Weekly* 20 March 1972: 61. Original and photocopy.

I50. K.R. "Stuff of Life at A Funeral." *New Haven Register* 28 May 1972.*

I51. Rogers, W. G. "Book of the Week." *Book Service for Newspapers* 20 May 1972: 1–2. Mimeographed ts. Two copies. Plus *NY Post* 16 May 1972—original and photocopy. *Wichita Falls Times* 21 May 1972, Magazine: 4—two copies. *North Carolina Leader* 17 May 1972: 5. Variously titled.

I52. Shaffner, Claire. "Southern Upmanship." *Charlotte Observer* 11 June 1972, sec. D: 5.

I53. Sion, Georges. "Decouvrir Eudora Welty." *Le Soir* 15 May 1974: 26.

I54. Spearman, Walter. "Life and Death in the Deep South." *Chapel Hill Weekly* 21 May 1972: 4.

I55. Symons, Julian. "Three novels—three cheers." *Sunday Times* [London] 18 March 1973.*

I56. Theroux, Paul. Rev. of *The Optimist's Daughter*. *Washington Post* 14 May 1972, Book World: 5—original and two photocopies.* Plus *San Francisco Examiner* 8 June 1972: 35.

I57. Thomas, Phil. "Eudora Welty Heroine Finds Life Linked." *AP Book Newsfeatures*, Book Reviews. Original and photocopy.

I58. Thomas, Sidney. "Novelist Captures Small Town South." *Atlanta Journal and Constitution* 4 June 1972, sec. C: 8.

I59. Thomas, W.H.J. "Current Reading." *News and Courier* [Charleston, S.C.] 21 May 1972, sec. D: 2.

I60. Trail, George Y. "Faulknerian theme lacks Faulkner's sympathy." *Houston Post* 11 June 1972, Spotlight: 19. Two copies.

I61. Wasson, Ben. "Welty novel is pure literary gold." *Delta Democrat-Times* [Greenville, MS] 21 May 1972: 25. Two originals and photocopy.

I62. Weeks, Edward. Rev. of *The Optimist's Daughter*. *Atlantic* June 1972: 111–12. Original and two photocopies.

163. Wharton, Will. "Welty's south: old judge, young wife." *St. Louis Globe-Democrat* 13–14 May 1972, sec. C: 4. Three originals.
164. Wilson, W. Emerson. "'Optimist's Daughter' probes life, death." *Wilmington News* [DE] 24 May 1972.*
165. Wood, Michael. "Cunning Time." *NY Review of Books* 29 June 1972: 8–9. Original and photocopy.
166. Wordsworth, Christopher. "Voice of the turtle." *The Guardian* 24 March 1973: 25.*
167. Yardley, Jonathan. Rev. of *The Optimist's Daughter*. *Boston Review of the Arts* July 1972: 57–58.
168. Yardley, Jonathan. "About Books." *Greensboro Daily News* 21 May 1972, sec. E: 3.

J. Reviews of The Eye of the Story (1978)

J1. Bargreen, Melinda. "A Collection of Welty." Seattle newspaper 27 Aug. 1978, "Sunday Magazine": 15.
J2. Baskin, Bernard. Rev. of *The Eye of the Story*. *The Spectator* [Hamilton] 17 June 1978. Photocopy.
J3. Barrett, Lynne. "What is good fiction, anyway?" *Greensboro Daily News* 11 June 1978.*
J4. Bitker, Marjorie. "Star Essays." *Milwaukee Journal* 28 May 1978. Photocopy.*
J5. Boozer, William. "The Welty Imagination is Ever-Present." *Nashville Banner* 29 April 1978: 5. Two originals.
J6. Broyard, Anatole. "On Literature's Porch." *NY Times* 22 April 1978: 17. Two originals, plus originals from *Seattle Post-Intelligencer* 14 May 1978, sec. G: 8, and from *International Herald Tribune* 3 May 1978.
J7. Bunke, Joan. "Pattern and passion." *Des Moines Register* 14 May 1978. Original and photocopy.*
J8. Burris, Mark. "Miss Welty Bridges Gap for Readers." *Richmond News Leader* 14 June 1978.*
J9. Rev. of *The Eye of the Story*. *Choice* Oct. 1978: 1056. Photocopy.
J10. Connor, George. "Other Facets." *Chattanooga Times* 11 June 1978. Two originals.*
J11. Cook, Carole. "Critic, Friend, and Teacher." *Saturday Review* 29 April 1978: 37–38. Original and photocopy.
J12. Curb, Randall. Rev. of *The Eye of the Story*. *Birmingham News* 27 August 1978.*
J13. Curtis, Cathy. "Near Ms." *Daily Californian* 19 May 1978, Friday Magazine: 16, 30.

J14. Enholm, Susan. "All about writers and writing." *Evening News* [Southbridge, MA] 26 July 1978: 9.

J15. Fox, Thomas. "Reflections on Fiction." Memphis *Commercial Appeal* 7 May 1978, sec. G: 6. Two copies.

J16. Frank, Michael R. "Welty eyes literature." *UCLA Daily Bruin* 11 May 1978: 18, 22.

J17. Glendinning, Victoria. "Eudora Welty in Type and Person." *NYTBR* 7 May 1978: 7, 43. Original and photocopy.

J18. Gribbin, Daniel V. "Fiction and Life in a Nutshell." *Roanoke Times and World News* 20 August 1978.*

J19. Hall, Wade. "The human dimension in criticism." Louisville *Courier-Journal* 7 May 1978: D 5.

J20. Hartley, Lodwick. "Selected writings by Eudora Welty." *News and Observer* [Raleigh, N.C.], sec. IV: 6. Photocopy.

J21. Houston, Levin. "Some Collected Works by Gardner and Welty." *Free Lance-Star* 24 June 1978, Town & Country Magazine: 6.

J22. Howard, Edwin. "From Two Masters of the Trade, Insight on Writing and Writers." *Memphis Press-Scimitar* 29 April 1978: 6. Two photocopies.

J23. Hyman, Ann. "'Eye of the Story' Is Literate, Entertaining Collection." *Times-Union and Journal* [Jacksonville] 9 July 1978: G 11. Photocopy.

J24. Johnson, Diane. "Two novelists offer homely wisdom and plain talk." *Chicago Tribune Book World* 30 April 1978, sec. 7: 3.

J25. Kendall, Elaine. "Mississippi's Welty Tips Off Fellow Writers." New Orleans *Times-Picayune* 10 Aug. 1978, sec. 7: 4. Original and photocopy. Plus review as published in *Durham Morning Herald* 30 July 1978 and photocopy of review from an unidentified newspaper.

J26. Klinkenberg, Robert P. "Writers prove exception." *Fort Wayne News-Sentinel* 10 June 1978: 14W.

J27. Leffler, Merrill. "From Eudora Welty, unique curtain-openers." Baltimore *Sun* 17 Sept. 1978.*

J28. Leighton, Betty. "A Feast for Anyone Who Hungers for Excellence." *Winston-Salem Journal* 25 June 1978. Photocopy.*

J29. Lowry, Beverly. Rev. of *The Eye of the Story*. *American Book Review* I.4 (1978): 4–5. Complete issue and original copy.

J30. Malone, Johnny. "Eudora Welty: A Garden of Southerly Delights." *Jackson Sun* [Tennessee] 3 Sept. 1978: 4A.

J31. Manning, Margaret. "Welty writes on writing." *Boston Globe* 22 May 1978.*

J32. May, John R. Rev. of *The Eye of the Story*. *America* 7 Oct. 1978: 232.

J33. McCabe, Carol. "So nice to have around the house." *Providence Journal* 25 June 1978.*

J34. McHaney, Thomas. "Words of Wisdom." *The State* [Columbia, S.C.] 28 May 1978, sec. E: 4. Photocopy.

J35. McKenzie, Alice. "'The Eye of the Story' Sheds Light on Fiction." *Clearwater Sun* 2 July 1978: 4F.

J36. Milazzo, Lee. "Eudora Welty: A literary artist." *Dallas Morning News* 30 April 1978, sec. G: 4. Five originals and photocopy.

J37. Morris, Robert K. "Eudora Welty as critic." *St. Louis Globe Democrat* 20–21 May 1978, sec. G: 5. Two copies.

J38. Mullinax, Gary. "4 decades of Eudora Welty, for others who love words." *News Journal* [DE] 28 May 1978.*

J39. Mysak, Joe. "Southern Belle surprises even the wariest of Yankee reviewers." *Summer Spectator* 15 June 1978.*

J40. Rev. of *The Eye of the Story*. *New Yorker* 22 May 1978: 139–40.

J41. Overmyer, Janet. "Eudora Welty Collection Is A Treasury of Prose." *Columbus Dispatch* 13 August 1978.*

J42. Paul, Kenneth. "Distributing Treasures." *Newsday* 21 May 1978. Photocopy.*

J43. Peter, Emmett. "Readable collection from the versatile Eudora Welty." *Sentinel Star* [FL] 21 May 1978. Two photocopies.*

J44. Powers, Ed. "Eudora Welty: still a prize-winner." *Cleveland Press* 29 June 1978.*

J45. Prothro, Laurie. "An author explains the heart of the matter." *Berkeley Gazette* 20 Oct. 1978, Weekend Vistas: 10. Original and photocopy.

J46. Rev. of *The Eye of the Story*. *Publisher's Weekly* 27 Feb. 1978: 149. Original and photocopy.

J47. Quinn, Ellen Ann. "On Writers and Writing." *Capitol Reporter* [Jackson, MS].

J48. Reefer, Mary. "She's a Generous Critic and Creator." *Kansas City Star* 18 June 1978. Photocopy.*

J49. Romine, Dannye. "Welty's 'Eye of the Story' Deserves a Celebration." *Charlotte Observer* 30 April 1978: 2F. Three originals.

J50. Rubin, Louis D. Rev. of *The Eye of the Story*. *New Republic* 22 April 1978: 32–34. Original and two photocopies.

J51. Serravillo, Lorraine. "The thunderclap at Welty's ears." *Christian Science Monitor* 17 May 1978: 23. Two originals.

J52. Shaw, Robert B. "A Storyteller's Appreciations." *Nation* 24 June 1978: 765–66. Photocopy.

J53. Sipper, Ralph B. "An Exploration of Welty's World." *San Francisco Examiner & Chronicle* 23 April 1978. Photocopy.

Final paragraph is photocopy of a ts.*

J54.   Skube, Michael. "Eudora Welty: The Storyteller as Critic." *Miami Herald* 7 May 1978, sec. E: 7.

J55.   Sparks, Christine. Rev. of *The Eye of the Story*. *Daily Press* [Newport News, VA] 6 August 1978, Panorama: 17. Original and photocopy.

J56.   Sperry, Ralph. Rev. of *The Eye of the Story*. *Best Sellers* Oct. 1978: 225. Photocopy.

J57.   Streissguth, Tom. "Book Score." *Daily Breeze/News Pilot* 28 April 1978. Photocopy.*

J58.   Thomas, Jane Resh. "There's beauty under her 'good, patient hands' . . . . " *Minneapolis Tribune* 14 May 1978. Two copies.*

J59.   Thompson, Francis J. "On the Morality of Fiction." *Tampa Tribune-Times* 25 June 1978. Photocopy.*

J60.   Wasson, Ben. "Rejoice—a new book by Eudora Welty." *Delta Democrat Times* [Greenville, MS].

J61.   "A Eudora Welty Collection, Filled with the Writer's Life." *Washington Star* 14 May 1978.*

J62.   "Welty's Tributes." *Chronicles of Culture*, p. 21.

J63.   Wimsatt, Margaret. "A Distaste for Cant, an Ear for Prose." *Commonweal* 29 Sept. 1978: 632–34. Photocopy.

J64.   Wright, Austin. "Eudora Welty's wisdom on writers and writing." *Chicago Sun Times Book Week* 14 May 1978.*

J65.   "Writing, Analysis 'Separate Gifts.' " *Indianapolis Star* 13 Aug. 1978.*

J66.   Yardley, Jonathan. "Pattern and Passion." *Washington Post* 7 May 1978, sec. E: 1, 6. Original and photocopy.

II. BIBLIOGRAPHIES
(Archives Series 31)
(Items are listed alphabetically by author or editor.)

A.   "Eudora Welty 1909-." *First Printings of American Authors*. Ed. Matthew J. Bruccoli. 4 vols. Detroit: Gale Research, 1978. I: title page, 407–09. Off-print.

B.   Hinds, Katherine Powell. "A Checklist of the Works of Eudora Welty, March 1954." Part of an unpublished master's thesis done at Duke University, 1954, pages [1]–5; separately published under name Katherine Hinds Smythe as "Eudora Welty: A Checklist," *Bulletin of Bibliography*, XXI (Jan.-April, 1956): 206–08. See IV.C below.

III. CRITICAL ESSAYS
(Archives Series 32)
(All items are listed alphabetically.)

A. Published Essays

A1.   Allen, John. "Eudora Welty: The Three Moments." 1974.
Ts, photocopy; pages [1]–20 and 3 pages of notes; paper read at Hollins College in Feb. 1974 and published in *VQR* 51 (1975): 605–27.

A2.   Bryant, J.A. "Seeing Double in *The Golden Apples*." 1974.
Ts, photocopy; pages [1]–21 and one page of notes; paper read at Hollins College in Feb. 1974 and published in *Sewanee Review* 82 (1974): 300–15.

A3.   Gross, Seymour. "A Long Day's Living: The Angelic Ingenuities of *Losing Battles*." 1978.
Ts, photocopy; pages [1]–27 plus 2 pages of notes; sent to EW by author 02.28.1978; EW's holograph notation on envelope reads, "*Essay on Losing Battles*|(a good one)|for Archives"; published in *Eudora Welty: Critical Essays*. Ed. Peggy W. Prenshaw. Jackson: Univ. Press of Miss., 1979. 325–40.

A4.   Gross, Seymour. "Eudora Welty's Comic Imagination." 1973.
Off-print; autographed by author; published in *Comic Imagination in American Literature*. Ed. Louis D. Rubin. New Brunswick, N.J.: Rutgers Univ. Press, 1973. 339–48.

A5.   MacKethan, Lucinda. "To See Things in Their Time: The Act of Focus in Eudora Welty's Fiction." n.d.
Ts, photocopy; title, pages [1]–63, two pages of notes; published as chapter 8 of *The Dream of Arcady*.

A6.   Magee, Rosemary. "Eudora Welty's *Losing Battles*: A Patchwork Quilt of Stories." *South Atlantic Review* 49 (1984): 67–79.
Tear sheets.

A7.   Manning, Carol F. "With Ears Opening like Morning Glories: Eudora Welty and the Love of Storytelling." n.d.
Ts, photocopy; title, pages i–ii, iv–vi, 253; part of typescript of book with the same title.

A8.   Mullen, Dale. "Some Notes on the Stories of Eudora Welty." *Mississippi Literary Review* I.1 (1941): 21–24.

A9.   Pei, Lowry. "Dreaming the Other in *The Golden Apples*." n.d.
Ts, photocopy; pages [1]-33; published in *MFS* 28 (1982): 415–33.

A10.   Prenshaw, Peggy W. "Woman's World, Man's Place: The Fiction of Eudora Welty." 1978.

Ts, photocopy; pages [1]–39; in envelope dated 03.28.1978; published in *Eudora Welty: A Form of Thanks*. Ed. Louis Dollarhide and Ann Abadie. Jackson: Univ. Press of Miss., 1979. 46–77.

A11. Rubin, Louis. "Everything Brought Out in the Open: Eudora Welty's Losing Battles." *Hollins Critic*, VII (June 1970): 1–7, 9–12.

A12. Vande Kieft, Ruth M. "Eudora Welty: The Question of Meaning." n.d.

Ts, photocopy; pages [1]–21; published in *Southern Quarterly* 20 (Summer 1982): 24–39.

B. Unpublished Essays

B1. Gohlke, Madelon S. "The Charmed Circle: Maternal Protectiveness in *Delta Wedding*." n.d.

Ts, photocopy; pages [1]–6.

B2. Seaman, Gerda and Walker, Ellen. *"The Ponder Heart."* n.d.

Ts, photocopy; title, pages [1]–32, 2 pages of notes.

B3. Williams, Nancy Clarke. Untitled. 1979.

Ts, photocopy; 17 pages; an essay about *The Golden Apples*, dated Dec. 79 and written by a student at the University of California, Santa Cruz.

IV. THESES

(Archives Series 33)

(All theses are listed alphabetically by author.)

A. Berry, Betsy. "Mythic Motifs in Eudora Welty's Short Fiction." Master's Thesis. University of Vermont. May 1971.

B. Foster, Mary Jane. "Family Consciousness in the Novels of Eudora Welty." Master's Thesis. Auburn Univ. Dec. 1975.

C. Hinds, Katherine Powell. "Eudora Welty: A Checklist." Part of a Duke University master's thesis.

Bibliography of Welty's works; see II.B above.

D. Jordan, Leona. "Humor in the Works of Eudora Welty." Master's Thesis. Mississippi State Univ. 1958.

E. Peterson, Linda May. "The Story Set: Definition of a Genre." Master's Thesis. Brigham Young Univ. Dec. 1978.

F. Yarrow, Deborah Thompson. "Family Versus Outsiders: Welty's Delta Women." Honors Thesis. Univ. of Southern Mississippi. August 1977.

V. DRAMATIZATIONS OF WELTY'S FICTION
(Archives Series 34)

A. The Ponder Heart
(Listed in order of production.)

A1. Fields, Joseph and Chodorov, Jerome. "The Ponder Heart."
Ts; 2 preliminary pages, Act I—pages [1]–57, Act II—pages [1]–55;
stored in brown folder with wing pins and with title embossed in gold
on folder; EW's holograph note on the ts reads, "Their early ver-
sion|some comments attached (by me)"; holograph revisions and
comments by EW.
A2. "The Ponder Heart." Univ. of Miss. production. 1977.
Ts, ditto; title page, Act One 1–25, Act Two 1–32; not the Chodorov
and Fields dramatization. See VII.B2 below.

B. A Piece of News and Petrified Man

B1. Evans, Emily Helen. Prompt book for dramatizations of "A
Piece of News" and "Petrified Man." 1965.
Ts; performed at Western Reserve University; prompt book includes
photographs of the production, newspaper clippings about it, a pro-
gram, press releases, a rehearsal schedule, and an audio tape of "'A
Piece of News' Dream Sequence."

VI. OTHER WRITINGS
(Archives Series 35)

A. Yarrow, Deborah Thompson. "The Monitor."
Ts, photocopy; pages [1]–8; pages [1]–8, plus an additional photo-
copy of page 3 and a ribbon copy of page 3; a short story inspired by
EW; 2 copies.
B. Yarrow, Deborah Thompson. Untitled.
Ts, ditto; draft of a novel, Chapters 1–4, 6; inspired by EW.

VII. EPHEMERA
(Archives Series 36)

A. Advertisements of books, articles about EW, articles mentioning
EW, best seller lists, articles about book publication, news photographs, brief reviews. (Listed in order of publication of EW's books.)

A1. *A Curtain of Green*: 3 items
A2. *Delta Wedding*: 19 items
A3. *The Ponder Heart*: 9 items
A4. *The Bride of the Innisfallen*: 4 items
A5. *Losing Battles*: 20 items
A6. *One Time, One Place*: 4 items
A7. *The Optimist's Daughter*: 6 items
A8. *The Eye of the Story*: 15 items
A9. "Bye-Bye Brevoort": Program of *The Littlest Revue*, 1955–56 season of the Phoenix Theater in NYC (the revue included EW's "Bye-Bye Brevoort"); photograph of Jackson's 1958 Little Theatre production; a program for and a newspaper article about the Jackson production. 4 items.
A10. Miscellaneous: 27 items

B. Playbills of, articles about, advertisements drawn from, reviews of dramatizations or other creative productions of Welty's fiction. (Listed in order of production.)

The Ponder Heart

B1.a. *The Ponder Heart.* Broadway production.
A scrapbook of ephemeral materials.
B1.b. *The Ponder Heart.* Various productions. 76 items.
Playbill from Country Playhouse, Syracuse, N.Y., has a holograph note from David Wayne to EW on the cover. (Wayne played Uncle Daniel Ponder in this July 9–14, 1956, production.)
B2. *The Ponder Heart.* Univ. of Miss. production. 1977. Album.
Album contains newspaper clippings, 14 photos of the production, a dittoed script.

The Shoe Bird

B3. *The Shoe Bird.* Jackson, Miss., production. 1968. 2 items.

A Seasons of Dreams

B4. *A Season of Dreams.* Jackson, Miss., production. Program.

The Robber Bridegroom

B5.a. *The Robber Bridegroom.* St. Clement's production. 1974. 5 items.
B5.b. *The Robber Bridegroom.* The Acting Company productions. 1975. 36 items.
B5.c. *The Robber Bridegroom.* Biltmore Theatre, New York City. 1976. 13 items.

B5.d.   Los Angeles production. 1976. 16 items.

C.   Photographs of dramatic productions. (Listed in order of production.)

The Ponder Heart

C1.   *The Ponder Heart*. Broadway production. 8 photographs.
C2.   *The Ponder Heart*. Jackson, Miss., production. 1956. 9 photographs.
Jackson (Miss.) Little Theatre, October 1956.
C3.   *The Ponder Heart*. Univ. of Miss. production. 1977.
See B2 above.

The Shoe Bird

C4.   *The Shoe Bird*. Jackson, Miss., production. 1968. 15 photographs.
Production of April 20, 1968.

Other Productions

C5.   *Petrified Man* and *Why I Live at the P.O.* Univ. of Illinois production. 1979. Album.
Performance done in conjunction with the presentation of an honorary degree to EW (5/20/79).
C6.   Dramatization of "A Visit of Charity." Unidentified production. 10 photographs.

APPENDIX A

Related Materials at the Mississippi Department of Archives and History

The Eudora Welty Collection consists only of materials donated to the Mississippi Department of Archives and History by Eudora Welty. The Department, however, holds many other items of interest to those studying Eudora Welty's work, and this appendix is a rather comprehensive but not an exhaustive list of such items.

I. AUDIO TAPES AND SOUND RECORDINGS

A. AUDIO TAPES

A1. OHP 056. Welty, Eudora. Interviewed by Charlotte Capers and Frank Hains. October 26, 1971. Jackson, Mississippi. Cassette. Transcript available.

A2. RG 68. Welty, Eudora. "A Seasons of Dreams." 1971. Jackson, Mississippi. Reel. (Also on video cassette.)

A3. OHP 046. Welty, Eudora. Interviewed by Charlotte Capers. May 8, 1973. Jackson, Mississippi. Cassette. Transcript available.

A4. OHP 176. Welty, Eudora. Mississippi Arts Festival Literary Seminar. May 12, 1973. Jackson, Mississippi. Reel. Transcript available.

A5. Welty, Eudora. Remarks in honor of Nash Burger. Delivered March 28, 1974 in NYC, but not by EW. Cassette. Text available, see Chapter 1, IV.C2.

A6. OHP 171. Welty, Eudora. Interviewed by Charlotte Capers. May 27, 1976. Jackson, Mississippi. Reel.

A7. OHP 368. Welty, Eudora. Interviewed by the Davis School Children. February 26, 1981. Jackson, Mississippi. Transcript available.

A8. OHP 384. Welty, Eudora. Interviewed by John Jones. May 13, 1981. Jackson, Mississippi. Reel. Transcript available.

A9. OHP 385. Welty, Eudora. Interviewed by Charlotte Capers. May 16, 1981. Reel. Transcript available.

A10. OHP 409. Welty, Eudora. Meeting with a University of Alabama class. May 28, 1982. Jackson, Mississippi. Reel.

A11.   OHP 410. Welty, Eudora. Interviewed by Charlotte Capers. February 8, 1984. Jackson, Mississippi. Cassette.

A12.   OHP 407. Welty, Eudora. Reading from *One Writer's Beginnings*. February 16, 1984. Jackson, Mississippi. Reel and cassette.

A13.   OHP 408. Welty, Eudora. Reading from an unpublished manuscript. April 12, 1984. Jackson, Mississippi. Reel. RESTRICTED.

A14.   Audio tape 11. Griffin, Robert J. *Losing Battles*. Everett/Edwards Instructional Tapes. Deland, Florida. 1972.

A15.   Audio tape 15. Vande Kieft, Ruth. "Eudora Welty." Everett/Edwards Instructional Tapes. Deland, Florida. 1976.

A16.   Audio tape 16. Vande Kieft, Ruth. "The Works of Eudora Welty." Everett/Edwards Instructional Tapes. Deland, Florida. 1976.

A17.   Audio Tape 40. Welty, Eudora. "On Story Telling." Jeffrey Norton Publishers. Guilford, Connecticut. 1961.

A18.   Audio Tape 44. Welty, Eudora. *The Optimist's Daughter*. Random House. New York. 1986.

B. Sound Recordings

B1.   SR 6. Welty, Eudora. Reading "Why I Live at the P.O.," "A Worn Path," "A Memory." Caedmon TC-1010, 1952.

B2.   SR 338. Welty, Eudora. Reading "Powerhouse" and "Petrified Man." Caedmon TC-1626, 1979.

B3.   SR 242. *The Robber Bridegroom*, original cast recording of the Broadway musical. CBS Special Products P-14589, 1977.

II. VIDEO CASSETTES AND FILMS

A. Cassettes

A1.   RG 68. A Conversation with Eudora Welty/Conversation 8. Moderator-Reynolds Price. Produced by MAETV. Jackson, Mississippi.

A2.   RG 68. A Conversation with Eudora Welty. Moderator-Frank Hains. Produced by MAETV. March 23, 1971. Jackson, Mississippi.

A3.   RG 68. "A Season of Dreams." Produced by MAETV. 1971. Jackson, Mississippi.

A4.   RG 68. "A Time and a Place." A conversation about Eudora Welty's fiction: Louis Rubin, Louis Simpson, T. Daniel Young, Peggy Prenshaw, Elizabeth Spencer. Part of *A Climate for Genius* series. Produced by MAETV, sponsored by Mississippi Library Commission, funded by the National Endowment for the Humanities. Sept. 18, 1975. Natchez, Mississippi. Transcript available.

A5.   RG 68. "One Time, One Place." Produced by MAETV. 1971. Jackson, Mississippi.

A6. "A Writer's Beginnings." A documentary about Eudora Welty for the program "Omnibus." Dir. Patchy Wheatley. Produced by BBC. July 24, 1987.

B. Films

B1. Film #51. Four Mississippi Women. Center for Southern Folklore. Memphis, Tennessee. n.d.
B2. Film #35. Writer in America: Eudora Welty. Produced and directed by Richard O. Moore. Perspective Films. Chicago, Illinois. 1978.

III. PRINTED MATERIALS — PRIMARY AND SECONDARY

A. First and limited editions of EW's works.
B. A collection of short works written by EW when she was a student at the Mississippi State College for Women. Compiled by Steve Pieschel. Photocopy. Originals available at the Mississippi University for Women, Columbus, Mississippi.
C. Some doctoral dissertations, some masters' theses, and all scholarly books about EW's work.
D. Many scholarly articles about EW's work. Some are listed in the card catalogue. Others are available in the "Welty, Eudora" subject files under the titles of individual Welty works.
E. A subject file consisting of scholarly articles, reviews, and ephemeral material about EW and her work. Subject file headings are:
E1. Welty House (Hinds County)
E2. Welty (Eudora)
E3. Welty, Eudora—Americana Awards
E4. Welty, Eudora—Biographical Material
E5. Welty, Eudora—Book Jackets
E6. Welty, Eudora—Newsletter
E7. Welty, Eudora—Undated
E8. Welty, Eudora yearly files 1930 Present
E9. Welty, Eudora. *A Curtain of Green*
　　　　　　　　　　The Robber Bridegroom
　　　　　　　　　　The Wide Net
　　　　　　　　　　Delta Wedding
　　　　　　　　　　The Golden Apples
　　　　　　　　　　The Ponder Heart
　　　　　　　　　　The Bride of the Innisfallen
　　　　　　　　　　The Shoe Bird
　　　　　　　　　　Losing Battles
　　　　　　　　　　One Time, One Place

The Optimist's Daughter
The Eye of the Story
The Collected Stories of Eudora Welty
One Writer's Beginnings

IV. WELTY, EUDORA. LETTERS TO LEHMAN ENGEL. RESTRICTED.

Microfilm. 816|W46e.

Originals available at Millsaps-Wilson Library, Millsaps College, Jackson, Mississippi.
(Open for research only with permission from Eudora Welty
and the estate of Lehman Engel.)

Correspondence from EW to Lehman Engel, 1941–1982. 78 items. Letters discuss personal concerns, EW's fiction, Engel's prose works, travels undertaken by EW and by Engel, the "Night-Blooming Cereus Club" of which both were members, production of "The Shoe Bird" as a ballet, Elizabeth Bowen's 1954 visit to EW in Jackson, the appearance of Leontyne Price at the Coliseum in Jackson, Mississippi, in 1967, and other matters.

IV. CHARLOTTE CAPERS COLLECTION. RESTRICTED.

The Charlotte Capers Collection contains the following material of interest to Welty scholars. (Open for research only with curator's permission.)

A. Accession #82.122, Box 3

A1. Post cards, birthday and Christmas cards, short letters from EW to Charlotte Capers, 1953–1985. 32 items. EW reports on travels to Europe, to England, to Canada, and within the U.S.A.; sends humorous verse in honor of specific occasions. (Charlotte Capers, a long-time friend of EW's, was director of the Mississippi Department of Archives and History from 1955 until her retirement in 1969.)

A2. Picture. "Eudora Welty & friends at Ann & Bill Morrison's [William Morrison was a Jackson architect, and his wife Ann is now Programs Coordinator at the Mississippi State Historical Museum], April 13, 1970." Jackson, Mississippi. Taken at party celebrating the publication of *Losing Battles*.

A3. Picture. "Santa Rosa Seven." 1978. Picture of a group of friends who had once vacationed together on Santa Rosa Island off the coast of Florida. Pictured are Karen Gilfoy, Patricia Carr Black, Charlotte Capers, Eudora Welty, Reynolds Price, Ann Morrison, Jane Reid Petty. (All except for novelist Reynolds Price are Jackson, Mississippi, residents. Gilfoy is a lawyer and a judge; Black is the Director of the Mississippi State Historical Museum; Morrison is Programs Coordinator at the Mississippi State Historical Museum; Petty is Managing Director at Jackson's New Stage Theatre.)

B. Accession #80.59

B1. Welty, Eudora. 9 photographs taken at the Medal of Freedom presentation, The White House, Washington, D. C., 1980. Photographs taken by Bill Ferris of the Center for Southern Folklore.

C. Accession #80.58

C1. Welty, Eudora, and Warren, Robert Penn. 3 photographs taken at the Medal of Freedom presentation, The White House, Washington, D.C., 1980. Photographs by Bill Ferris.
C2. Welty, Eudora, and Winter, William. 2 photographs taken at a dinner party, the Governor's Mansion, Jackson, Mississippi, July 17, 1980. Photographs by Bill Ferris.

D. Accession #81.069. Presentation Copies of Eudora Welty's Works

D1. *A Curtain of Green*. First Edition. Signed.
D2. *The Robber Bridegroom*. First Edition. Signed.
D3. *The Wide Net*. First Edition. With inscription.
D4. *Delta Wedding*. First Edition. With inscription.
D5. *Music from Spain*. Levee Press Edition. With inscription.
D6. *The Golden Apples*. First Edition. With inscription.
D7. *The Golden Apples*. First Edition. Signed.
D8. *The Bride of the Innisfallen*. First Edition. With inscription.
D9. *The Shoe Bird*. First Edition. With inscription.
D10. *A Sweet Devouring*. Albondocani Press (1969) Edition. With inscription.
D11. "A Flock of Guinea Hens Seen from a Car." Christmas Card Printing. With inscription.
D12. *A Pageant of Birds*. Albondocani Press (1974) Edition. With inscription.
D13. "Women!! Make Turban in Own Home!" Palaemon Press Edition. With inscription.
D14. "Four Photographs by Eudora Welty." A broadside published by Lord John Press, 1984. Signed.
D15. *The Ponder Heart*. Hebrew Language Edition. With inscription.

E. Periodicals

E1. "Jackson Communique." *The New Yorker* 18 Feb. 1985: 33. An interview with EW. Complete issue.
E2. Capers, Charlotte. "Distinguished Dame—Eudora Welty." *The Tattler* March 1985: 6–7. Rpt. from *The Tattler* Sept. 1966. Complete issue. (*The Tattler* is the Junior League magazine of Jackson, Miss.)

V. PICTURE COLLECTION

The picture collection contains numerous photographs of EW. See the following call numbers:

PI| ART| 82.47
PI| LIT| 84.21
PI| LIT| 82.48
PI| LIT| W45.4
PI| COL| 82.142
O| 810| M678
PI| LIT| 82.149
PI| PER| 81.24
PI| LIT| 82.62
PI| ED| 81.23

A Handlist of Eudora Welty
Manuscripts in Other Collections

by Noel Polk

Listed here are the significant Welty prose manuscripts, not including letters, in collections other than the primary one at the Mississippi Department of Archives and History. I am particularly grateful to Cathy Henderson, of the Humanities Research Center of the University of Texas, for her extensive help in checking my notes on the fine Welty collection in the HRC, a collection second only to that in the Mississippi Department of Archives and History. I am also very grateful to Suzanne Marrs and Seetha Srinivasan for their sense that this handlist had a place in Dr. Marrs' superb catalogue of the Archives' collection.

I. BOOKS

A. THE ROBBER BRIDEGROOM (1942)

1. Typescript setting copy, 102 pages ([1]–102, complete). Some minor editorial intervention, some handwritten authorial changes. Subtitle "A Tale" deleted from page [1]. Dated 6/16/42 in an editorial hand. (Dartmouth College)
2. Carbon typescript of A1. A few authorial changes. (Texas)
3. Carbon typescript of A1. Same pagination except for the addition of a title page and a couple of blank sheets. Adhesive-bound in green cardboard covers. Some authorial revision. Title page reads: 'THE ROBBER* BRIDEGROOM | A Tale | By Eudora Welty | 1119 Pinehurst Street | Jackson, Mississippi'. (Texas)

B. THE WIDE NET (1943)

1. Carbon typescript, 148 pages (paged as below). Bound with wing pins in a green folder. Title page reads: 'THE WIDE NET | Short Stories | by | Eudora Welty'. Stories are paged and numbered separately. (Texas)

a. Front matter, 4 pp. ([i–iv]).
b. FIRST LOVE 21 pp. ([1]–21, complete).
c. THE WIDE NET 25 pp. ([1]–25, complete).
d. A STILL MOMENT 14 pp. ([1]–14; complete?).
e. ASPHODEL 12 pp. ([60]–71; complete? Page [60] originally bore a typed numeral 69, which was then erased).
f. THE WINDS 18 pp. (72–73, 3–18; complete?). Page 72 is numbered only in pencil; page 73 is numbered in hand over a typed #2.
g. THE PURPLE HAT 8 pp. (91–98, complete).
h. LIVVIE 16 pp. ([1]–16, complete).
i. AT THE LANDING 24 pp. (115–138, complete). Pages 116–118 are renumbered in pencil over typed numbers 2–4 respectively.
j. Blank end sheet.

C. DELTA WEDDING (1946)

1.   Galley proof, 81 pages (1–81, complete). Two copies of galley 36. No authorial alterations, but occasional corrections by editor. All galleys date from 8 December through 15 December [1945]. (Yale Beinecke)

D. THE GOLDEN APPLES (1949)

1.   Working papers, primarily carbons (ca. 410 pp). (Texas)
a. Seven preliminary sheets: chapter titles, list of main families, acknowledgments, statement of fictionality of characters, quotation of all of Yeats' "The Song of Wandering Aengus." First title page reads: 'THE GOLDEN APPLES | by | Eudora Welty | March 9, 1949'. Second title page reads: 'THE GOLDEN APPLES | Some Aspects of Morgana | by | Eudora Welty'.
b. Chapter 1. SHOWER OF GOLD   Carbon and ribbon typescript, 18 pp. ([title, 1]–5, 5A, 6–16, complete). Sheets from at least two different versions. Lots of authorial alterations.
c. Chapter 2. JUNE RECITAL   Carbon and ribbon typescripts, 88 pp. ([2 title pages], 1, 1, 2–57, 57A, 58, 59, 59, 60–65, 65A, 68–84. It is difficult to tell whether this is complete or not). There are lots of pages from various versions: pasteovers, half-pages, partial pages pasted to newspaper backing, many pen and pencil revisions. The first, carbon, title page reads: '2. | June Recital'. The second, brown title page originally marked in ink: 'III | 1920 Golden Apples'. 'The' was added in pencil to this title and everything but the title and the date crossed out; a chapter number, 2, was assigned, and the title changed to 'June Recital'. The second page 1 was originally headed in typed ribbon ink, 'Golden Apples, Silver Apples'; this title was erased and 'Golden Apples' inked above the deletion. The inked title was further deleted in pencil and the title 'June Recital' pencilled above it. It

also bears the inked designation 'III 1920'. 'Golden Apples, Silver Apples' also appears as a rejected title on the otherwise blank verso of p. 11. Page 2 bears Welty's sketch of a house, apparently the one Loch Morrison sees next door.

d. Chapter 3. SIR RABBIT   Carbon typescript, 16 pp. ([title, 1]–15, complete). Some authorial alterations.

e. Chapter 4. MOON LAKE   Carbon typescript, 51 pp. ([title, 1]–50, complete). Some authorial alterations.

f. Chapter 5. THE WHOLE WORLD KNOWS   Carbon typescript, 28 pp. ([title, 1]–27, complete). Some authorial alterations.

g. Chapter 6. MUSIC FROM SPAIN
  i. Carbon typescript, 54 pp. (1–54, complete). Some authorial alterations. This appears to be the copy from which g.ii, following, was typed. Two inked lines at top of page 1, '6. 1942 | VI. 1942', are deleted in ink.
  ii. Carbon typescript, 49 pp. ([title], 1–10, 10A, 11–47, complete). Some authorial alterations.

h. Chapter 7. [THE WANDERERS]
  i. Carbon typescript, 50 pp. ([title], 1–14, 15A, 15B, 16–33, 33A, 34, 34–48, complete). Carbon typed title reads: '7. | The Golden Apples'. Typed title on page 2, '*The Humming-Birds*' deleted in pencil, 'It's The World That's Turning' inserted in pencil, then also deleted. At top, in ink, in Welty's hand: 'VII present | time'. Some authorial alterations.
  ii. Carbon typescript, miscellaneous leaves, 37 pp. (1–5, 8–11, 14–20, 23–36, 28–36, [37–38 on one leaf], 39–40, 46–47, 52–54). Some authorial alterations. First page has typed title '*The Kin*' deleted and 'It's the World That's Turning' added in pencil, then that title also crossed out and in pencil is added 'The Golden Apples'. Above this title, in Welty's pencil, is added: '(new pages for) | 7.'.
  iii. Ribbon typescript pages, 4 miscellaneous leaves (25, 26, 37, 38–A). Some authorial alterations.

E. THE PONDER HEART (1954)

1. Working Vari Proof of the *New Yorker* text, 128 pp. (1–128, complete). Some authorial alterations. Double-spaced, narrow columns, ragged right margins. Printed at top of galley 1: 'GALLEY ONE—JULY 20, 1953——7-X—Q-MG MID NOVEMBER TO MID | DECEMBER 1953——WORKING VARI-TYPE—VT-805-H | THE PONDER HEART'. (Texas)

2. Galley proofs of book text, 41 leaves (1–41, complete). Some authorial, but mostly editorial, alterations. Dated September 21–25 [1953]. (Texas)

3. Page proofs of book text, 150 pp. ([7]–156, text complete on 50 galleys, 3 pages per galley, plus 6 pages printed front matter and illustrations, and 6 pages typed front matter). (Texas)

F. THE BRIDE OF THE INNISFALLEN (1955)

1.   Working papers and early drafts (Texas)

a. THE BRIDE OF THE INNISFALLEN Typescript, 42 pp. ([1]–42, complete). Some authorial alterations. A very e. ·ly version of this title, earlier than the *New Yorker* text. Dated by Welty April 1951 and inscribed to Elizabeth Bowen.

b. THE WAND Typescript, 10 pp. ([1]–10, complete). A very early version of "Circe," earlier than the magazine text, with significant differences from all other versions. Inscribed to Elizabeth Bowen.

2.   Typescript setting copy, 265 pp. (1–265, complete. Page numeral #1 written in in pencil). Some authorial alterations. Pages numbered as below, then renumbered in pencil, beginning with page 35. (Texas)

a. NO PLACE FOR YOU, MY LOVE 34 pp. (1–4. Page numeral #1 written in in pencil).

b. THE BURNING 23 pp. ([1]–23; renumbered 35–57).

c. THE BRIDE OF THE INNISFALLEN 50 pp. ([1]–50; renumbered 58–107).

d. LADIES IN SPRING 24 pp. ([1]–24; renumbered 108–131). Typed title 'Spring'; 'Ladies in' added in ink by author. P. 24 is typed in a typeface different from the rest of the text.

e. CIRCE 11 pp. ([1]–11; renumbered 132–142). This story typed in same typeface as p. 24 of LADIES IN SPRING, and different from the rest of the text.

f. KIN 61 pp. ([1]–61; renumbered 143–203). Pages 1, 43–46, 50, 51 are typed with same typeface as CIRCE. Page 27 is typed in a third typeface, different from the other two.

g. GOING TO NAPLES 62 pp. ([1]–62; renumbered 204–265).

3.   Carbon typescript of setting copy, containing some authorial corrections which differ from the setting copy. Some of these corrections are not on the ribbon typescript, but are incorporated into the book. Same typed pagination as setting copy, same number of pages, plus five pages of front matter. Adhesive-bound in tan boards with green marbled pattern. (Texas)

4.   Miscellaneous typescript leaves, 22 pages, variously numbered, in a third typewriter face. These pages represent later versions of pages, or portions of pages, 13–15, 19, 23–24, 33–42, 44–46, 47–49. Page 47 has an editorial note: 'New ending for gal 25'. It is this version of galley 25 which is on the galleys at Texas (see 6, below) though the implication is that these are corrections for the galleys. So these papers posit an earlier set of galleys than Texas' set. The revisions on the carbon of the setting copy (3 above) correspond to retyped pages described here; so, Welty apparently sent the setting copy to Harcourt but kept tinkering with the carbon, and incorporated the changes she had made into the new typed pages at the galley stage. (Texas)

5.   Front matter, 22 pages. (15 pp. proof and 6 pp. typescript versions). (Texas)·

6. Galley proof, 56 sheets (9–64, incomplete). Some authorial alterations, with the typed insertion affixed to galley 25 (see 4, above). Dated October 11–18 [1954]. Note on verso of final galley indicates that this is a 'revised galley'. (Texas)

7. Advance sheets, 134 pp. ([i–vii], 1–127, complete). No authorial marks of any kind. (Yale Beinecke)

8. Page proof, 75 sheets (3–46, 84–207, incomplete. First 29 pages separate, remainder printed on 48 galleys, 3 pages per galley). Page proofs for the title story missing. (Texas)

G. The Optimist's Daughter (1972)

1. Xerox of typescript setting copy, 170 pp. (Texas Restricted)

II. CONTRIBUTIONS TO PERIODICALS AND OTHER WORKS

A. "How I Write"

1. Carbon typescript, 14 pp. ([1]–14, complete). Page 5 is a ribbon. This was used as setting copy for this essay's appearance in *Virginia Quarterly Review*. With printer's, editor's, and some author's marks. (Virginia)

2. Galley proofs, 4 sheets (90–93, complete). Dated January 8–9 [1955]. (Virginia)

B. [Presentation to William Faulkner of the Gold Medal for Fiction]

1. Manuscript, 5 pp. (1–5, complete). On Hotel Algonquin stationery. (Texas)

2. Typescript, 2 pp. ([1–2], complete). Some authorial revision. (Texas)

3. Typescript, 2 pp. ([1]–2, complete). Appears to be professionally typed, perhaps for newspaper release. At top of p. [1]: 'PRESENTATION TO WILLIAM FAULKNER OF THE | GOLD MEDAL FOR FICTION | BY EUDORA WELTY | At the Ceremonial of the American Academy and the | National Institute of Arts and Letters, May 24, 1962'. (Texas)

C. [Associated Press Release Written upon the Occasion of William Faulkner's Death]

1. Typescript, 2 pp. ([1]–2, complete). Signed at the bottom of page 2: 'Eudora Welty | Written at request of Associated Press July 6, 1962'. (Texas)

D. Some Notes on Time in Fiction

1. Typescript, 13 pp. ([1]–13, complete). Some authorial changes, and shows signs of extensive revision toward the end. Setting copy for this essay's appearance in the *Mississippi Quarterly*. (Mississippi State University).
2. Galley proof, 4 sheets (3–6, complete). (Mississippi State University)

E. [On The Ponder Heart]

1. Typescript, 4 pp. ([1]–4, complete). Essay written apparently as a press release in conjunction with the production of *The Ponder Heart* on Broadway. Dated 'Jackson, Miss., Jan. 11, 1956' on final page. Some authorial revision. (New York Public Theatre Library)
2. Carbon typescript of a retyped and somewhat modified version of the above, probably professionally typed, 3 pp. ([1]–3, complete). Marked 'Exclusive to Otis Guernsey / for release Sun. Feb. 19, please' and titled 'BROADWAY MEETS THE SOUTH—AND VICE VERSA / by Eudora Welty'. (New York Public Theatre Library)

F. [Reader's Report]

1. On page 27 of the typescript of KIN is a blind-typed text—obviously it was used as a back-up sheet for the ribbon copy of the reader's report—of a reader's report on THE TRUE HISTORY OF OUR FLAG by Lawrence Phelps Tower. The report appears to be signed and dated 'EW | 7-13-54'. (Texas)

WORKS CITED
IN INTRODUCTIONS

Brookhart, Mary Hughes and Suzanne Marrs. "More Notes on River Country." *Welty, A Life in Literature*. Ed. Albert J. Devlin. Jackson: Univ. Press of
Mississippi, 1987. 82–95.

Bunting, Charles T. "'The Interior World': An Interview with Eudora Welty."
The Southern Review 8.4 (1972): 711–35.

Devlin, Albert J. "Jackson's Welty." *The Southern Quarterly* 20.4 (1982): 54–91.

Engel, Lehman. *This Bright Day*. New York: Macmillan, 1974.

Ferguson, Mary Anne. "*Losing Battles* as a Comic Epic in Prose." *Eudora
Welty, Critical Essays*. Ed. Peggy W. Prenshaw. Jackson: Univ. Press of Mississippi, 1979. 305–324.

Kuehl, Linda. "The Art of Fiction XLVII." *Paris Review* 55 (1972): 72–97.

McDonald, W. U. "Artistry and Irony: Welty's Revisions of 'Lily Daw and the
Three Ladies.'" *Studies in American Fiction* 9 (1981): 113–21.

———. "Eudora Welty's Revisions of 'A Piece of News.'" *Studies in Short Fiction* 7 (1970): 232–47.

———. "Welty's 'Social Consciousness': Revisions of 'The Whistle.'" *Modern
Fiction Studies* 16 (1970): 193–98.

McHaney, Pearl Amelia. "A Eudora Welty Checklist, 1973–1986." *Welty, A
Life in Literature*. Ed. Albert J. Devlin. Jackson: Univ. Press of Mississippi,
1987. 266–302.

McKenzie, Barbara. "The Eye of Time: The Photographs of Eudora Welty."
Eudora Welty, Critical Essays. Ed. Peggy W. Prenshaw. Jackson: Univ. Press
of Mississippi, 1979. 386–400.

Mann, Charles. "Eudora Welty, Photographer." *History of Photography* 6.2
(1982): 145–49.

Meese, Elizabeth. "Constructing Time and Place: Eudora Welty in the Thirties." *Eudora Welty, Critical Essays*. Ed. Peggy W. Prenshaw. Jackson: Univ.
Press of Mississippi, 1979. 401–10.

Mississippi Department of Archives and History. Eudora Welty Collection.
Manuscripts: "Beautiful Ohio," Archives Series 1; "Stories," Archives Series 2; "The Delta Cousins," Archives Series 4; "The Flower and the Rock,"
Archives Series 5; "The Ghosts," Archives Series 7; "Losing Battles," Archives Series 11; "An Only Child—Omitted Pages," Archives Series 12;
"One Writer's Beginnings," Archives Series 17; "The Robber Bridegroom,"
screenplay, Archives Series 21. Photographs: Negatives and Prints. Correspondence. Z301. Reference to the Eudora Welty Collection made by permission of the Mississippi Department of Archives and History.

Polk, Noel. "A Eudora Welty Checklist, 1936–1972." *Eudora Welty, A Life in Literature*. Ed. Albert J. Devlin. Jackson: Univ. Press of Mississippi, 1987. 238–65.

Prenshaw, Peggy W. "Woman's World, Man's Place." *Eudora Welty, A Form of Thanks*. Ed. Louis Dollarhide and Ann J. Abadie. Jackson: Univ. Press of Mississippi, 1979. 46–77.

Russell, Diarmuid. "First Work." *Shenandoah* 20 (1969): 16–19.

Samway, Patrick H. "Eudora Welty's Eye for the Story." *America* 23 May 1987: 417–20.

Thompson, Victor H. *Eudora Welty: A Reference Guide*. Boston: G. K. Hall, 1976.

Tiegreen, Helen Hurt. "Mothers, Daughters, and One Writer's Revisions." *Welty, A Life in Literature*. Ed. Albert J. Devlin. Jackson: Univ. Press of Mississippi, 1987. 188–211.

Warren, Robert Penn. "The Love and the Separateness in Miss Welty." *Kenyon Review* 6 (1944): 246–59.

Welty, Eudora. *Acrobats in a Park*. Northridge, Calif.: Lord John Press, 1980.

——. "At The Landing." *The Wide Net*. New York: Harcourt, Brace, 1943. 178–214.

——. "The Burning." *The Bride of the Innisfallen*. New York: Harcourt, Brace, 1955. 28–46.

——. "The Burning." *Harper's Bazaar* March 1951: 184, 238, 242, 243, 244, 247.

——. "Clytie." *A Curtain of Green*. New York: Doubleday, Doran, 1941. 155–71.

——. "Death of a Traveling Salesman." *A Curtain of Green*. New York: Doubleday, Doran, 1941. 231–50.

——. *Delta Wedding*. New York: Harcourt, Brace, 1945–46.

——. "Flowers for Marjorie." *A Curtain of Green*. New York: Doubleday, Doran, 1941. 189–203.

——. *In Black and White*. Northridge, Calif.: Lord John Press, 1985.

——. "Looking Back at the First Story." *Georgia Review* 33 (1979): 751–55.

——. *Losing Battles*. New York: Random House, 1970.

——. "Magic." *Manuscript* 3 (Sept.-Oct. 1936): 3–7.

——. "Music from Spain." *The Golden Apples*. New York: Harcourt, Brace, 1949. 161–202.

——. *One Time, One Place*. New York: Random House, 1971.

——. *One Writer's Beginnings*. Cambridge, Mass.: Harvard Univ. Press, 1984.

——. *The Optimist's Daughter*. New York: Random House, 1972.

——. Personal interviews. July 1985—January 1988.

——. "Place and Time: The Southern Writer's Inheritance." *Times Literary Supplement* 17 Sept. 1954: xlviii.

——. *The Robber Bridegroom*. New York: Doubleday, Doran, 1942.

————. "Some Notes on River Country." *The Eye of the Story*. New York: Random House, 1978. 286–99.

————. "Some Notes on Time in Fiction." *The Eye of the Story*. New York: Random House, 1978. 163–73.

————. *Twenty Photographs*. With "A Word on the Photographs" by Welty. Winston-Salem, N.C.: Palaemon Press, 1980.

————. *Welty*. Ed. Patti Carr Black. Introduction by Black. Jackson: Mississippi Department of Archives and History, 1977.

————. "The Whistle." *A Curtain of Green*. New York: Doubleday, Doran, 1941. 107–15.

————. "A Worn Path." *A Curtain of Green*. New York: Doubleday, Doran, 1941. 273–85.

Westling, Louise. "The Loving Observer of *One Time, One Place*." *Mississippi Quarterly* 39.4 (1986): 587–604.

————. *Sacred Groves and Ravaged Gardens*. Athens, Ga.: University of Georgia Press, 1985.

A Writer's Beginnings. Dir. Patchy Wheatley. BBC. July 24, 1987.

INDEX

*"Rev." denotes review by Eudora Welty.

237